INTERNATIONAL CONFERENCE ON LEARNING TO LIVE TOGETHER

International Encyclopaedia of Learning to Live Together - 1

INTERNATIONAL CONFERENCE ON LEARNING TO LIVE TOGETHER

By

Dr. Digumarti Bhaskara Rao
M.Sc., M.A., M.A., M.Ed., Ph.D.
Dean, Faculty of Education
Member, Academic Senate
Ex-Chairman, Board of Studies in Education
Member, Research Advisory Committee
Acharya Nagarjuna University
D-43, S.V.N. Colony
Guntur - 522 006 (India)

First Published – 2005

Reprinted – 2026

ISBN: 978-81-7141-848-0 (Set)

ISBN: 978-81-7141-989-0

Published by:

DISCOVERY PUBLISHING HOUSE

4383/4B, Ansari Road, Darya Ganj

New Delhi-110 002 (India)

Phone: +91-11-23279245; 23253475; 43596065

E-mail: discoverybooksindia@gmail.com

discoverypublishinghouse@gmail.com

namitwasan9@gmail.com

web: www.discoverypublishinggroup.com

Printed at:

Infinity Imaging Systems

Delhi

FOREWORD

The development and reform of school curricula is an ongoing preoccupation for educational authorities in all countries. The approach of the new millennium has given new urgency to efforts by governments to provide all citizens with access to quality education, at least for the basic level, while improving and widening access to secondary education. More than ever before, governments are being called upon to equip children and young people through education with the capacity to lead meaningful and productive lives in a world of bewilderingly rapid and complex change. Existing curriculum content and pedagogical methods are increasingly being called into account, as pupils leave schools ill-prepared for the world of work and adulthood, unready and unmotivated to carry on learning throughout their lives. The meaning and role of education, of teaching and learning, are constantly being redefined in an effort to meet the real needs and demands of individual and society.

The implication of globalization for societies around the world is at the heart of present concerns to improve and upgrade education systems. While globalization is often defined primarily in terms of its economic dimensions, the Report to UNESCO of the International Commission on Education for the Twenty-first Century—the *Delors report*—sees the most important consequence of this complex phenomenon to be its socio-cultural and ethical dimensions as regards the growing interdependence and interrelationships between peoples and cultures the world over: 'the far-reaching changes in the traditional patterns of life require of us a better understanding of other people and the world at large today; they demand mutual understanding, peaceful interchange and indeed harmony'.[1] However, the report stresses

1. Delors, J., et al. *Learning: the treasure within.* Paris, UNESCO, 1996, p. 22. (Report to UNESCO of the International Commission on Education for the Twenty-first Century.

that 'learning to live together'—one of the pillars of education—will only occur through the possession of self-knowledge and understanding, and appreciation of one's own origins and culture.

It is now widely recognized that designing a curriculum is mainly a national concern, normally shared between educational protagonists at the central, local and school level. The principle of subsidiarity suggests that curriculum issues should not be addressed at the supranational level. Indeed, experience shows that, until quite recently, international exchanges and co-operation in curriculum development were limited, being restricted to professional associations of curriculum specialists. However, two recent trends have contributed to bringing international attention to bear on curriculum matters:

1. The globalization of economies and societies raises a new challenge, requiring the adaptation of educational content to meet both national demand and international concerns;
2. The diversification of actors, both national and international, involved in the delivery of education (in particular with the growing use of information and communication technologies—ICTs), as illustrated by the significant share of non-formal education, have resulted in the emergence of new concepts and norms for educational content; as indicated by such terms as the 'common core', 'universal values', 'basic life skills', etc. Once again, this means sharing responsibility for educational content, as well as presenting us with new opportunities for international co-operation.

It is against this background and in an effort to respond to the numerous contemporary concerns about the content of education, that the International Bureau of Education (IBE), designated as the UNESCO institute responsible for strengthening the capacity of Member States in curriculum development, is focusing its new programme activity on the adaptation of the content of education to the challenges of the twenty-first century. The IBE's programme is divided into two components: (i) integrating the concern of living together into the content of education; and (ii) adapting the content of education in order to cope with some of the challenges raised by a globalized world.

The IBE programme of co-operation in 'research and studies', 'training and capacity building'; and 'the exchange of information and expertise' is based upon two major assumptions:

(a) Although different Member States of UNESCO have very uneven and heterogeneous experiences in the design and adaptation of their educational content, there is room for beneficial exchanges between countries;

(b) Although there are some common views on how to address the demand that content should be modified, a great deal remains to be done to improve the process of adaptation.

The approach to implementing the programme followed by the IBE is based on the assumption that the programme proposes to include: (a) an international platform of information on educational content; and (b) a number of regional and sub-regional co-operation projects. The preparation of such programmes is carried out through regional workshops.

This sub-regional workshop took place in 1999 in New Delhi to cater to the concerns of South and South-East Asia. The purpose of the workshop was:

(a) To collect information about the status of educational content in the region—a 'fact-finding' exercise;

(b) To encourage the assessment of experiences, both among Asian countries and a selected number of countries from other parts of the world; and

(c) To explore and map out some areas for potential co-operation among the participating Member States.

Two key phrases of the IBE's new programmes were incorporated into the umbrella theme of the course, which was *The adaptation of content to the demands of the globalization and the need for learning to live together.*

This publication is a compilation of the various presentations made during the workshop. Both through the diversity of topics covered and the list of issues raised, it offers a rich and varied picture of the challenges facing Asian countries seeking to adapt educational content to meet the social demand of the coming decade.

The IBE would like to thank all of the contributors, both from the participating countries and from other parts of the world, who have shared their information and experience during the workshop. Indeed, the distinction between 'faculty' and 'participants' proved to be of little relevance in this workshop, where all contributors learned from each other.

On behalf of the International Bureau of Education, I would like to express our deep appreciation to the Government of India—and in particular to the Central Board of Secondary Education—for its generous support of the workshop. India both financially supported and hosted the meeting and contributed significantly to the debates and to enriching the information shared among the participants. Finally, I should mention with thanks the financial and intellectual contribution of the Deutsche Stiftung für internationale Entwicklung, which ensured the success of the workshop.

Jacques Hallak
Assistant Director-General,
Director of the IBE.

PREFACE

Education is gearing towards preparing individuals to live in together since ancient times. However, the notion of 'learning to live together' is clearly shaped only very recently by the UNESCO's International Commission on Education for the Twenty-first century. The Commission emphasized that education had a treasure within and developed a vision of education for the 21st century based on four pillars namely, Learning to know, Learning to do, Learning to be, and Learning to live together. The first three pillars are essential for the sound development of persons, communities or individual nations, but the fourth pillar, learning to live together, is of a different, more global nature: its omission may result in the annihilation of all educational, cultural, health and developmental efforts through war, terrorism, deterioration of resources, pandemics, etc.

The theme for which the UNESCO convened from 5 to 8 September 2001 in Geneva the 46th session of the International Conference on Education (ICE), organized by the UNESCO's International Bureau of Education, was "Education for All for Learning to Live Together: Contents and Learning Strategies—Problems and Solutions".

The ICE brought together over 600 participants from 127 countries, including, in particular 80 ministers and 10 vice-ministers of education as well as representatives of inter-governmental and non-governmental organizations. The themes of ICE are very relevant all over the world with regard to the necessity and complexity of living together as well as to the role and limitations of education in this respect.

This book, Learning to Live Together, is in four volumes, namely, Volume 1: International Conference on Learning to Live Together, Volume 2: Globalization and Living Together, Volume 3: Curriculum for Learning to Live Together, and Volume 4:

Science Education for the Contemporary Society. This multi-volume book will make all the partners of education aware of the entire spectrum of learning to live together and involve them in making the 'learning to live together' a reality.

I am very much grateful to Ms. Cecilia Braslavsky, Director of the UNESCO's International Bureau of Education and Secretary-General of the 46th Session of the International Conference on Education for her kind co-operation in this academic endeavor. I am thankful to Mr. John Fox, Head of the Publications Unit of UNESCO-IBE for according me the permission to reproduce the material from various documents that appeared in this book. I am thankful to all the contributors and editors of various documents incorporated in this book. I am also thankful to the UNESCO's International Bureau of Education, UNESCO, Indian Ministry of Human Resource Development, Indian Central Board of Secondary Education, Ministry of Education of Cuba, Caribbean Network of Educational Innovation for Development, Organization of Ibero-American States, The Oman National Commission for UNESCO, UNESCO-Principal Regional Office for Asia and the Pacific, Thailand Ministry of Education, and The Chinese National Commission for UNESCO.

Sai Soudha **Dr. D.B. Rao**
D-43, S.V.N. Colony
Guntur-522 006
Andhra Pradesh
India

CONTENTS

Part—1

Education for All for Learning to Live Together: Contents and Learning Strategies—Problems and Solutions

* Pre-conference documents of the 46th session of the International Conference on Education © International Bureau of Education.

International Conference on Education for all for Learning to Live Together: Contents and Learning Strategies—Problems and Solutions

This document is a starting point whose priority aim is to "pioneer" the work of the International Conference on Education. It particularly strives to take on board what has already been achieved and the need to take further steps within a process of dialogue, commitment and action by national and international actors whose three fundamental references are: the Dakar Forum Action Plan, the Report of the International Commission on Education for the Twenty-First Century and the Jomtien World Conference on Education for All.

It is therefore in a spirit of an exchange of information, dialogue, debate, expression of opinion (even controversial) and enrichment of thinking that the reader is invited to take this reference document.

Introduction

The theme of the forty-sixth session of the International Conference on Education (ICE) was decided at the thirtieth session of UNESCO's General Conference and was expressed as follows: "Within the context of the four pillars of education as defined in the Delors Report—particularly "learning to live together"—the Conference will examine, more precisely, how to enable each learner to master the knowledge, skills and attitudes necessary for the intellectual and moral development of individuals and society." This theme is an integral part of the research and promotion of better alternatives for a quality education for all throughout life and across all the activities in which humans are involved.

Its background is the overview document of the forty-sixth ICE (ED/BIE/CONFINTED 46/5), drafted with the help of a working group of the IBE Council and approved at the forty-seventh Council Session. This draws on a wide range of documentation, reports of meetings, programmes, projects and educational practices brought together by UNESCO, and more precisely by the IBE's INNODATA and BRIDGE Projects. It has also benefited from the messages of ministers and the contributions of many researchers, decision-makers at various levels and educators, who have participated in the Netforum, between March and June 2001. It has also been enriched—in a still preliminary way—by the first National Reports received during the preparatory phase of the ICE.[1]

Moreover, this document is indissociable from the proposed workshop documents (ED/BIE/CONFINTED 46/4) for the six workshops organized during the ICE. The ICE itself will be an opportunity to gain a greater understanding of how to analyze problems, ideas and practices so that all may find the best solutions to make progress in local, national and international educational dialogue and action of learning more successfully to live together.

In dealing with the theme: "Education For All For Learning To Live Together: Contents and Learning Strategies—Problems and Solutions", the forty-sixth session of the ICE wishes, through wide-ranging and open political dialogue, to make a contribution to thinking in this field so as to advance the development of more relevant learning, whose aim is the achievement of all human rights as well as human development.[2]

Throughout the world, the themes dealt with during this session are very topical. Education leaders are aware of the existence of the complex and varied problems of living together and of the limits of education in this respect.

What emerges from the majority of National Report drawn up for the forty-sixth session of the ICE, with different emphases according to each situation, is that living together raises many questions. On the one hand, education leaders tell of new trends and their influence, such as: globalization, democratic progress, the existence of economies operating at different speeds and social disruption, marginalization and violence, the desire to belong to the world and at the same time to strengthen each distinct identity. They also mention the challenges of participating in the knowledge society and the opportunities offered by new information and communication technologies. On the other hand, they propose major innovations in syllabuses, methodologies and learning situations, as well as more open and wide-ranging policies for teaching languages, scientific literacy and the use of new technologies, citizenship training and education in a larger context, both from the viewpoint of content as well as that of practices in school life.

These perspectives reveal that learning remains a source of hope as a human right, whose achievement will make a contribution to other rights and human development, for which the ability to live together is an unavoidable condition.

Meeting this challenge is the major issue for the planet as a whole at the start of the twenty-first century. To do so, we need to make progress in our understanding of the challenge itself, its significance and its specificities in the context of current trends of development, of solutions in the making, and perspectives for promoting and improving them.

I. TOWARDS A CONCEPT OF LEARNIN TO LIVE TOGETHER

The search for harmony is an old aspiration. Sometimes, it is fulfilled, but the history of humanity shows how difficult it is to satisfy this desire for any length of time or to any extent. It is not possible to conclude that this difficulty is only due to shortcomings in education. Yet, it is possible to state that it has a role to play in helping to overcome it.

At the start of the twenty-first century, there seems to be general agreement on the fact that Learning to Live Together also entails *"wishing and knowing how to live together"*.

Wishing and knowing how to live together entails knowledge, as intolerance and rejection are often borne of fear which in turn feeds on ignorance on the one hand, and on untolerable injustices in terms of access to human rights and development, on the other hand.

It is therefore necessary to learn to discover and get to know other peoples, generations, genders, social classes and groups of people, their cultures, needs, aspirations, sufferings, religions, traditions and motivations. To be able to do so also requires learning to know oneself better, acknowledging our own strengths and weaknesses.

One must also have and experience the right to information, knowledge and methodologies to learn throughout life and in the context of all of life's experiences. This involves a basic education which guarantees both skills, in terms of the systems of codes, communication and research, organization and analysis of information on the environment, technologies, society, as well as spiritual expressions in all their forms.

But the intellectual dimension is not enough in itself. The possibilities and difficulties of Learning to Live Together also have an effect on affectivity and the emotional life.

Wishing and knowing how to live together involves affectivity and the emotions which, combined with relevant knowledge, can build values, attitudes, behaviours which we know are not part of an individual's natural baggage. In this way, one must learn self-respect and self-esteem which are at the root of any possible acceptance of others, of respect and empathy for them to be capable of solidarity. It is self-respect and self-esteem which bring about listening, dialogue, the non-violent resolution of conflicts and cooperation rather than confrontation.

Learning to Live Together is part of the "construction of meaning" for the type of education which children and teenagers feel they need. Wishing and knowing how to live together is both a personal and social challenge which needs to be developed by, including the renewal of the idea of the general goods, the rules of life in society, the rights and responsibilities of all. *Wishing and knowing how to live together involves the ability to "work together"*, to carry out joint projects to improve day-to-day existence and build a better future together.

But the very idea of living together itself changes with time and in different cultures, as does the learning required to be capable of doing so and necessary forms of education for its promotion. Consequently, the question being raised at the start of the twenty-first century is to know what are the specifities es of the current environment in the face of the challenge of Learning to Live Together, to what extent is current education able to meet its task and in which directions are ongoing changes moving and which are desirable for the future.

Over recent decades, for example, there have been major changes in the perception we have of the right to education.[3] Whereas the Universal Declaration of Human Rights states that everyone has the right to education. The Declaration adopted at the World Conference on Education for All at Jomtien (1944) states that every person—child, youth and adult—shall be able to benefit from a basic education which meets their basic learning needs. Ten years on, the Dakar Forum stressed the challenge of developing "quality education for all". What are the basic learning needs for Learning to Live Together at the start of the twenty-first century? What kind of education will meet these needs? What are we doing to improve them?

II. BASIC LEARNING NEEDS FOR LIVING TOGETHER IN THE FACE OF GLOBALIZATION

Learning to Live Together in the twenty-first century needs to be developed in a world characterized by a number of increasing interdependency. One of the concepts used to define this interdependency is that of globalization, of which some of the most significant characteristics are economic globalization, the emergence of democratic government, the rise of a new economy alongside its precursors accompanied by a worsening of social inequalities, change in cultural landscapes, and the dynamism of the sciences and technologies.

Economic globalization is the most visible symbol of these interdependencies. There are those who highlight its potentially positive effects: access to markets without frontiers, an increase in trade, an increase in capital, etc. Others stress the accompanying risks: the dominance of the economic over the political, widening of the gap between rich and poor, weakening of the regulatory role of the State in the area of public policies (education, social, health, etc.) and difficulties for civil society, even though it may be very active, to find replacement, particularly in the poorest sectors.

These processors of globalization are not entirely new. They have been in motion for several centuries. But what defines them in their current state is their extremely rapid pace of expansion and their consequences both objective and subjective, that is the "subjects", people in their daily lives and their deepest feelings. These are the characteristics which have brought globalization in recent years to the fore, and have led to some symbolic events and violent classes between its supporters and its opponents.

Clearly, we are witnessing, in all societies, the emergence and spread of a sentiment of anxiety as regards the future. Globalization is both a source of hope and uncertainty, whether in the field of work, social security, or culture, since the mechanisms likely to master economic, political and cultural interdependence through building strong personal feelings of belonging and security are not in place. We are witnessing the growth of societies at risk and of an "anxious majority" with increasingly inward-looking attitudes, yet which calls for "globalization with a human face".

Building such a "globalization with a human face" will only be possible if we also globalize the will and ability to live together more successfully by capitalizing on its opportunities and by seeking to eliminate its risks.

The impact of globalization on basic learning needs and on instructional possibilities lead to various reflections. These reflections suggest the hypothesis that there are some learning needs for living together more successfully shared by different cultural and social contexts.

> The first learning need for living together more successfully is developing the ability to take on board rapid changes in all areas of human activities: political, economic and social, cultural, scientific and technological.

From this general need, it is possible to identify other learning needs for living together more successfully: some are more closely linked to social participation: others concern participation in the learning society and its interdependencies. Both broad discussion units of the forty-sixth session of the ICE and both major debates will provide the opportunity to intensify the exchanges and analyses of the problems and solutions to meet these needs.

1. Learning needs for living together and social participation

Contemporary society is characterized by, among others, the emergence of democratic systems and by fundamental socio-economic and cultural changes involving the challenges of renewing the concepts and commitments in terms of citizenship, social cohesion and tension between strengthening both world culture and local cultures.

From the emergence of democratic government to a renewed citizenship

Quantitatively, democracy has made enormous advances over recent decades. "The number of States whose leaders have been elected according to party systems and multiple candidatures has increased from 22 in 1950 to 119 in 2000".[4] The creation of democratic governance has generated enormous expectation. But although the creation of a system for popular participation in decision making is a necessary first step, it is only one facet of building democracy. Democracy is also measured by the way in which it operates and by its ability to contribute to creating conditions which enable equitable participation in human development.

Democracy consists of a certain number of fundamental elements, including: respect for the dignity of all human beings, their right to have an influence on institutional, social, professional and political life; the Rule of Law; holding of free elections: freedom of opinion and expression and dialogue between citizens, social partners, political parties, the State and civil society.

Democratic functioning is based on individual behaviour. Democracy involves the right to become a citizen and the possibility of widening areas of citizenship. However, this democratic functioning is also based on collective behaviour and democracy also consists of the process of participation in institutions, including in educational institutions, according to the rights, responsibilities and abilities of all men and women. These forms of expression are an integral part of the economic, social and cultural realities and specificities of every people—its tradition and its history—and change frequently. Democratization and the condition of citizenship are thus processes which have to be learnt from the earliest of ages and throughout life. They are never irrevocably definitive nor are they fully satisfactory conditions. "Old democracies", for instance, are often apathetic, disinterested and inward-looking.

Youth from very diverse societies seem to waver between disenchantment for politics and dynamism in the associative and public way they intervene in social, cultural and religious movements which attract a growing number of them, institutions and increasingly diverse people.

> The second learning need for living together is developing the ability to became a citizen through participating in political life and in public institutions in the broad sense of the term, and to reinviting them.

Concern over an education in democratic citizenship is increasingly present in all education systems.

Some decades ago, when the relationships between democracy, citizenship and education were being sought, the first was exclusively related to learning institutional forms of public regulation. In this context, the learning challenges essentially consisted of training electors, representatives and civil servants of a State of Law.

In current conditions, ambitions with regard to educational contributions to citizenship are growing. So that known forms of democratic participation and new forms of engagement strengthen it, discover new ways of institutionalization and became established in the appropriate spaces, people need to have the appropriate knowledge, abilities and values to do this, which call for devoting more time to their training and to developing new concepts. What can and must learning do? How can it exploit the fact that school is a privileged environment, where everybody spends a number of years and contributes to forming a "micro-society"?

Possibilities and limits of learning for social cohesion is the face of wars, violence and inequalities.

Democratic progress has not always been successful in establishing or maintaining peace. Peace, the end of discrimination of all kinds and social cohesion do not come about naturally and definitively. One needs to prevent, mitigate and cure the worst causes, namely: unemployment, poverty, exclusion, discrimination, marginalization and violence of all kinds.

During the nineties, there were over 150 armed conflicts.[5] Although war has always been a tragedy in itself, those which have impacted on our time have some distinctive characteristics. It is above all internal conflicts, with nationalist, ethnic or religious connotations, whose victims are first and foremost civilian populations.

According to UN statistics, 90 per cent of the victims of current conflicts in the world are civilians, of which a large proportion are women and children. More than two million children have been killed, millions of others wounded or disabled for life, 12 million left to their own devices after losing their homes, in the last decade alone. Children and the young often pay a particularly heavy price, not only as victims, but also as actors, "volunteers" or enlisted by force. UN estimates that there are at least 300,000 children in the world who take part in armed conflicts. Girls are also enlisted. They sometimes account for 25 to 35 per cent of recruits.

Military life does not only cause immediate destruction, it also jeopardizes a possible return to civilian life. Unsustainable burdens, malnutrition, appalling sanitary conditions, diseases (including AIDS), wounds and impairment greatly undermine their future. Witnesses and sometimes actors in atrocities, they are traumatized for life and their re-education is long and difficult.

Humanity is directly concerned by such war situations in general and the condition of children in particular, not only because it is "immoral that adults want children to make war for them and that there is just no excuse, nor acceptable argument to arm children", but above all because they reveal a profound crisis of values, as much on the local, as national or international level.

But war is not the only form of violence prevalent.

Violence is also caused by unjust and unacceptable inequalities. According to reports by UNDP, inequalities between poor and rich countries and individuals have grown in unprecedented proportions. The ratio between the income of the richest and poorest countries was approximately 3:1 in 1820, 35:1 in 1950, 44:1 in 1973, and finally 72:1 in 1992. The gap between the rich and the poor is also growing within many countries. In some countries of the North, it has grown by more than 16 per cent. Economic growth is stagnating where the population is on the rise, with quite serious consequence on the possibilities for distributing available social wealth. A new concept has appeared in industrialized countries: that of "new inequalities" or "new poverty", which affects social groups who until recently were not affected and which have been called the "working poor". In countries considered as rich, this new category of people who live below the poverty line can be up to 20 per cent of the population. Several social classes are involved, but the phenomenon particularly affects immigrant populations. When urban concentration is added to the equation, the risk of possible escalation in violence rise.

A FUNDAMENTAL ELEMENT TO TAKE INTO CONSIDERATION IN THE CONSEQUENCES OF GLOBALIZATION IS THAT OF MIGRATION

As a whole, "the number of long-term international migrants has never stopped growing. According to the UN Population Division, only 75 million people fitted this definition in 1965; it was 84 million in 1975 and 105 million in 1985. In 1990, the last year for which there are detailed international statistics, it reached an estimated 120 million. On examining data from some countries of immigration, there is evidence that there has been a steady rise in international migrations during the nineties. As of the year 2000, there were an estimated 150 million international migrants."[6] The growing diversity of international migrations—whether of workers or refugees, asylum seekers and displaced persons—has had far-reaching economic, demographic, health and social consequences. The effects of migrations take many forms and can be positive and negative. They contribute to a greater cultural diversity expressed, for instance, in gastronomy, entertainment and sports. However, community tensions can occur when migrants and local inhabitants of the host country find themselves at the centre of a growing phenomenon of urbanization, which leads to the creation and development of an overpopulated megalopolis which is split up according to the social class or the origin of its inhabitants, where the living conditions become very difficult and where ghettoes, homes for the poor, violence and exclusion can grow.

Violence in the form of discrimination based on race, gender and religion is ubiquitous. For instance, in some countries unemployment rates for the coloured adult population are much higher than that of the adult population. Worldwide, women occupy only 14 per cent of parliamentary seats. Religious minorities are confronted by physical aggression on the part of extremist groups.

It has been estimated that, worldwide, one woman in three has been the victim of violence on the part of their partner and that approximately 1.2 million women and young women under the age of 18 are forcibly sent abroad into prostitution.

It is therefore necessary to highlight the fact that Learning to Live Together means understanding the need to belong, for respect and cohesion and adhering to this, which at the same time rejecting social polarization discrimination and violence.

As regards the need to ensure social cohesion, the onus very specifically falls on the rich, as much in terms of countries, communities or individuals. The fight against poverty also concerns those who benefit most from our common wealth, who wish and learn to live together to preserve peace and their own capacity for self-development.

THE AIDS EPIDEMIC

In Africa and, increasingly in South Asia, the difficulties to overcome are multiplied the HIV/Aids epidemic. In the worst affected African countries, it has been forecast that 10 per cent of teachers will die over the course of years to come. During the same timeframe and in the same countries, those orphaned by HIV/Aids will account for more than 20 per cent of all school-age children. The epidemic is likely to drastically reduce school attendance of girls, forced to stay at home to care for the sick. There is a tendency to explain that HIV/Aids is spreading due to the lack of information on contraception methods, but it also needs to be stressed that it is spreading due to a lack of the capacity to live together: to care for and respect oneself, to better respect others. This should be a central aspect of orientation of preventive education, today in the fight against HIV/Aids and tomorrow for better health and a better quality of life for all.

Furthermore, although ignorance, poverty or human distress often provide fertile ground for conflicts, it cannot be forgotten that the political or military "war lords", are rarely illiterate. This is true for inventors, dealers and manufacturers of increasingly sophisticated and light-weight arms which are therefore better suited to child soldiers. What purpose has education, up to higher educations, served in such cases? History has shown that most of the time same intellectuals assume a large part of the responsibility for conflicts themselves and the general climate in which they breed.

> The third learning need for living together more successfully is the capacity to defend and promote human right for all and in all spheres: the rights to life, liberty and to one's own safety, to work, to health, to one's own well-being and to that of one's family.

Although it seems idealistic to think that this type of situation might be reversed only by changes in the field of education, it remains particularly desirable, in this context, do design educational structures and processes which, at least, attempt to offer equivalent training possibilities, given the diversity of starting points for individuals.

It can also be asked how for education itself has contributed to promote propaganda, to feed intolerance and to stoke up hatred. The results of certain studies on school textbooks in a country in which there has been war show, for instance, that the reading book, designed for third grade primary school pupils and used before the conflict, contained 17 per cent of text on the subject of war; out of this, 73 per cent portrayed war positively and only 25 per cent came out against war and for peace. In this same country, the new reading book with post-conflict editing only contained 8 per cent of text on the same subject on but the majority of this was still in favour of war.

Education's role in strengthening social cohesion has its critics. Some believe it is for society as a whole and economic and social policies in particular to deal with such issues. Others, on the contrary, think that although education cannot act alone, the aim of social cohesion is part of schooling's fundamental educational mission and that educational policies can play a crucial role. Education often participates in maintaining social disruption: all the studies show that there is a direct causal link between criterion of birth (and therefore of the socio-economic background) and successful schooling. By selecting at too early a time, by sometimes teaching right from the first years of school an education of failure rather than of success, by not giving sufficient importance to differences in pupil ability (their origin, their culture and their expectations), by omitting to "give meaning" to activities, education leads, even in the most developed countries, to a high rate of failure or abandon, often synonymous with economic and social marginalization and with violent reactions both inside and outside these establishments. Costly corrective and compensatory measures then need to be taken; some, such as "continuation education" are undoubtedly indispensable and beneficial. Yet the fundamental question which still needs to be raised with all the education actors is surely this: what can be done to ensure that all pupils take full advantage the first time round"?

Learning to Live Together in the face of pressure between belonging to a "world culture" and supporting cultural diversity

Dissemination of cultural processes at international level is as important as that of political, economic and social processes.[7] Opinions on the characteristics and impact of the cultural dimension of globalization are often deeply-held and controversial.

Some believe that contemporary developments will necessarily lead to "one market = one language = one culture", to the detriment of diversity. Opening up and building a world culture could bring about the threat of uniformization which would endanger the diversity of cultures and lead to the predominance of one single culture. Others describe the emergence of a world culture as a permanent process of construction and renewal, which is not entirely dominated by the culture of a single country or linguistic area. They appreciate enrichening blends, for instance in the field of music.

Firstly, the development of cultural globalization is linked to the evolution of mass popular culture and comprises both an opportunity for strengthening identification with the world and the risk of dictating cultural content only concerned with commercial gain and far-removed from seeking to live together. It also invovles the risk of forgetting human group practices, expressions and values which are not closely linked to decision centres or which do not have the ability as others to access the "cultural marketpalce". Lastly, it runs the risk of individualistic withdrawal, with consequences on the intolerance and refusal both of the promising aspects of a world culture with growing humanist values and the humanist heritage of other cultures.

It seems that in the present context of vitality of each local and national culture needs to be reconciled with its integration in world culture. The fact that, for instance, the supremacy of English on the Internet is starting to be partly eroded shows a trend in this respect. In 1998, 75 per cent of content on the Internet was in English, which dropped to 60 per cent in 2000. It has been forecast to fall below 50 per cent in 2003.

What is also obvious is that twenty-first century Man will need to be "both rooted in their own culture whilst respective to others". They also need to build a strong identity (dispose of languages, structures, spatial and temporal reference points. codes, values) whilst being open to other cultures.

This requires the construction and deconstruction of both dependence and freedom as regards community, national and global traditions, whilst rediscovering and cultivating shared universal values which would contribute more to wishing and knowing how to live together.

> The fourth learning need for living together more successfully is therefore to know and to be able to strengthen an identity both rooted in the best community, nation and global traditions, whilst carrying out their renewal for the common good.

What can education bring to this field? Frequently education has played a role of cultural homogenization. In some cases, programmes, textbooks and even thinking on school life have been imported regardless of cultural differences. In others, educational proposals only took into consideration local or national cultures. How can these two extremes be avoided?

What role do the media, the family and religious leaders play as educators in the tension between the possibilities or restrictions of belonging to the "would culture" and to the direction in which it is moving, as well as to the enrichment and acceptance of creative diversity?

Essentially, the challenge is to learn to discover that, in the world, there are other people who speak, feel, think and act differently, not only because they belong to other cultures, but also because they share the same need to seek well-being, justice and beauty.

There is also a need to learn to discover that these "others" are not stereotypes of people wholly good or wholly bad, and that they are not part of a homogenous whole. These "others" are human beings in constant interaction with their social, material and symbolic accomplishments. They are part of a culture, in all its grandeur and failings. And this culture changes meaning depending on how and from where it is perceived.

This involves contributing to an education which will give them the tools to find in others parts of themselves, the best of themselves, to provide all men and women with opportunities to build a "multicultural common identity" together which respects diversity.

2. Quality Education for all and participation in the knowledge society to bring about the learning society

The world today is characterized by the emergence and development of a "learning society", in which research, production and access to knowledge is a major challenge.

The question of languages: a strategic dimension to Learning to Live Together

Languages are essential not only for access to information, but also in terms of affective education and working together. Learning languages is therefore a strategic dimension of Learning to Live Together. But there are an increasing number of new and growing demands which interfere with teaching languages.

The defence of the right to community identity, on the one hand, and the presence of the global economy and technology as leading forces with their own laws and rules, on the other, can, in some circumstances have a pincer effect, which fosters a certain type of language teaching which may become devalued. The two arms of the pincer are not in themselves qeustionable.

After years of acculturation of peoples from all over the world and research which shows the importance of the first language in the learning process, its presence in school cannot be ignored. Children learn their first language, very often their mother tongue, within their family and community. They learn through affectivity. Many studies show that access to higher forms of thinking and other languages is helped if this access involves their mother tongue.

Given the undeniable presence of a globalized economy and technology, it would be unrealistic to suggest that people in the twenty-first century should not be able to learn languages which facilitate regional and international communication. Lastly, the challenges of building citizenship through strengthening political, social and legal institutions, which are still national, compel the teaching of national languages.

> The fifth learning need for living together more successfully is access to linguistic diversity based on the ability to better understand one another, to better understand other and to become more able to build a "shared common identity" which includes cultural diversity.

Meeting this need is more difficult in situations of great poverty, where languages often do not even exist in written form and there is less available school time than in more comfortable situations. There is a need to combine school policies with economic, social cultural and, very specifically, language policies.

But intervention in terms of teaching is also required. From this viewpoint: What do we mean when we talk about language teaching? Do we mean reading and writing of signs? In the past, language teaching was above all based on deciphering signs. But there is growing consensus on the need to place emphasis on understanding and the ability to communicate. More precisely, when deciding on education on living together, greater importance needs to given to the fact that learning each language provides a new opportunity for dialogue.

Moreover, at a time of learning throughout life, is it indispensable to teach all the required languages during the first years of basic education?

When the teaching of languages, especially the mother tongue and national language, combine pleasure and emotion, reason and personal, community, national and world memories, it makes a great contribution to Learning to Live Together. Children, the young and adults who can use language to resolve conflicts can avoid using force. Those in favour of peace, justice and the truth need the ability to develop stronger arguments, in which language plays a central role alongside scientific knowledge and modern information means.

The question of sciences: a paradigmatic case of permanent reconstruction

Sciences in general—and life sciences in particular—are evolving at a rapid pace. Being "scientifically literate" seems to be becoming an absolute necessity in our age, to better understand, respect and master the relationships with the planet of which humans are a part.

A scientific education adopted to the twenty-first century is discovering that it has to comes to terms with some new and more complex issues.

Knowledge—and more precisely science and technology-related knowledge—is updated at an increasingly rapid pace: in one generation, and even less in some fields, knowledge becomes obsolete. At the same time, the world and science are becoming more and more complex and relations between the various disciplines more and more interdependent.

Scientific discoveries and technologies have direct consequences for some basic aspects of people's daily life such as health, food or reproduction. They also directly impact economic output and distribution as well as the possibilities of sustainable development through atmospheric pollution, the greenhouse effect, waste-related issues, the supply of water, etc.

Developments in science and technology, which bring hope and progress but are equally a source of concern, have a more ethical dimension than before (assisted reproduction, genetic modification of plants, animals and even human beings, increasing sophistication of arms—"clean bombs"—and their use—"surgical strikes"—).

> The sixth learning need for living together more successfully is to be able to access knowledge—including know-how—and to evaluate the impact of scientific progress on the environment, our daily lives at community, national and world level.

Today, science is a reality which affects everyone and which raises a fundamental problem for education. What do people need to be able to participate in a more enlightened way in debates and decisions whose main challenge can be stated as: what is humanity's place in all this?

Traditionally, school has often ignored scientific literacy and has attempted to pass on "learning products". There was a need to pass on rather academic knowledge, which was considered as true for all of the learners' lives, organized within a discipline framework itself considered as stable.

How can scientific literacy by achieved in the context of learning for all? How is it possible to build a strong social conscience with such an imperative? How can teaching sciences be made interesting and meaningful for learners and educators?

The growth of information and communication technologies: possibilities and limits

The revolution in communications paved the way for new "expert systems" for transmitting and accessing information, which are often more efficient at carrying out this task than educational system and schools. It is therefore vital that educational institutions examine the risks and opportunities that such new expert systems present.

Information and communication technologies (ICTs) may bring huge potential for improving access to and the quality of education: the possibility of overcoming geographic distances, providing self-learning, training teachers, accessing global information in all fields... They are increasingly required in the context of societies where rapid change, the growth in knowledge and the demands of high-level and constantly updated training are in permanent demand. But ICTs widen the gap between those who already have access to education and those who do not. "In poor countries, and under present conditions, technologies may not be affordable; paradoxically, the new reality is that poor countries cannot afford not to fully use them."[8] ICTs, moreover, are an integral part, both in terms of cause and effect, of globalization.

The extent of inequalities as regards access to information flows is huge, not only in terms of what is known as the "digital gap" or "digital divide" (information technology and the Internet) but also in terms of access to older and more traditional means of communication or information such as the telephone or television.

The "digital divide", as regards access, is a reality at world level. Whereas OECD countries in 1998 had access to 490 main telephone lines, 594 televisions and 255 personal computers, including nearly 38 Internet Hosts per 1,000 people, developing countries had access to 58 main telephone lines, 162 televisions and only 0.26 personal computers with Internet hosts per 1,000 people. The situation in East and South Asia (excluding India) and in Sub-Saharan Africa (excluding South Africa) is contrasted further still.[9]

But there are tangible differences as much within regions as within countries and even within developed regions, primarily according to social class, gender and age. For instance, high income populations have access to more than 48 personal computers with Internet hosts per 1,000 people, whereas low income populations have access to only 0.02.[10]

In addition to the purely quantitative or material aspect of access, the digital divide widens the "knowledge divide", particularly as regards access to up-to-date information.

> The seventh need for living together more successfully is to have access to new information and communication technologies and to develop the skills use to them for learning and working together.

Thinking on the relationships between ICTs and education started at the end of the sixties, when it was said there would be a "scientific revolution in teaching" due to "teaching machines". The revolution never happened, for at least two reasons: the limits of the technology at the time and the reactions of still very strong traditional system and what was, still a weak, innovative, teaching method. With the rise in audiovisual technologies and above all of the television, the demise of schooling (and that of the book at the same time) was also predicted. Reality showed that educational systems, as a whole, have more or less stood the test of time, despite massive advertising campaigns for technical equipment and technologies—past or present—have yet to drastically change learning and teaching.

ICTs, for some, may offer the chance of training real learning communities, based on co-operation and interdependnce instead of competition and individualism. Others believe, on the contrary, that ICTs strengthen individualism and restrict socialization in real situations (" I've got loads of friends on the Internet but none at school").

As far as teachers are concerned, studies show that they are proportionally an above-average group in terms of access and personal use of ICTs (particularly the Internet). But they are not a homogenous group. Will new technologies provide the opportunity to sideline schools and teachers? Is this necessary? It would appear very difficult to think of an education in living together more successfully based on machines, even if they are interactive. How can affectivity be taught and socialization developed outside the process of institutionalization and interpersonal relationships?

Furthermore, a whole line of thinking in open on the relations between the alternatives offered by ICTs and the cost of education. Initial costs of installing new technologies are very high, but then the cost of a quality education for all would fall significantly, enabling more equitable access to the learning society.

Learning for All in the Face of Social and Economic Pressure

Learning does not exist in a vacuum, isolated and somehow sheltered from the events of the political, economic and social world. It is confronted with the realities of its local, national and, to an increasing extent, world environment. The Report of the International Commission on Education for the Twenty-First Century identifies some of the tensions to overcome:

- *"the tension between the global and the local:* people need gradually to become world citizens without losing their roots and while continuing to play an active part in the life of their nation and their local community";
- *"the tension between the universal and the individual:* culture is steadily being globalized, but as yet only partially. We cannot ignore the promises of globalization nor its risks, not the least of which is the risk of forgetting the unique character of human beings; it is for them to choose their own future and achieve their full potential within the carefully tended wealth of their traditions and their own culture which, unless we are careful, can be endangered by contemporary developments";
- *the tension between traditional and modernity:* how is it possible to adapt to change without turning one's back on the past, how can autonomy be acquired in complementary with the free development of others and how can scientific progress be assimilated? This is the spirit in which the challenges of the new information technologies must be met";
- *the tension between long-term and short-term considerations;* [...] Public opinion cries out for quick answers and ready solutions, whereas many problems call for a patient, concerted, negotiated strategy of reform. This is precisely the case where education policies are concerned";

- ***the tension between, on the one hand, the need for competition and, on the other, the concern for equality of opportunity.*** This is a classic issue, which has been facing both economic and social policy-makers and educational policy-makers since the beginning of the century. Solutions have sometimes been proposed but they have never stood the test of time. Today, the Commission ventures to claim that the pressures of competition have caused many of those in positions of authority to lose sight of their mission, which is to give each human being the means to take full advantage of every opportunity. This has led us, within the terms of reference of the report, to rethink and update the concept of lifelong education so as to reconcile three forces: competition, which provides incentives; co-operation, which gives strength; and solidarity, which unites";
- ***the tension between the extraordinary expansion of knowledge and human beings' capacity to assimilate it.*** [...] Since there is already increasing pressure on curricula, any clear-sighted reform strategy must involve making choices, providing always that the essential features of a basic education that teachers pupils how to improve their lives through knowledge, through experiment and through the development of their own personal cultures are preserved";
- ***the tension between the spiritual and the material.*** Often without realizing it, the world has a longing, often unexpressed, for an ideal and for values that we shall term 'moral'. It is thus education's noble task to encourage each and every one, acting in accordance with their traditions and convictions and paying full respect to pluralism, to lift their minds and spirits to the plane of the universal and, in some measure, to transcend themselves. It is no exaggeration on the Commission's part to say that the survival of humanity depends thereon".[11]
- lastly, during the forty-fifth session of the International Conference on Education at Geneva, in 1996, Mr. Delors added a further tension, common to many countries and whose importance for education policies is not to be underestimated: ***"the tension between the market economy and the market society"***. There is, according to Mr. Delors, a worrying shift underway since, in such a society, the policy—and therefore the concern for the common good—is relegated to the background, in favour of, in the very short term, shareholders' dividends only, often regardless of medium/long term investments and, above all, of a "social market economy".

The essential question for decision-makers and education leaders is how to exploit the positive aspects of such increasing interdependencies and how to grasp their perverse consequences in order to provide more opportunities for social participation and access to the learning society.

Faced with new realities, learning finds itself directly challenged since, by nature, it is supposed to allow people and society to learn to master their destiny. A tool for developing a sense of belonging at family, local, regional, national and global levels, it should be able to provide everyone with a desire for social cohesion which would foster freedom and creativity, as well as individual training to deal with an increasingly wide range of personal decisions in an environment characterized by doubt and a range of tensions.

Are the learning structures, contents and strategies we are attempting to promote able to meet all of the learning needs for living together more successfully?

III. EDUCATIONAL RESPONSES TO THE BASIC EDUCATIONAL NEEDS FOR LIVING TOGETHER IN THE TWENTY-FIRST CENTURY

Analysis of political, social economic, cultural, scientific and media trends and interdependence help us form our definition of the basic requirements for Learning to Live Together, but it is by examining educational trends that we gain a better understanding and collective appreciation of the means by which they may be maintained.

In the previous pages, we have proposed several approaches to the different ways in which basic learning needs are being shaped by the most visible changes at the beginning of the twenty-first century. We have identified a number of transverse issues, which are linked to the two major debates, to the two principal discussion units and to the six workshops of the ICE's forty-sixth session. In the following pages we will propose a number of hypotheses on the ways in which education is facing upto these requirements. These hypotheses will either be confirmed or subject to review after the Conference.

Quantitative advances for learning to live together

The latest country and world reports on education show that schooling rates have progressed. The estimated total of children without schooling has fallen from 127 million in 1990 to 113 million in 1998. The number of literate adults has increased from 2.7 to 3.3 billion in 1998. Currently global literacy rates are 85 per cent for men and 74 per cent for women.

Despite these advances, late access to schooling, grade repeats and leaving school before a sound educational base is complete—with all the familiar consequences for self-esteem—together with adult illiteracy, continue to be major problem. The number of children without minimal skills for getting by in life remains high and there are an estimated 880 million adults who cannot read or write. In addition, two-thirds of illiterate adults are women, the same proportion as ten year ago.

RESPONSES TO THE EDUCATION NEEDS OF THE YOUNG FOR MORE SUCCESSFUL EARNING TO LIVE TOGETHER

Learning to live together requires more time and a better basic education than has been previously available. The concept of basic education does not equate with that of primary education: it describes the type of education necessary for a better quality of life and lifelong learning in an increasingly complex world replete with both positive opportunities and obstacles. It involves the idea of the "platform" or "foundation", of "soundness" but also of "usefulness for living" and of "motivation for continuing to learn". The number of years provided by traditional primary education is not enough for building this platform. Also, what should we do for young people who have not managed to complete their curricula?

When we refer to a better quality of basic education for the twenty-first century, the option "of doing the same thing for longer" will not do. We must plan for a different education. Which is no longer a simple improved version of what has been inherited from the past. This perspective is particularly important for secondary education.

Institutions operating similar timetables despite their varied situations, overloaded syllabuses, compartmentalized disciplines, mainly focused on encyclopaedic knowledge, forty minute course units and a uniform offer, irrespective of the diversity of students' personalities and their stage in life—for example for young adults—are no longer convincing as adequate learning environments for Learning to Live Together.

The young people themselves are aware of both aspects of the issue. To obtain more basic instruction time, they try to extend their time in the educational system; so that in different regions of the world, they are striving to gain access to secondary education, while showing in different ways their increasing discontent in this respect. Surely the various forms of violence prevalent among them or directed against teaching staff are a clear illustration of this phenomenon?

If we succeed in inventing new basic education models, tailored to the needs of young people and directed towards learning "to live together more successfully", especially in poverty situations, will we not also enhance economic, social and political development and strengthen values? Are there positive lessons to be drawn from this area of innovative experiences and successful educational and intersectorial policies?

For all the advances achieved reducing inequalities, significant educational disparities persist; they mainly concern poor or isolated communities, ethnic minorities, women and girls.

Empirical data indicate that although advances have been very substantial in some countries or regions, in others population growth, rapid changes, wars or other complex socio-economic, political and educational factors have obstructed the education access process.

New problems are also appearing in countries which are not considered poor, such as ghetto-schools for immigrant children or for children from well-off families and a marked trend towards "specific" schooling with the effect that the population's opportunities for encountering the daily life of "different people" are becoming increasingly rare.

Educational integration must be assured so that—while respecting freedom of choice—every person may have opportunities to access enriching educational experiences, among their different peers, for lifelong learning firmly focused, in each individual's personal career, on values of humanity, community and solidarity.

Two questions arise in this respect. The first concerns the external conditions needed for ensuring this integration. According to the first national reports received as part of the preparatory work for the ICE's forty-sixth session, during the 1990s, several countries were especially concerned to implement educational policies and tools aimed at counteracting disadvantageous socio-economic conditions through partnership programmes with communities, provision of low-cost teaching means, creation of 'priority education zones', etc. But it is becoming increasingly apparent that such measures are not sufficient.

The second question concerns the limitations of educational reforms based on the 'institutional architecture' and management methods. The possible impact of these reforms seems to have been overestimated. Research provides examples analysing the limitations of measures aimed at decentralization, unilateral promotion of educational self-management, change in education system study programmes and encouragement of privatisation.

So we need to develop a different educational offer in order to satisfy the learning requirements for living together more successfully.

1. Acknowledging the challenge involved in improving quality of education for learning to live together.

THE DAKAR FORUM AND QUALITY OF EDUCATIONAL FOR ALL

The Dakar Forum and the 2000 Education for All Assessment which preceded it emphasised *'quality education for all'*. In the decade since Jomtien substantial progress has been made in many places regarding access to education—although many inequalities and disparities still exist between regions and countries and also within many countries. But the effects of this quantitative expansion on the development of individuals, communities and societies have fallen far short of the ambitions and objectives set at Jomtien. The Dakar Forum stressed the need for developing quality education, as a component which cannot be separated from access, equality and equity. Many different factors contribute to improving quality; the Dakar Forum identified several, including the importance of, *"organizing the contents of basic education in order to attain society's needs and values":* "The economic, social and other changes sweeping through human society in recent years have forced a reconsideration of what knowledge, skills and values are needed for successful living. The movement toward more open and democratic societies has created a need for learning that goes beyond the academic curriculum and factual knowledge to emphasize problem-solving and open-ended enquiry. The expansion of communication and information technologies necessitates more inter-active and exploratory forms of learning, and the increased pace of change has put a premium on the need to engage in continuous learning over a lifetime. There is also a new urgency to ensure that education at all levels and in all places reinforces a culture of peace, tolerance and respect for human rights."[12]

So the issue is not only to provide an educational offer "for all", but "quality education for all" and also to improve this quality by taking better stock of its complexity.

Quality of education is becoming an increasingly central question on world and national education agendas. It has become very apparent that better access to education unaccompanied by quality learning, was a "hollow victory".

Although a great deal had been said and written about quality of education over recent decades, the concept remains difficult to define. By way of simplification, we can say that some writers place more emphasis on quantitative results while others stress the conditions and learning processes leading to them. The two angles are of course closely linked.

From the perspective of the promotion of human rights and development, quality of education may be defined as the ability to learn to live together, both from the viewpoint of results in terms of acquired skills and willingness for living together, and the conditions and processes which contribute to this acquisition.

Knowing how, being able and wishing to participate, master languages, be scientifically and technologically literate are undoubtedly indicators of quality of education for all for living together more successfully. The investigation field for collection data on these indicators is very complex; research into education finds itself before an immense challenge. It has made it possible to know more concerning acquired skills relative to conceptual learning and concerning a number of representations. But it is proving much more difficult to establish whether education has enabled individuals to acquire skills relating to their emotional side and willpower.

In addition, results from research into acquired skills do not seem to have yet been sufficiently applied, either in learning management processes, schools and other institutions or educational environments or at political decision-making levels.

From the management of learning processes and high-level decision-making viewpoint, the research results are a step forward for enhanced Learning to Live Together. Comparative analyses of available studies from different world regions agree on the importance a number of factors which help to shape a favourable school environment for learning, such as: consensus on the meaning of education, the desire to attain clearly defined and mutually agreed standards and goals, teacher motivation, access to good teaching materials, community and parent participation, planning in partnership, quality of management, staff continuity, placing better teachers in school primary grades, training strategies and maximum exploitation of school time. They also agree on underlining the importance or "a relevant curriculum" of "carefully prepared and co-ordinated syllabuses" and of "dynamic and solid support from the competent educational authority".

Therefore, the curriculum appears to be one of the most important guiding resources which countries can use to ensure "dynamic and solid support from the competent educational authority".

So it is perfectly understandable that questions concerning curricula, are in one form or another, the focus of education thinking, debate and policies worldwide. What should we teach? How do we organise educational processes? How do we reconcile the demands involved in all the educational needs for more successful living together? How do we make progress when there is so much disparity between countries? Over the last decade, some countries have made great progress, others less, and others none.

2. Towards a new curriculum design

At the beginning of the 1980s, study programmes and syllabuses were, in most countries and in a certain sense, meagre, rigid mechanisms. They referred to only some of the elements involved in educational processes and did so by defining rigid methods. As awareness grew of the need to take into account changes in courses and the complexity of education, they were drawn away from the regimentation of pyramidal, hierarchical systems designed to maintain a type of stratification and an outdated socioeconomic, political and cultural ethos.

Reading the first national reports submitted to the forty-sixth session of the ICE, we find that most countries are endeavouring to make progress in the design of a new type of guidance material: the curriculum. The curriculum is conceived both as a contract between what society expects from education and what education managers agree it should offer in terms of teaching contents and educational support, and as a working tool in schools and classrooms. A contract and a tool which are difficult to construct and even more difficult to use creatively to influence school life, but also a contract and a tool which are very influential, for example in the production of teaching material, such as text books, CD-ROMs etc. This influence also extends to the media and to a number of Internet productions.

In the late 1980s and early 1990s, in their enthusiasm to do away with former dictates and to take on board diversity, some new curricula were based on very expansive and at the same time very open ideas. As it turned out only some schools were able to adapt to such systems. According to a number of national reports, the direction "to leave schools free" to choose their contents and teaching methodologies in some cases detrimentally affected schools and education, putting under-trained teachers into more difficult working conditions, without the resources to cope with very complex and rapidly-changing situations.

So the apparent result was not the creativity expected but, in some cases, to a decline in the quality of learning for students. Concerned by some of the said processes—in particular the widening of inequalities—, numerous authorities responsible for designing curricula have decided, in recent years, to implement a new type of curricular structure, which focuses both on creating guides for teachers and students, and on innovative coaching processes intended to facilitate what is increasingly known as "curricular development" in schools.

In this respect, a number of national reports stress the need to move towards curricula capable of fostering the integration, sense of belonging and creativity of each school and each teacher.

These trends are emerging at the same time as a movement towards giving greater legitimacy and better quality to official curricula by modifying their definition processes and their proposals.

3. Rewriting curricula together in order to learn to live together: promoting participation in curricular decisions

Some national reports prepared for ICE's forty-sixth session show that, in recent years, curriculum drafting processes have favoured or tried to combine three basic logics: an expertise logic, a strategic logic and a project logic.

The expertise logic is characterised by the fact the curriculum's preparation is entrusted to experts (or to a single expert) who advance in a very precise direction, without encountering obstacles when preparing the curriculum (or if they do so they can redirect them, either by applying their political or scientific influence). The strategic logic consists in seeking a balance between divergent tends and interests, in contexts in which the curriculum represents a power stake for the actors involved. The project logic emphasises the fact that the actors construct the curriculum gradually, following a drawn out process, based on participatory stages for preparing projects.

The new elaboration mechanisms attempt to take into account several factors, for example the fact that currently a great deal of knowledge is not acquired from school but from other institutions with either physical or symbolic output (media, businesses of all kinds, associative movements, etc.). Their principal focus consists in involving new actors in the curriculum definition processes. Unfortunately, we still have insufficient detail on the characteristics in learning terms of these mechanisms, from all the authorities and professional teams involved.

Those countries which try to combine the expertise, strategic and project logics, through this combination mobilize all the actors involved more effectively and make a more definitive commitment towards achieving results.

Choosing to reform curricula by associating authorities, experts, social partners and teachers is not an easy task. Which tensions need to be overcome? Which strategies put in place? What are its costs? What relation is there between the costs of the various processes and their benefits?

4. Proposals for Learning to Live Together in the new curricula

From a brief analysis of the first national reports prepared for the ICE's forty-sixth session, the new curricular strategies—in the regions where the most promising processes are underway—comprise a series of general features and a set of guidelines specific to each field of knowledge.

On initial examination the general features seem to show a convergence of basic education systems towards training in "skills", identifying a number of basic contents (in the broad sense, namely content-products, content-processes and content-values), setting standards for these contents, seeking out a structure encouraging inter—and multi-disciplinary teaching practices rather than fragmentation, promoting a new form of educational support (including school life methods and characteristics) which places students at the centre of the learning process and accords importance to team work and acknowledgement of student diversity.

Awareness of the accelerating obsolescence of encyclopaedic knowledge and the conviction that it is very important to "learn to learn" are prompting an intense effort to identify and construct "skills". This trend is a reaction following on the realization of the limits of widely spread and still very prevalent traditional teaching methods.

In some countries "skill" is understood as the ability of individuals "to do, think and at the same time to create value"; skills produce the development which motivate the creativity and values bound up with living together, by also fostering those abilities which enable us to deal both with daily life and higher intellectual aptitudes.

The new outlook stresses the need to concentrate on acquiring and mastering learning and know-how defined in terms of skills and key skills, rather than in terms of contents divided up into disciplines organized in a certain number of teaching periods. By concentrating on learning in order to find the best ways of managing teaching, by promoting "learning acquired by doing", we will be in a position give meaning to knowledge and to guide the selection and organization of teaching contents. As one national report puts it, the challenge is to contribute to "transforming information into wisdom and well-being".

The very structure of syllabuses and study programmes would be transformed, together with teaching stages, evaluation and role of teachers, organization of school time and even management of the system. To react against fragmentation of learning, some curricula are encouraging the creation of fields instead of disciplines. For example they purpose to replace history, geography and sociology by a field known as "social sciences". These trends are in some cases opposed, by both recognized educationalists and by teachers, especially at secondary level.

Making learning the focus of curricular recommendations sets up new challenges for teaching methods. Some reports pose the question of how renewal may be implemented and the potential risk of "emptying" educational practices. They also ask how teachers' experience is to be considered, at times connected with possibilities of using traditional teaching methods, which produce a result, albeit limited.

Other changes refer to the way in which each knowledge area should be approached. Many countries have seen progress in the implementation of communicative approach for language teaching, and in bilingual or multilingual teaching. In mathematics, formalist proposals are giving way to contents linked to probability, statistics and to applications of mathematics for forming interpretation models. In social sciences, proposals aimed at the teaching of processes have gained ground, at the expense of simple transmission of ideas. Efforts devoted to initiating boys and girls in multiperspectivity and respectful confrontation of ideas (in particular in social sciences such as history and geography) have been redoubled. The Concept of Scientific Literacy is developing. Environmental perspectives have advanced. In physical education, militaristic methods are being increasingly abandoned in favour of more wide-ranging training (sport for all, health, etc.). In artistic education greater stress is being placed on personal production and creativity given the realization that artistic and creative skills will in the future play a growing role in the individual, social and professional life of persons.

Several national reports recognize that the changes in these ways of approaching knowledge areas seem as difficult to carry out in practice as the four general changes mentioned above.

Curricula, capable of becoming effective guidelines and tools for more successful Learning to Live Together should take into consideration factors concerning education objectives, learning strategies and the criteria for choice and organization of contents, while promoting systematic changes and modernising the framework for each discipline and each level.

In several cases, the processes underway to renew learning proposals take into account innovations introduced in programmes, countries and educational institutions, or even in other regions. Almost all the national reports presented as part of the ICE's preparatory work refer to "good practices". But they also refer to the difficulties encountered in promoting changes which affect all schools and their relations with the media, families and society in general. The forty-sixth session of the ICE will provide the opportunity to examine a number of these "good practices" and to reflect on their conditions for success, their problems and their transferability.

5. Progress and obstacles in school life for Learning to Live Together

A wide range of actors and sectors involved in education are increasingly questioning the slowness, difficulties and limited character of large-scale changes in education. Some of the ideas, concepts and practices which are beginning to influence education for learning more successfully to live together are not at all new. They date back several decades or even a century: interest and motivation, the activity of the student, primacy of learning over teaching, group work, individualization of learning, co-operative work, the role of the teacher as a mediator of knowledge rather than as a simple transmitter, etc. How has it happened that it has taken so long to introduce changes of this type? Why have commitments made not been carried through to their conclusion more often?

To answer these questions, several hypotheses may be advanced: insufficient financial resources, absence of political concern for the importance of educational changes, apathy and disinterest on the part of teachers or, conversely, lack of emphasis on their key role in educational systems and, consequently, in any effort to improve the quality of education.

Undoubtedly, factors connected with all the above dimensions, and with others, are present in each situation in which change takes place. Each situation is marked by the "spirit of the time", and also interrelates with other contexts, through mechanisms of interpenetration of ideas and expertise, but is in its turn unique and complex. This is why each situation requires at the same time unique solutions which consider its complexity, make advantage of interpenetration and experiences, without however succumbing to fads or transferring without a critical attitude proposals originating from other contexts.

Each education system and each educational institution constitutes a very complex universe of elements linked by multiple relationship and able, in interaction with their environment, to adapt, evolve, learn and to self-organise. But each education system and each school also present, in their functioning a certain number of specific elements which seem to strongly condition their capacity—or their incapacity—to learn more successfully to live together.

Can we assume that the ability to network within the system, with other partners, with society and with other systems is the key to the various capacities for change? Or is it the capacity of ministries to guide changes and the technical capacities of planners, technicians, educationalists and teachers which make the difference? Are the same factors always involved? Do they affect all the levels in which changes are desired: in the system, in the schools, in the relation between the education system, schools, media and society?

IV. HOW TO MOVE FORWARD IN LEARNING MORE SUCCESSFULLY TO LIVE TOGETHER: SOME SUGGESTIONS FOR BROADENING THE DIALOGUE

Education for all for learning more successfully to live together encounters,—albeit with significant nuances—certain common challenges and the same type of fundamental problems worldwide. Education for who? For what? With which contents, which learning strategies and which teaching methods? With which structures? With which human and financial solutions?

A number of results derived from analysis of education systems have underlined how much, despite the differences due to their geographic location, to their history and their surrounding culture, educational systems resemble each other. Likewise, several researchers have brought to the fore increasingly marked transactional trends, for example in terms of curricula. But are these conscious convergences? Do these convergences have any meaning for learning more successfully to live together in a world where diversity and also inequalities are still very pronounced?

We may also justifiably wonder whether the issue of Learning to Live Together in a world characterised by both increasing interdependence and reaffirmed diversity, has yet found its place on the international agenda. Significantly the

Human Rights 2000 report does not bring up the question of the quality of education for living together more successfully. Would it not be desirable to have a more marked proactive attitude, with a view to taking into account more systematically and more clearly the requirements of an education for living together as a cornerstone of education for all?

There is also the question whether we have sufficient empirical knowledge on the skills which are essential for living together more successfully and on the curriculum characteristics and processes which would allow us to attain this objective.

In the words of the Dakar Framework for Action, "UNESCO will continue its mandated role in co-ordinating FFA partners and maintaining their collaborative momentum". Particular importance is accorded "to the information of the monitoring report from the UNESCO International Institute for Educational Planning (IIEP), the UNESCO International Bureau of Education (IBE), the UNESCO Institute for Education (UIE) and, in particular, UNESCO Institute of Statistics, and inputs from Regional and Sub-regional EFA Forums."[13]

How might the monitoring report be expanded regarding quality of education and in particular contents and teaching support for learning more successfully to live together?

There is still limited data for evaluating how education contributes to a training for living together. There are of course some analyses of students' acquired skills and of the curricula proposed to teachers, but very few are comparative. A priority area of international co-operation could be research into education and its application for the follow-up of processes of change and as a support for education policies.

We have much less information on how curricula are drawn up, put into practice and no their real impact at classroom level. In addition, what research there is concerns almost exclusively the countries of the North, where educational research has a long tradition.

Generally management of knowledge on education, even in developed countries, is far from satisfactory. A recent OECD study points out that for education, research and development costs are about 0.3 per cent of GDP; by way of comparison they from 5 to 7 per cent of sales for pharmacy. This same study also brings to the fore a problem of method. In health and engineering, there is a progression from basic research focused on innovation, applied research which gives it expression, and finally the transfer to the user, to a model in which technique can take precedence over science, in which the user takes part in the design. In education this type of interaction is extremely rare.

Politically, education remains basically a national responsibility; and Dakar Forum reiterated this. However, an important question remains. Is it reasonable for each country to continue, most of time, to advance alone, to seek answer alone, to try out solutions alone, when so many experiences are present elsewhere and the world, while diverse and multiple, is at the same time single world? Is it ethical—and pragmatic—to only globalize trade and problems? Is it not time to put in place a better international strategy allowing us to try to resolve together a number of common problems?

UNESCO's mission consists in simultaneously promoting the universality of certain values and in preserving the diversity of cultures. Should we therefore be considering an "international learning for living together"? As was stressed in the UNCESCO *Prospects* issue on the ICE's forty-sixth session: " We must learn to accept the reality of the different character of others and the fact that it is improbable that they will change by themselves simply to please us. Learning to live with others implies that they have the right to remain others, also from the point of view of choice and organization of learning contents, educational environment and educational supports for succeeding in living together".

But should we not also reaffirm the need to acquire, through education, values which are part of humanity's common heritage? While there is no question of reaching uniform contents or methods, should it not be possible to systematically exchange tested experiences, applied criteria, fertile practice, tools created for curriculum development, in order to help different actors find their own solutions more easily?

Training for development, and especially curriculum implementation is often too abstract and focused on the transmission of information rather than the building of skills.

This training has demonstrated its limitations. How do we change outlook and contribute to training which takes better account of required skills and the experiences of others?

In many different areas numerous actors are involved in promoting education for living together. Reinforcement of partnerships is always to be desired and considered as a solution. What are the conditions for their success? How can we introduce and develop these partnerships?

Political dialogue on issues of education contents, learning strategies and teaching methods is still too frequently limited and above all uninventive in its methodologies, both within each country, and among the world's countries and regions. The succession and even simultaneous holding of international conference may begin to engender weariness and demobilization. How can we use new technologies more effectively to reinforce political dialogue? How can we enrich it by using elements taken from compilation and analysis of innovation processes, whether in everyday school life or in promotion of successful policies for more successful Learning to Live Together?

This forty-sixth session of the ICE could be the point of departure for a reinforced, deepened and renewed dialogue on all these issues crucial for the future of the planet. For while the primary responsibility rest with each of the member states, there is also an international responsibility to improve quality of education for all the world's population.

The challenges of the twenty-fist century are not those of 2020 or 2050, but already those of 2001. So it is important to act now.

REFERENCES

1. Bibliographical references, the list of conferences, meetings and seminars, as well as of those participating in the Netforum, will be jointly published in a document which will be distributed during the ICE. Messages of ministers, programmes, projects and "good practices" may be consulted at the Conference website: (www.ibe.unesco.org).

2. UNDP, *Human Development Report 2000,* Paris, Brussels, De Boeck & Larcier, Départment de De Boeck Université.

3. UNESCO, *World Education Report 2000. The right to education: towards education for all throughout life.* Paris, UNESCO Publishing, 2000.

4. World Forum on Education, Final report, Paris, UNESCO, 2000, p. 32.
5. See UNDP, *2000 World Human Development Report*; International Peace Research Institute, Oslo. *Causes and Dynamics of Conflict Escalation* (Report of a research project), June 1997; Dan Smith and PRIO, *The State of War and Peace Atlas*, New York; Harmondsworth, Penguin, 1997.
6. International Organization for Migration, *The State of Migration in the World in 2000*, Geneva, IOM and UN, 2000, p. 5.
7. Javier Pérez de Cuéllar *et al.*, *Our Creative Diversity*, Paris, UNESCO Publishing, 1996. (Report on the World Commission on Culture and Development).
8. World Education Forum, *Final Report*, Dakar, UNESCO, 2000.
9. UNPD, "Human Rights and Human Development", in: *2000 Human Development Report*, p. 201.
10. *Ibid.*
11. J. Delors *et al.*, *Learning: The Treasure Within*, Paris, UNESCO Publishing and Odile Jacob, 1996, p. 12 onwards. (Report to UNESCO of the International Commission on Education for the Twenty-First Century).
12. World Forum on Education, *Final Report*, Dakar, UNESCO, 2000 p. 20.
13. World Forum on Education, Dakar Framework for Education, "Education For All: meeting our collective commitments". Adopted by the World Forum on Education, Dakar (Senegal), 26-28 April 2000, p. 10 point 19.

2

Document to Assist the Discussions during the Workshops of the International Conference of Education

WORKSHOP 1

CITIZENSHIP EDUCATION: LEARNING AT SCHOOL AND IN SOCIETY

Introduction

The concept and implications of citizenship are dependent on culture and context. The term itself is connected to the tradition of a Western democratical concept. However, the substance is based on common global values about ways of living together, as expressed in the Declaration of Human Rights.

Different dimensions and levels of citizenship

Citizenship is carried out in different contexts and holds different interrelated dimensions: politically, socially, culturally. *Political* citizenship is fundamentally identified as a set of constitutional rights and obligations, but also implies active engagement in and a sense of responsibility towards society and the common good. The *social* dimension is based on a common socio-cultural context and refers to the mutual relations between the members of the community and the way they live together. The *cultural* dimension refers to the awareness of a common cultural heritage that defines the community in relation to the surrounding society.

Citizenship, as well, is found and intended at different levels: locally, nationally, regionally and globally.

This fact feeds potential conflict for the individual due to a clash between the interests within the different communities. This could, for example, be the case, if a cultural community is in opposition to the general political community in connection with the creation of a nation state or a political region. The challenge of multicultural coexistence is more evident than ever. The common problems of our earth—the environment, war, ineqality—require a sense of global citizenship, but the obstacles are numerous and can only be met by the furthering of leaning to live together.

- How is it possible to learn to handle the different types of citizenship?
- How is it possible to learn to handle possible conflicts between the different contexts, dimensions and levels?
- Are any groups excluded from participating in the community—be it local, national, international or global?
- How can possible marginalisation be counteracted?
- How is it possible to support a global consciousness that underlines for instance that environmental questions can be perceived locally, but also must be understood globally?

Responsibility for development of citizenship as an individual and a collective concern.

The motivation for developing democracy and constituting citizenship has often been linked to an expectation of development of economical welfare. In established democracies active citizenship is seen as a central concept and ideal in a societal development aiming at "a better life for all" and active citizens form a part of the social, cultural and economical capital of the communities. Learning to Live Together or civic education is a corner stone in development of citizenship. It is both an individual concern and a collective concern. *Individual* because it presupposes competencies that enables in individual to relate expediently to his or her surroundings. *Collective* both because it is a goal of the society to develop citizenship and because citizenship is implemented through collective actions.

It is of great importance to emphasize that citizenship implies both rights and obligations. The citizen has civil, political and social rights. However, citizenship cannot be understood as a private life style but rather as a way of living together in which you share the responsibility for the society. You cannot, as a citizen, focus on what is better for yourself. You must estimate the interests of the community: the common good. Citizenship is via involvement, participation and the ability of dealing with disagreement the best tool to create understanding of the dilemmas encompassed in the ideal: the common good.

- To which extent is it a task for the school system or for the private upbringing to educate us for living together?
- Where are the limits for the school system—as a tool for the state—in the effort of influencing the learners?
- Should there be coherence in the goals for the education between the individual/the family/the community and the school system?
- How is it at international and global level possible to encourage that the responsibility of Learning to Live Together is accepted by the communities at local and national level?

The learning of citizenship through formal, non-formal and informal contexts

Citizenship is being developed through the acquisition of knowledge, skills and values. Learning take place in different learning environments. According to the type of society, economical structure and culture there is a large diversity in the way the citizens are being qualified. To learn how to maintain a work function is in some societies a concern for the educational system, in other societies it is mainly learned within the context of the family or the local community. The acquisition of basic skills (reading, writing and arithmetic) is being considered a responsibility for the school, even in areas where there is little or no possibility to implement the ideals.

The knowledge that form the basis for values and attitudes is being learned more diffusely in a complex pattern encompassing the three forms of learning: formal, non-formal and informal, that supplement and reflect each other.

Formal education takes place within the educational institutions, it is structured, aimed at well defined age groups and leads to recognised certification of skills and qualifications.

Non-formal education learning is taking place outside formal educational institutions, it is structured and supplementing a formal educational system. It does not lead to formalised certification, but possibly to factual recognition of skill and qualifications, for example in workplace or in trade unions. But it also takes place in leisure time activities, e.g. sports and music, in nursery schools, in evening schools and in voluntary association etc.

Informal learning is incidental, it takes place alongside formal and non-formal learning as an unintended or 'hidden' curriculum. It is possibly not even recognised by the learner—it forms tacit knowledge and the learning goes on all the time in the family, in the media, in religious life, in the street or at the market.

The individual's learning opportunities are directly dependent upon the settings and curricula that school and community make available. Education for citizenship should not be seen isolated within the formal education systems. When it comes to the ability of living together learning is deeply anchored in the social practice within the family, on the job, associations etc. where non-formal and informal learning environments are being found. They contain elements that furthers citizenship due to their connection to practice of everyday life—be it organised, intended learning or unconscious learning. The social practice unites the cultural, social and political aspects of citizenship.

The concept of 'lifewide learning' reflects a wideness in the learning uniting the experiences and recognitions of everyday life with the learning taking place in the more intended form. The concept of 'lifewide learning' stresses that learning can be of any form and take place any time throughout life and therefore also includes the concept of lifelong learning. By that formal, non-formal and informal learning are put into an organic connection with each other, thus complementing one another. Within the formal educational systems citizenship is therefore developed both through formal and informal curricula as well as through democratic participation in the learning environment.

- In which ways can the formal school system further responsibility and active participation of the learner?
- In which non-formal and informal learning environments can it be furthered?
- What is the significance of different role models—peers, parents and educators?
- Do co-operation/networks between different formal and informal learning environments further citizenships?

The practice of citizenship: increasing critical participation

To learn citizenship and democracy in practice implies active participation, critical judgement as well as an actual possibility to influence on or to be affected by the situation. The learning environment inviting the learners to express themselves and their views and an open and friendly school and classroom climate has proven essential in the formal educational system.

It is crucial that practices of living together is supported by knowledge of human and social sciences in order to understand different cultures, traditions and societies and learn from the history. This implies understanding of one-self in the light of one's history and culture, and in the light of that of others. Knowledge of this kind makes an important difference to our attitudes and actions.

Skills and competencies for practising citizenship is a matter for generally speaking all subjects, as Learning to Live Together must be seen from all aspects of life. We learn aspects of differences of cultures and different images of the world in both mathematics, physics, in the field of languages etc. Civic education deals with moral issues that take place in all parts of life. Thus civic education can be seen as a cross-curricular matter related to all subjects and to no one in particular.

It is vital for the learning and participation that the curriculum is relevant to the learner and builds upon the learners actual knowledge and experiences. The content of subjects like civics, history, geography, biology etc. must ideal with issues of relevance, and sometimes taboos, to put the learners in a position to meet the challenges of the changing demands of society. We are entitled to know our own historical and cultural background—even though it contains dark sides—in order to understand ourselves as a part of it and at the same time to be able to act towards the future Learning based as debate and discussion, critical thinking, familiarity with problems and ability of solving problems will enable learners to involve their own creativity in bridging the gap between education and everyday life. Thus, the role of the educator must be reconsidered. It is a challenge for the educator to keep the authority intact and at the same time ensure an open class climate and provide access to different sources of knowledge.

- How can education in citizenship be included in the concrete subjects taught in school?
- Is it necessary to develop specific subjects or a particular interdisciplinary approach?
- Which elements should be included?
- Which role must the educator play? What kind of authority should the educator exercise?
- Which pedagogical frameworks furthers the understanding of citizenship?
- Which requirements must be made to the teaching materials?

Assessment of learning to live together should include qualitative dimensions

Civic education is about practices and attitudes to common human values like moral responsibility, avoiding marginalisation and exclusion, furthering participation and sustainability. It could be considered essential to be able to assess practices of and attitudes towards citizenship, civic education and learning to live together. How is it possible to measure such dimensions and qualities in education?

We need some supplementary indicators—of a more quantitative substance—to be able to see the development in educational methods, in learning strategic, in contents etc. The following questions pinpoint a number of issues to be included in the supplementary indicators for analysing citizenship educations in the different school system and societies.

It is of vital significance to emphasize these and other relevant issues for assessing practices and attitudes towards citizenship and civic education. It is not evident, though, how to measure practices and attitudes. When trying to compare different educational systems in order to discuss new ways and new pedagogical frameworks, a quantitative approach is the most dominating, but more qualitative approaches could also be essential.

- How and to which extent is a global perspective an integrated part of the education at different levels?
- How and to which extent is a cross-cultural aspect an integrated part of the educations at different levels?
- How and to which extent is active participation being practiced in education?
- How and to which extent is moral responsibility present in attitudes and practices?
- To which extent does the educational system make a conscious effort to prevent marginalisation and exclusion?
- How and to which extent is sustainability practised as part of the educations at different levels?

WORKSHOP 2

SOCIAL EXCLUSION AND VIOLENCE: EDUCATION FOR SOCIAL COHESION

Introduction

Compulsory, standardized, public schooling has traditionally been a central vehicle for the creation and consolidation of a common sense of belonging, identity and social cohesion within the model of the nation-state. Yet, schooling sometimes fails in this essential function, reflecting and even exacerbating existing social and political tensions and conflicts. The efficiency of formal education as an instrument of integration and social cohesion is thus being increasingly called into question as rapid structural changes associated with the multiple processes of globalization weaken traditional models of social, political and economic organization. Concerns with the deterioration of social cohesion are most often related to observed increases in inequalities in income distribution both within and across countries, increasing social exclusion and an apparent rise in the incidence of violence in all societies. Indeed, the combination of socio-economic disparities, social exclusion, and easily politicized cultural factors such as ethnicity, language, and religion, often lead to violence and to the breakdown of social cohesion. It may be argued that manifestations of physical violence are indicative of the breakdown of social bonds associated with the multiple processes of social exclusion at the cultural, political and economic levels. *How do the content and processes of formal education relate to processes of social exclusion and to patterns of violence associated with the breakdown of social cohesion?* After the necessary epistemological clarifications of the terms 'social exclusion' and 'violence', this paper sketches out some ideas relative to the causes and consequences of diverse manifestations of violence from the perspective of their dialectical links with the content and process of education. More specifically, the discussion will be organized around the following clusters of guiding questions:

- What *consequences* does societal violence have on education? How much of, and in what ways does societal violence translate into the learning experience in schools? In what way is societal violence related to school-based violence?
- To what extent and how does formal education act as a *catalyst* or precipitating factor in the process of social disintegration and the outbreak of violence?
- How can education effectively contribute to strengthening or rebuilding social cohesion and to *preventing* violence at school and in society at large?

Epistemological issues

Any attempt at identifying and exploring these interrelations, however, requires clear definitions of what is meant by such terms as social exclusion and violence. As a multidimensional notion conceived to capture the various political, social and economic processes of social disadvantage, the notion of social exclusion may be seen as encompassing a series of exclusions that may be economic in nature (exclusion from employment, means of production, land.....), political (denial of security, representation, citizenship, rights....), or social (exclusion from education, health services, or housing...). Although the concept of social exclusion clearly overlaps with more conventional conceptual frameworks such as poverty, inequality, and deprivation, educational exclusion is often seen as being central to other processes of exclusion. As far as violence is concerned, a wide definition covers a wide array of human interactions ranging from the use or the threat of the use of force, to armed conflict and even to other forms of denial of human dignity associated with extreme poverty. In addition to the crucial distinction between the overt forms of violence of gangs and armed struggles, and covert forms of structural and symbolic violence, it is necessary to distinguish between patterns of violence at interpersonal and inter-group levels.

Armed conflict and educational exclusion

A significant number of countries in which declining school enrolments were observed during the 1980s were already recognized as being affected by chronic political instability, insecurity and armed conflict (Berstecher and Carr-Hill, 1990). During the past decade of international effects toward EFA. Political violence was progressively recognized as an "emerging challenge" (Amman, 1996) and the "needs of (...) children and adult affected by armed conflict" came to figure in the Dakar Framework for Action (2000).

- What proportion of the reported 113,000,000 school-age children who are not enrolled in school reside in areas affected by political violence and armed conflict?
- Are education for all goals attainable given the apparent spread in internal armed conflicts around the world?
- To what extent have educational interventions been successfully integrated into the design of emergency relief responses? What types of partnerships have proved effective in responding to educational needs of populations in conflict-affected areas?

Education as a catalyst for violence

What role does education play as a catalyst to the multiple socio-economic, cultural and political processes that may be associated with the weakening and general breakdown of social cohesion and the outbreak of violence? The growing recognition that education is often a target of political violence, has prompted a greater concern with the ways in which the content and process of education may actually contribute to precipitate the outbreak and development of violent conflict. The Dakar thematic assessment study on education in emergencies (2000) recognized that "weaknesses in education structures and content may have contributed to civil conflict" and that "an education system that reinforces social fissures can represent a dangerous source of conflict".

- What case studies have been researched to establish causal links between the content and the processes of education and internal strife?

Education and social exclusion

How does formal education contribute to the multiple social processes of seclusion at the economic, political and cultural levels? Authoritarian education systems, for example, are explicit instruments of political domination and exclusion often based on discrimination and denial of cultural and political rights. However, education systems also contribute to perpetuating economic disparities and inequalities as is illustrated by the continued denial of access to basic education for a significant proportion of children in many regions of the world. The recent shift in focus from supply to demand-side considerations when dealing with the issue of access to basic education, indicates that issues pertaining both to household poverty and to the quality of education have become key to understanding why over 110 million primary school-age children in the developing world continue to be denied access to school. Exclusion from education may be seen as "part of an intricate web of human rights violations" (Dakar, 2000), and the widespread and increasing failure of schooling to ensure socio-economic integration of individuals and groups to the labour market, to adequate levels of consumption, for example, questions the efficiency of formal education as an instrument both of redistribution and of upward mobility.

- How does the failure of schooling in its integrative and distributive functions contribute to undermine the legitimacy of existing power structures?

School-based violence

Although not new, the phenomenon of school-based violence points to a social problem of increasing importance in countries both in the North and South as is reflected in the increasing media coverage of this complex phenomenon. Physical and symbolic manifestations of school-based violence are multiple and include bullying between youngsters, intimidation and physical aggression towards teaching personnel, vandalism, racketeering, and sexual violence. Any serious attempt to understand this particular category of violence goes well beyond the confines of the school itself to include wider social considerations relative to the strains of economic crisis and transition, cultural alienation and social exclusion. The symbolic and cultural violence of schooling largely reproduce and perpetuate structural inequalities. Learners from minority, immigrant, and other possible disadvantaged groups are often less-well equipped to adjust to the normative and social demands of school culture that is anchored in middle class values. In this perspective, anti-school violence may be interpreted as a response to the violence of the educational process itself and to the inability of schooling to adapt to changes in the wider social environment. Finally, school-based violence may also be a reflection of violence in wider society, as active or passive participation of youth in domestic and political violence has direct repercussions on their learning experience in school.

- Is not each manifestation of school-based violence different in nature thus calling for differential responses?
- How do the frustrations of unfulfilled expectations among youth confronted with unemployment, failed cultural integration and disintegration of popular cultures translate into violence at school?
- To what extent is violence towards school by youth a product of, and a response to, the school experience

and the symbolic violence imposed on students belonging to minority and other disadvantaged groups?

Education for social cohesion

While the content and unintended consequences of schooling may act as precipitating factors in the breakdown of social cohesion and in the possible outbreak of violence, formal education also has an important role to play in strengthening or rebuilding social cohesion. Differences must, however, be made between educational systems as victimise of social and political violence and the potential role of education in the reproduction of exclusion and social and political violence.

- What successful strategies exist in terms of curriculum design and educational management that overcome the tensions inherent to contradictory aims such as selection and competitiveness versus egalitarianism, standardization versus respect for particularisms, centralization versus decentralization, nation-building versus universalism?
- What conditions are necessary for education systems to minimize, if not prevent, wider social and political tensions?
- How can education contribute to rebuilding social cohesion, particularly in the wake of violent civil conflict and confrontation?

In the case of school-based violence, measures taken to prevent or reduce the incidence of violence are commonly articulated around information, prevention, and repression. In addition to the necessary external controls of repressive measures, preventing violence aims to develop a commitment to norms and values embedded in social networks may inhibit the recourse to violent behaviour.

- To what extent can the schooling system alone be expected to be effective in preventing or reducing the incidence of school-based violence?
- What successful strategies have been documented in differing contexts of school violence?
- What types of partnerships have obtained positive results?

WORKSHOP 3

COMMON VALUES, CULTURAL DIVERSITY AND EDUCATION: WHAT AND HOW TO TEACH?

Introduction

To learn to live together in today's increasingly globalized world, we need to develop the skills and values to live in a very diverse cultural and linguistic environment. Once we may have seen such diversity as a feature of far-off societies, but it has now become part of our own daily life. Right in our own homes our lives are being touched by otherness, by different cultures. The new information technologies that are becoming omnipresent put us in touch with people of different cultures and languages, while our home countries are welcoming immigrants and travellers from other regions and countries. So, to learn to live together in the twenty-first century, we need to recognize this new situation and accept our creative diversity, while also overcoming the last vetiges of colonialism.

This situation poses serious challenges for education, in particular because of its different focus, and these challenges are particularly significant when the time comes to decide what is to be taught and how.

Shaping curricula to suit more diverse environments

In speaking of learning and curricular contents, one thing that must be recognized is that there is no one true vision of the world and of things in general. Rather, our viewpoints are strongly imbued with the particular cultural traditions to which we belong and with the knowledge and experience we acquired in childhood when we learned to be part of our family and of our immediate local community, apprehending the world in the context of that belonging and learning to encode and decode it in a certain way and from a certain standpoint. Thus, an Aymara-speaking boy or girl from the South American Andes learns that any past action lies in front of him or her, since these are experiences already lived through and which are "visible" to the child; future events, in contrast, lie behind us, since they have yet to happen, and so are "invisible". If schools ignore the

Aymara child's spatio-temporal perceptions when dealing with those aspects of the curriculum that pertain to time and space, that is, if teachers adhere strictly to the Western world's traditional conception of time and space, they run the risk, in the first place, of a communication breakdown, since the two parties have different understanding of the same phenomena, and, in the second place, they reject a way of knowledge that is equally valid and just as much a product of human experience. Accordingly, the learners' self-image and self-esteem, instead of being strengthened, are eroded.

The example of the Aymara children is only one of many we could cite, among rural people and city-dwellers alike, around the world.

- How can we reconcile, and/or forge links between, the interests and expectations of specific cultural communities and those of other communities which, for socio-historical reasons, have become national or mainstream cultures?
- How might the curricular presentation of content from the Western tradition be combined or made compatible with content from other cultural traditions?

An openness to diversity

Just as the relevance of the school curriculum to children from minority group, whether they are indigenous people or not, appears questionable, the curriculum also now needs to be rethought for the whole population. As was suggested at the beginning of this paper, there is a growing need to develop the necessary skills to learn to see one's own knowledge as culturally conditioned, to discover that there are other ways of thinking and apprehending the world, different from one's own, and that there is no longer any room for one absolute truth. Only in this way, by displaying openness and flexibility towards what is different and unknown, will the learners of the twenty-first century be able to discover the wealth in diversity and so become individuals with the ability to live in harmony with those of other origins. To that end, it will be necessary to provide that conditions for new, less hierarchical, more respectful relations between teachers and students, in particular when the teachers do not belong to the same cultural and linguistic community as their students.

In this new context, education will need to adopt an intercultural point of view in which, together with the reaffirmation of one's own culture, openness, curiosity and understanding towards others is promoted, so that people will grow up with a variety of tools on which they can lay their hands at various purposes. In addition to the affirmation of one's own knowledge, these tools should include the positive affirmation of the relations between persons, societies, cultures and languages.

- Can we conceive of diversity in school and in the curriculum in terms of complementarity rather than opposition?
- What might be the characteristics of a new school curriculum based on the knowledge of one's own culture but providing the opportunity to discover and assimilate knowledge from other cultural traditions? Would such a formula be appropriate only for learners from minority or marginal groups, or would it also be of benefit to members of the majority culture?
- Would the suggested complementarity overcome ethnocentric tendencies of the curriculum and hence prepare learners to live in a world that is increasingly interconnected and interdependent?
- What difficulties or conflicts could arise as a result of possible differences in outlook, interests and expectations between older and younger students?
- What role should members of each minority community play in the management and development of the education programme? Should they be at the teacher's side in the classroom to present local knowledge, thus bringing the community to the school, or should the school instead reach out of the community in search of knowledge that traditionally is not taught in school?

Diversity and the development of new shared values

An intercultural focus such as we propose would have to begin by promoting the development of values directly related to the issue dealt with here: the diversity we should be sharing with all human beings. A development of this type should ultimately lead us to conceive of diversity as wealth and the promise of harmonious relations between men and women of different cultures and languages. Among the values that all men and women of the twenty-first century should share are tolerance of what is different or unfamiliar, respect for others, and the will to seek unity in diversity. In the last analysis, what is needed is a change of attitude and disposition towards what is different, together with acceptance of plurality as something valuable in itself.

- What values could be considered common or shared if our goal is international understanding and respect between members of different societies and cultures?
- How could plurality be made intrinsically valuable? What can be done, in schools and in society, to achieve this goal?
- Can schools by themselves achieve these objectives, or must their efforts be supplemented by those of there stakeholders in society?

Interculturality and learning

This intercultural focus would include the realization that learning, to be meaningful, must build on learners' existing skills, knowledge and experience, so that they can sensitively and intelligently build bridges between their own vision and knowledge and those of others, and seek complementarity rather than opposition. It should also be remembered, however, that there is not just one way of learning and that learning can also be influenced by specific cultural practices of the socio-historical group to which the learners belong. For that reason, various forms and styles of learning need to be identified and characterized.

Aspects such as those just mentioned are particularly pertinent to the pedagogical style chosen by teachers, and have far-reaching implications for initial and ongoing faculty training as well as for the standards governing the relationship between the school and the community in which it is located. Today more than ever this last aspect calls for special attention if what is sought is, on the one hand, a kind of learning that is rooted in its culture and society and, on the other, a school and kind of education that meet local communities, specific and general needs.

New and more creative links must also be forged between the school and the community. For example, assistance networks need to be organized to provide support for teachers, work and to enable the various members of the community to foster a more comprehensive education for their children. In this way, teachers could seek support from various professionals (artists, physicians, technicians, farmers, etc.) and get them involved in the learners, education, whether the latter are children, young people or adults.

- How, using this same approach—taking creative advantage of diversity—could we go beyond curriculum content to deal with other aspects such as methodology and evaluation?
- Could one not also, for example, take advantage of the variety of situations and opportunities afforded by every classroom to foster cooperative learning and genuine evaluation?
- Starting today, what skills would teachers need to develop in order to bring forth a new type of education that would take account of our "creative diversity" and enable us "to learn to live together"?
- What new skills do school administrators, teachers, the community and learners need to develop to manage the conflicts that will inevitably arise as we eagerly seek complementarity between vision that are often contradictory and historically separate?

Diversity in teaching and openness to the community

Finally, in order to make plurality a value and permanently instill curiosity and respect for otherness and difference in all members of the future society, we need to go beyond school as an institution. In that effort, we need to involve other stakeholders in society and embark on ways of learning and teaching which, in different spaces and from different points of view, will promote the development of values and skills such as we have described in this paper. People living today and future generations need to develop this attitude of openness to others and the ability to process new ways of interpreting and transforming reality. Only then will they be prepared to live in the increasingly interconnected and interdependent world that globalization has brought us.

- Will the school of the twenty-first century be able to make itself over into meeting-point and forum for these different world visions, or will it be necessary to design alternative, non-school spaces where our creative diversity can be optimally processed?
- How can we overcome our societies' arbitrariness and lack of values and build a world based on shared values, one such value being the diversity that has always characterized humankind?

WORKSHOP 4

LANGUAGE(S) TEACHING AND LEARNING STRATEGIES FOR UNDERSTANDING AND COMMUNICATION

Introduction

Language is a major factor in human society because it is fundamental in forming and expressing both individual and group identities. Language is also a tool of prime importance in communication among individuals and between groups. When considering ways of improving 'learning to live togehter', the role that language and language communication play in human interaction, should certainly be considered.

Mankind has developed thousands of languages, most of which are mutually unintelligible. Most individuals are born into and brought up in only one language. The languages of many individuals, however, have no or only a very small place in education; many nations and communities are plurilingual and, therefore, have grave internal communication problems to cope with; and, on the international level, the languages of both the majority of nations and their individuals have no status.

Although for each individual person his or her own language is a unique and priceless commodity—not in the least because of the close connection between language and culture—and although diversity of languages and cultures may be equally highly priced, it is this diversity that at the same time causes grave problems, both for individual persons and for societies.

There are language communication problems at a variety of levels and in a variety of domains. When it comes to 'learning to live together better', the most pressing problem-areas from a politician's point of view may well be: (1) the different 'status' of languages, nationally and internationally, (2) the importance of language(s) of instruction, (3) foreign language(s) instruction, and (4) language learning and teaching strategies. In each of these areas important developments may be observed and many political decision wait to be taken.

Linguistic diversity: conflicts and consequences

Only very few countries are truly monolingual; some 'pretend' to be monolingual—usually by ignoring or underplaying the existence of minority languages. Multilingual countries display great variety in their choice of the language(s) for national intercourse. Often a choice is made for one language, occasionally two or three. The language chosen is usually spoken by a majority of the population. But, sometimes either one of the few 'international' languages—often English—or a more neutral, 'lingua franca', are adopted.

Whatever the choice, the main objective is usually to achieve improvement of the national communication process by reducing and simplifying linguistic variety. Often, a related but not always articulated objective is building a more homogeneous nation and fostering the national identity. Reduction of cultural variety is often the result.

The promotion of a language—nationally and internationally—has a lot to do with exercising economic and political power. Even if it is common to defend the view that no one should be treated as inferior because of the (minority) status of his or her language, it is a fact that in a multilingual communicative setting mother-tongue speakers of the preferred language are at an advantage over the non-native of that language. However, the national or international supremacy of a language is usually the outcome and not the cause of economic and political power. It is generally acknowledged that 'simplification' of multilingual situations—nationally or internationally—, however much accepted as a necessity, holds a threat of both linguistic and cultural uniformity. On the other hand, fighting the loss of diversity by (over-)stressing the need for diversity, may lead to intolerance and rejection of other cultures. Moreover, statements regarding the dramatic loss of linguistic and cultural variety are not always devoid of rhetorical exaggeration. However closely linked language and culture are, partial or—for that matter—full loss of a language does not necessarily mean a concomitant loss of (part of) the related culture; as every individual language has the capacity to express various (sub-)cultures, so every individual (sub-)cultures may be expressed in different languages. In a similar way, the monopoly position that a language may be accorded in international and global communication, may be overrated 'Global' languages are normally used for specific purposes only, in a restricted number of language use situations. And the more they are used by speakers of more and more different language backgrounds, the more the non-natives will take over the 'ownership' of the particular, 'global', brand of the language in question. The natives, consequently, will feel themselves 'disowned' and to them the—more and more culturally 'neutral'—new brand of their language may eventually appear as foreign as it may do to the non-native users of it.

The preceding insight is of particular relevance, it seems, for the internal communication policy of international organizations, like the European Union, in which many different languages come together. If for practical reasons a drastic restriction of the number of working languages is required, a reduction to just one implies less undue preference to the native speakers of that language than is often supposed.

- Which are the consequences related to 'learning to live together' that can be drawn from the diverse 'status' of languages?

The importance of the language(s) of instruction

A major factor determining success at school is the language in which the instruction is given. In general, it is a serious handicap to be instructed in another language than one's own. But because of a great many and a variety of reasons and circumstances instruction through the mother-tongue is very often not made available to pupils. Sometimes this is inevitable, sometimes it is by design. Languages may be so small but there are no instructional materials and/or teachers to give instruction in them. In other cases pupils, indigenous and/or immigrant, may have to be made acquainted quickly with the national language surrounding them, to make sure that they will be able to function as citizens of the country. Where there is a choice, in primary education one most profitably starts with instruction through the mother-tongue; then, instruction in the non-native national language is introduced by its side; and, eventually, all instruction is given in the national language only. Pupils being instructed in a non-native language right from the start usually fall behind seriously.

However, there are other reasons for deliberately abstaining from using the mother-tongue. It may be that for all further and higher education pupils will later have to go to educational institutes abroad. Or, instruction is given in a major foreign language because one hopes to achieve a higher level of command in it, more quickly than is habitual.

To sum up, there is no model that may be advocated as the best for all countries. Each set of circumstances requires its own assessment, which may lead to different outcomes.

- Which considerations should be taken in the choice of the languages(s) of instruction in basic education related to relevant factors holding for that specific situation?
- Is there a particular model which can be the best for all educational systems?

Controversial foreign language(s) instruction

The many factors that are at play in foreign language(s) policy, also in their combination, differ widely from country to country. There is the internal language situation of the country, but also of the country in its relations with neighbouring countries and with the international organisations in which it participates. There are factors which may be called socio-economic (e.g. foreign trade), and also many psychological and educational factors. As with 'language(s) of instruction' issue, there is not one model-solution applicable to all situations for foreign language(s) instruction.

What each individual country must do, is to define its own needs pattern in the first place and, on the basis of that, develop a proper foreign language learning and teaching policy. Needs are of various types (individual vs. societal, but also commercial vs. cultural) and the weighting of these categories one against the other is a separate issue; should one attach greater weight to the commercial needs of the country and its citizens than to the cultural needs? Under all circumstances, the point of departure should be the needs of the country itself. No foreign language should be taught 'for its own sake', for instance to prevent it from becoming extinct.

The policy drawn up eventually should encompass all sectors—'school' and 'out-of-school'—of the educational spectrum. Each sector may have to play its own specific role. Too often the burden of teaching has been laid in secondary education. In recent years, more and more primary education has been given a role to play. That in itself is a good thing. But, too often, it seems, early learning of foreign languages is put forward as an argument in cases, where one is just desperately looking for a panacea for failing secondary school teaching.

Finally, since a large part of the vast effort in foreign language teaching is necessitated by the requirements of international mobility of students and workers, there is also a growing need for measuring language competence—and for quality assurance—across languages and across national educational systems. In the search for ways to get to grips with the problems of international comparisons, in the Europeans context important progress has recently been made by the development of the Common European Framework and the European Language Portfolio.

- Which elements should be taken into consideration when an individual country is to define, in the first place, its own needs pattern (related to foreign language teaching) and, on this basis, develop a proper foreign language learning and teaching policy?

- What are the advantages of a national teaching policy for foreign language that encompass not just secondary education but all educational sectors?
- What are the conditions requried for full international mobility related to systems of certification and of quality assurance for foreign language competence?

Language learning and teaching strategies

Learners are involved most directly at the level of the classroom. In first language teaching (FLT) and foreign or second language teaching (SLT) the three main didactic questions to be tackled are: (a) what to teach?; (b) how to teach? and (c) how to assess learner achievements? Hardly ever are 'best practices' available that are applicable to all actual FLT or SLT situations. Much, therefore, depends on the qualifications of the body of teachers. Teachers must be properly trained and, among other things, should have a minimum of insight into the latest state of affairs in didactic theory. SLT-teachers should have a high level of competence in the language they have to teach. However, native language competence in itself does not qualify a person to teach the language to non-natives. A few points are of special interest with regard to each of the three questions.

What to teach? 'Needs' are of prime importance in particular when the final objectives of the curriculum are defined. 'Psychological' and 'educational' factors play their part especially when the day-to-day classroom programme has to be given shape. They are factors that, for example, have to do with characteristics of the learner, of the teacher, of the subject matter and of the educational context. Some of the issues that have a special educational policy relevance are the following.

As with other school subjects, not everything that is in the final objectives of the curriculum does actually have to be learned or taught in school. Often learners will pick up part of the programme objectives outside of school. A case in point is the influence of the omnipresence in Dutch society of the English language, which alleviates the school's task to a great extent.

In second language competence the objectives to be achieved for the (sub-skills of reading, writing, listening and speaking, are not necessarily the same. There has even been a long tradition of teaching reading only. Of late, 'partial competences' have again come under consideration, especially in countries where SLT claims large proportions of curricular time. In the latest curricular changes in Dutch general secondary education the obligation for English, French and German as final examination subjects for all pupils has been re-instituted. However, the obligation for the latter two languages concerns only the reading competence. Such a restriction of the final objectives to one skill should not lead to the misconception that the other skills cannot have a place in the classroom at all or that the particular partial competence can and should only be learned and taught through that skill.

How to teach? In SLT the prime concern is the acquisition of competence in the language. Contrary to what may be the case in FLT, an understanding of the structural make-up of the language will normally not be part of the objectives now-a-days. In discussions of the didactics of SLT the contribution that the learning of explicitly formulated rules of grammar can make to the acquisition of the desired competence, has always been—and still is—a moot point. A full and fully automatized command of the underlying rule—system is a prerequisite for high-level performance in a second language. In first language competence such a command seems to be a given thing that comes about in a 'natural' way, without any learning of explicit rules. In SLT there have always been, in one form or another, the opposing theories of the 'grammar-translation' method and the 'direct method'. So much is clear, neither theory can lay claims to universal validly for all learners under all circumstances.

The form that classroom teaching takes, greatly depends both on the characteristics of the learners, the teachers and the subject matter and on their interaction. No specific setting is exactly like any other setting, which means that there is a great deal of variation of 'best practice' in actual teaching. Some principles, however, hold under all circumstances. As a rule, skill acquisition requires a great deal of actual practice by the learners; not the avoidance of mistakes but the attempt at second language communication should be the principal concern. The learners should also be presented with lots of second language material, preferably authentic. The learning tasks set should at all times be challenging; the demands put on the learners should tax them to the utmost.

How to assess learner achievements? Assessment of both on-going learning performance and final achievements is necessary. Procedures, tests and examination formats applied should result in a valid and reliable assessment of the progress made by the learners. In theory, for tests to be valid they do not have to require genuine skill performance—think of the very common multiple-choice format—but the backlash that examination requirements and formats may have both on the learners and on classroom teaching, posses serious problems. Assessment matters should be handed with great care, especially in cases where the body of teachers is not adequately trained or well-informed.

- What are the main objectives of curriculum for the first foreign teaching language that should be guaranteed for all learners? Which strategies can be developed to help schools in this task?
- Can any teaching theory-i.e. 'grammar-translation' method or 'direct method'—claim to universal validity for all learners under all circumstances?
- What are the risks of assessment, seeing that, to be valid, procedures chosen do not have to represent faithfully the skills defined in the objects?

WORKSHOP 5

SCIENTIFIC PROGRESS AND SCIENCE TEACHING: BASIC KNOWLEDGE, INTERDISCIPLINARITY AND ETHICAL PROBLEMS

Introduction

All States recognize the importance of science in training individuals, but also as a driving force for sustainable development in all its aspects, in particular economic, social and ecological. It is therefore all the more urgent that access not be reserved for a small elite but that everyone, the world over, can reach a sufficient level of "scientific literacy".

However, is science education, in terms of its content and its learning methods and strategies, designed and implemented in such a way as satisfactorily to meet a range of challenges:

speed of change, complexity and interdisciplinary, ethical and social factors, citizenship issues?

All the studies that have been done on these subjects tend to show that **there is a significant gap between the scientific education actually provided and the needs of individuals and societies.** Giordan's conclusions are a good statement of the indictment: "*Science teachings as now practised is not producing the results we have a right to expect. Assessments that have been made over the last twenty years and more clearly show this. The knowledge imported is forgotten in a few weeks. The same difficulties are encountered at university level as in kindergarten. What purpose was served by the intervening years of schooling? Nor is this situation the most serious. It is only the visible symptom of a large malaise that is engendered by today's programmes. Science teaching is no longer suited to the society for which it is supposed to be preparing citizens. It burdens the mind with useless detail while keeping students in ignorance of important keys to understanding. It offers no insights into the challenges of the day. It does not introduce students to the ways of reasoning they will need in tomorrow's world. As a result of this mismatch, most young people give up on science. By failing to answer their questions, by treating subjects in the abstract, it generates boredom and kills interest, as is clearly shown by the fact that fewer and fewer questions are asked as the curriculum progresses. What is worse, scientific and technological education is a great contributor to exclusion. Because of the social role imposed on science teaching, many adolescents and young adults see in it only a way of screening them out.*" [Translation.]

Many countries have already undertaken—or are about to undertake—an in-depth reform of scientific and technological education, to resolve such problems as: the inflexibility of science education, the segmentation of content, the lack of applied knowledge, teachers' limited ability to manage change, inadequate teaching methods, the isolation of science from its environment and unsatisfactory evaluation of science education. The strategies adopted may differ from one country to the next, but the choices facing public authorities seem virtually identical.

A number of common factors or converging points of view appear when it comes to the necessary vision of science education reform. Osborne summarizes them as follows: "*Science education should be make up of a 'triumvirate' of knowledge and understanding of scientific content, the scientific method and science as a social undertaking (communities' social practices)."* [Translation.]

By taking this approach, education systems will be able to confront and resolve a number of *problems* concerned both with issues peculiar to the scientific disciplines themselves and with horizontal issues.

Problems to be solved

For the **scientific disciplines** themselves:

— the **scope of disciplines dealt with:** Should this be limited to the exact sciences (physical sciences, life sciences, earth sciences) or take in a wider field, including mathematics, information science and the technological disciplines, human sciences and social sciences?

— **basic knowledge:** What is the basic knowledge requried in the main fields in the discipline and the main teaching levels? How ought these to be defined, organized and evaluated?

— the **impact of science on contemporary societies:** How does the development of science and technology influence the development of our societies? What must one know and be able to do to understand and master this development?

— the **acquisition of methods and modes of reasoning:** A number of intellectual processes are characteristics of, or necessary to, scientific research. They are requried for work on scientific content, but when mastered they can be put to other than scientific uses. Among these processes are, for example: the ability to observe, to compare, to describe, the experimental method, the practice of research (documentary in particular) and criticism of information, and rigour in reasoning. Mastery of all these processes is doubtless desirable, but how can one do without experimental practice and the hypothetico-deductive method?

As regards **horizontal issues:**

— the **question of ethics** is particularly relevant to life sciences and biomedicine. But must it not also extend to issues pertaining to the environment, pollution, wastes, and water resources management?

— the **question of citizenship:** Does the impact of scientific development on societies not bring with it an absolute need to possess a certain store of up-to-date knowledge so that one can understand, relate to and engage in the societal debates directly or indirectly related to these developments?

— the **question of access to and use of ICTs:** In view of the explosive growth of ICTs and their impact on all aspects of economic, social and cultural life through access to communication networks and information sources that were unimaginable even 10 years ago, are ICTs not already a major issue for the educational procees?[1]

Possible solutions

In designing and implementing reforms, **a number of questions** arise: the curriculum and its construction, educational choices, the teacher, the role of the extracurricular sector.

1. **On what should be definition of the curriculum be based?**

   - If what is sought is not exclusion but universal access to scientific literacy, can curricula and programmes continue to be handed down from on high—that is, set by the tertiary sector and academia, which bring pressure to bear on lower levels, as when the ambition was to turn all students into "little scientists"?
   - Who is to determine what basic knowledge is necessary? Is any knowledge universal? Should required knowledge be decided at the national, regional or local level?

2. **Can we, and should we, continue to do "science teaching" in the traditional sense of the term?**

   - Where the goal is to build skills and not to accumulate knowledge that is quickly forgotten or becomes obsolete, what educational choices are required?

- Though there can be no question of abandoning scientific and technical knowledge, should we not seek to inculcate it through a set of intellectual disciplines: documentary research, experimental and systemic processes, verification and cross-referencing of information, and the use of modelling, argument and simulation? Shouldn't we also cast a critical eye on the knowledge being manipulated?

3. **"Inquiry into science, the links between scientific knowledge, culture and society, or between knowledge and values, is just as important as knowledge itself. For example, one may *inquire into the solutions proposed by technology and their limitations." How does transgenic maize constitute progress? Or the mobile phone?* (Giordan).**

- If the goal is to train citizens to debate social issues, shouldn't we first develop open minds that can reflect on themselves and the world and, rather than just solve problems, ask the right questions? Shouldn't we emphasize equally an interest in science and related issues, the desire to learn about these and the motivation to study them?

4. **In that case, does the role of the teacher not undergo considerable changes?**

- How is the teacher to move beyond his or her traditional role of dispenser of knowledge to become a facilitator of learning, a resource person, a catalyst of critical thought and, ultimately, an awakener of consciences and a guardian of ethics? What new skills will the teacher's educational mission require in future?

5. **Finally, we need to think about the role of the extracurricular sector and the educational environment.**

The extracurricular sector is a source of wealth that has so far been underused in science education and, in particular, has not been integrated into a coherent, complementary pedagogical undertaking.

The prime example of this, of course, is the **media** as a whole: the press (periodicals, scholarly and popular non-fiction books) and the audiovisual media (radio, TV, videocassettes, CD-ROMs, multimedia encyclopaedias, etc.) or everything that is accessible online (Internet).

Another example: **associations,** clubs and other groups. Another great source is **resource centres** such as museums, botanical gardens, terrariums, planetariums, observatories or various science parks such as exist in many countries and, increasingly, offer not just exhibitions to visit and things to see but also interactive knowledge-forming activities.

It may also be asked whether it would not be better for schools to be more open to visits by **scientists themselves,** not all of whom are aloof, inaccessible know-it-alls—far from it.

- In general, don't academic institutions—particularly in the sciences—too often still muddle along on their own, without any real connection to their environment, the society around them?
- Finally, societies have hidden stores of traditional knowledge and know-how in a great number of fields (medicine, agronomy, climatology, knowledge of natural perils, psychology, etc.).
- Does the fact that such knowledge may be hard to verify make it a threat to modern science?
- How could such knowledge contribute, not only to the enrichment of the scientific skills of the younger generation, but also to an open and critical approach to such fundamental cultural concepts as "tradition" and "modernity"?

WORKSHOP 6

NARROWING THE GAP BETWEEN THE INFORMATION RICH AND THE INFORMATION POOR: NEW TECHNOLOGIES AND THE FUTURE OF EDUCATION

Introduction

Technology offers enormous potential to improve learning, teaching, access, quality, management and delivery. However, the promise of such potential is still a subject of rigorous debate and testing.

The envisaged role of ICT must be seen within the context of globalization. More and more the elements of globalization (increased movement of people, goods and capital, liberalization of markets, increased pervasiveness of technology) are impacting on how governments are interpreting the 'Education for all' goals, and planning for it. In wanting to implement the goals, many governments are seeing the need for greater equity, quality and efficiency in the education system as the top priority.

As the demand grows for more education with less and less money becoming available to governments to meet the demands, there is a drive to greater efficiency. Technology has traditionally been seen as the promised tool that can enable greater efficiencs in the education system. Today, the area of efficiency is not only seen in the education management and administration, but also in the quality of the learning and teaching process. This workshop, in attempting to address the information and technology divide within the education context, would need to focus on the following and other related issues.

Creating enabling policies to address inequalities related to ICT

The use of ICT within the education and training system is dependent on having access to the information and telecommunication infrastructure within the country.

- Is the ICT policy and regulations supportive of its use within the education and training system?
- Are other policy and regulations within a country hampering the use of ICT within the education system?
- For example, are the import duties restricting the importation of hardware and software necessary for the education system?
- Are there innovative ways of increasing access to ICT infrastructure?
- What type of policy and regulatory framework would best enable ICT infrastructure to be developed and introduced into the education system?

Many myths have emerged about the technology. A classic example of how technology has impacted on the notions of information is to create a divide between the information-rich and information-poor. The issue of the information divide is clearly who is determining what constitutes information rich and what constitutes information poor. At present there is an explosion of information from mainly the developed world.

- Is this divide a reality or a myth?
- Does this imply that the information and knowledge from the developing world does not constitute worthy information and hence the country is information poor?
- Are there policies that can encourage the development, documentation and use of indigenous information and knowledge?

Integrating the people and the technology into the education system

While needing the hardware and software to address the information divide, perhaps the most important requirement is the needs of the 'warmware', the people involved in applying the technology to support the education and training system. This include the learners, educators, education managers, and parents.

- What are the strategies to ensure that the people involved in using ICT to support the education system are involved in the process?
- How can one encourage parents to become involved in the sue of ICT in the home and use this to instill positive values that inform the child and future generations?

The teachers are another vital group within the education and training system that requires support in their efforts to embrace ICT.

- What successful strategies are being employed to encourage teachers to use ICT in the classroom?
- Is the requirement training in ICT or is there a need for other forms of training, e.g. information literacy and management skills, new teaching strategies to include ICT, etc.?

Some would argue that technology is more likely to support and enhance learning in certain subjects. Subjects like science, math, electronics, health and support areas like laboratories and libraries are likely to benefit from the use of ICT.

- Does this statement reflect the reality in developed and developing countries.
- Are the innovative strategies that support or dispute this statement?

Choosing technologies that enhance learning and teaching

The process to make decisions on the need for technology is a difficult one. This, coupled with the wide selection of choices and opinions available to support and deliver learning, has made such decisions more difficult. While noting that personal computers were first introduced into the USA and Canadian secondary school system in 1982 and into the primary school system in 1983, one issue is what is the evidence that it has added value to the education and training system in countries and within institutions.

- Given the wide range of technologies, how does one decide which technologies are worth investing in?
- Is there a need to relook at older technologies such as radio and television and using it more imaginatively than was done earlier?
- Will one type of technology meet the needs of all sectors or should we be selective in the use of appropriate technologies for clearly defined proposes (e.g. radio to bring about non-formal education and the Internet and/or CD ROM for say professional development programmes?
- The investment in the hardware, software and people are costly, but is it worth it?
- What are the education gains that have been made through the introduction of educational technologies?
- How is the technology used in the classroom, the school, and the education system?

Distance Education

All countries face demands for more education either as a part of lifelong education or for more primary-schools places, for the expansion of junior-secondary schools, and for more and better qualified teachers. Several countries have committed themselves to using distance education as one means of addressing these needs.

Distance education can use a range of technologies. For much of the twentieth century it was dominated by print and this remains central to many developing countries distance education efforts. A second wave included extensive use of broadcasting, including an era of large-scale television projects. But today, countries are beginning to use more advanced technologies, like video-conferences for teachers, while comptuer-based technologies have been used in distance education at tertiary level and at times within the school system.

Two words of caution are, however, necessary. First, the more sophisticated and the more interactive the technology, the higher the unit cost is likely to be. Second, the greatest educational problems are often found in the most remote areas, where electricity supplies may be irregular or non-existent, telephones scarce and liens difficult to maintain. In such areas, the servicing of electronic equipment tends to be difficult, costly and slow. Sensible choices between technologies need to reflect both geography and economics.

Economic opportunity, educational demand, and strong political will are necessary for the establishment of distance education. One important problem is to what extent are distance education institutions able to become part of the regular education system and are accepted as such. As for the different types of distance education, most of them spring from different views about the role and functions of the state. There are countries with a tradition which leaves opportunities for non-governmental organizations and the private sector to play a significant role in education. These differences in culture and in organisational structure have a bearing on the audience that can be reached through distance education.

Two main questions are always present in the field of distance education: its outcomes and its cost. Even when there are few reliable figures about distance education costs, the evidence is consistent that, given adequately large numbers, the cost of distance education is likely to compare favourably with those of conventional education, provided the unit cost is per student. Large numbers bring down unit costs but, if we measure in terms of the cost per successful student, it is more difficult to establish the economic case for distance education.

- Which policies and strategies are necessary for the inclusion of distance education into the education and training system?
- What are the main realistic choices between technologies for the establishment of distance education institutions considering economic opportunity and educational demand?

REFERENCE

1. ITC-related questions will be taken up in Workshop 6.

3

General Overview of the Forty-sixth Session of the International Conference on Education

The Context

1. At its 160th session (October 2000), the Executive Board of UNESCO proposed that the Organization's activities should fall under the general theme of "contributing to peace and human development in the era of the globalization of education, science, culture and communication".

2. The proposals by the Director-General, Mr. K. Matsuura, concerning the medium-term strategy for 2002-2007 and the draft programme and budget for 2002-2003 correspond to his wish to focus on those areas were UNESCO can make a difference: access to basic education for all; protecting public service education; fighting against the standardization and impoverishment of educational contents; improving knowledge-sharing; helping bridge the digital divide; protecting and promoting cultural diversity in the face of globalization.[1]

3. The Education for All Movement received a new impetus following the Jomtien Conference in 1990. A policy dialogue took place between various partners going beyond educational authorities, in order to face the challenge of tackling "fundamental learning needs". The conceptual achievements of Jomtien were further developed by the International Commission on Education for the Twenty-first Century, chaired by Jacques Delors, which expressed the needs as four key concepts: "Learning to know, learning to do, learning to be and learning to live together".

4. Ten years after Jomtien, and five years after the report of the Delors Commission, the world situation on Education for All, as established by the Forum on Education for All (Dakar, Senegal, 26-28 April 2000), shows that there has been significant progress in many countries in access. However, the quality of learning and the acquisition of values and skills fall far short of the aspirations and needs of individuals and societies. **Thus, we must intensify exchanges and dialogue on matters concerning the quality of education and particularly aspects which may contribute to finding better solutions for "learning to live together" in its broadest sense.**

5. While pursuing the work undertaken in the context of major conferences and congresses (Adult education, 1997; Higher education, 1998; Technical and vocational education, 1999), UNESCO will grant priority in the field of education during 2002-2003 to basic education for all. The Dakar Forum has recently approved a Framework for Action that represents the commitment of the partners for education for all. Beyond recalling the national responsibility, the need for regional co-operation and new opportunities for financing, three fundamental characteristics of the Framework are: the recognition of education as a human right, reinforcing the call for the struggle against social exclusion via education; and the call to "improve all aspects of the quality of education and ensuring excellece".[2]

General introduction

Some ten years ago, in a book with a rather provocative title *Educate or perish*[3] Joseph Ki-Zerbo, a historian, thinker and teacher, described the dilemma of modern Africa (not to mention the rest of the world): there is no alternative but 'to educate' and to do so rapidly and properly. *'Our entry into the Third Millennium is marked by upheavals that call into question the certainties of yesteryear and will therefore oblige societies to reinvent the meaning of life, and to create the foundations of a world ready for action.*[4] We have now entered the third millennium. Is not the dilemma still valid? *'Is it better to live together in the twenty-first century or to vanish?'* Is this not the vital stake over which an education of quality should aim to triumph?

The theme adopted for the forty-sixth session of the ICE places the matter of 'living together' at the centre of the debate. There are in each of UNESCO's Member States.

- **Problems:** the first step is to identify them, to accept them and to share them;
- but there are also **solutions** to share them, to spread knowledge about the best practices, and to evaluate the possibility of transferring them into other contexts represent an indispensable second step.

The main **objectives** of the forty-sixth session of the ICE will be:

- to examine and to discuss in an open and profound manner those aspects connected with **the quality of education for all;**
- to launch **a new phase of international dialogue** on the contents, methods and structures of teaching.

In terms of **outcomes** (or of products), the Conference should enable us:

- to identify **controversial questions** or the **lessons to be drawn** on the subject of educational contents and methods;
- to adopt the **Conclusions** and **proposals for action** allowing the **policy dialogue to be intensified** and **the methodology to be enriched,** so as to progressively develop individual and, above all, communal competencies enabling us to adopt short-and long-term perspectives on these questions, thanks to greater efficiency, effectiveness and participation on the part of high-level decision-makers.

With its **theme** reflecting those of the recent World Forum on Education, and the responsibility of honouring the commitments undertaken in Dakar, the Conference is also intended to be **innovatory in its organization and dynamic** (see below). The context of UNESCO gives it **a global dimension** and it should draw the greatest possible benefit from what represents its real worth: **the inter-regional dimension,** by which means each region may benefit from the experience of the others.

The context

Education remains everywhere an unfinished and on-going enterprise, where successes exist side-by-side with failures and shortcomings. This was clearly evident at the Dakar Forum that, moreover, made this realization into a sort of leitmotif: "*even though a great deal of progress has been made towards achieving EFA, much remains to be done*".

Ten observations and considerations

1. **Globalization, of which a world-wide economic market is the most obvious symbol, has had a powerful impact on both developed and developing countries.** But reality has shown us repeatedly that a true debate and dialogue on these matters is extremely difficult and often ends up in confrontation. Some point out the potentially positive effects of globalization: access to all markets without frontiers, an increase in trade, an increase in capital, etc. Others stress the accompanying risks collapse of markets, the dominance of the economic over the political, widening of the breach between rich and poor, replacement of a 'market economy' by a 'markets society', weakening of the regulatory role of the State in the area of public policies (education, social, health, etc.)
2. **Globalization,** in principle a synonym of openness, **could present the world with the threat of cultural uniformity,** which would threaten the diversity of cultures or would drive people, according to some studies, to affirm their identity and their nationality, with the inevitable intolerance and rejection of other cultures. The same is true of languages, of whose importance we are aware in the creation and expression of an individual's cultural identity and its value as a tool for communication, numerous studies have shown that there is a positive correlation between spoken language/teaching language and success at school. Finally, we are aware of the important role that language and an awareness of other languages could play in the fields of international understanding, dialogue and learning 'to live together better'.
3. **Quantitatively, democracy has made enormous advances over recent decades.** "*The number of States whose leaders have been elected according to the party system and multiple candidatures has increased from 22 in 1950 to 119 in 2000.*"[5] Significant progress has been recorded in several countries and regions in terms of equity and quality, thanks to the

greater involvement of communities and citizens in the educational process. But, in numerous places, democracy has not always resulted in a better quality of education, in greater social solidarity and in 'living together better'; education has suffered too, since there is often a close connection between school breakdown and social breakdown.

4. **But, advances in democracy have not always resulted in establishing or in maintaining peace either.** Over recent years, many countries on all continents have been the victims of vicious civil wars, ethnic conflict, racism, xenophobia and violence. There is a further cause for concern: a high level of schooling among the population has not contributed to avoiding these disasters. *"The Institute for Research on Peace of Oslo (IRPO), which surveys conflicts, has shown that the 1990s witnessed numerous armed conflicts (ninety-eight between January 1990 and December 1996) and that these were mainly civil wars, and not wars between States.' According to IRPO, typically a certain number of elements were always present, such as: poverty, soil improverishment, lack of access to fresh water, a high population density, a heavy external debt, a decline in export revenues, etc.*[6] It therefore seems that the poorest countries are also the most vulnerable. But reality also shows us that conflicts and open warfare also exist in economically advanced regions or countries possessing a free democratic system.

5. **The rapid development of ITCs over the last few years** (Internet and multimedia did not figure in the Jomtien discussions just ten years ago!) **also presents education with new and extremely complex problems.** ITCs could represent an enormous potential to improve access to education and enrich its quality: overcoming geographical distance, providing self-education, teacher training, access to all kinds of information on a planetary scale. Increasingly, these technologies appear to be a necessity in the context of societies where rapid changes, the growth of knowledge and the requirement of a high level of education constantly brought up to date become a constant obligation. But the ITCs widen the gap between those who already have access to education and those who do not.

'In poor countries, and in the present circumstances, these technologies may not be available; but paradoxically, the new reality for these countries is that they cannot allow themselves not to be full-time users!'[7]

6. **Science in general and the life sciences in particular are evolving extremely rapidly.** To be 'scientifically literate' has become an absolute necessity in our day and age, not only to acquire working methods and to develop one's thinking, but particularly to understand and to master the world around us. Furthermore, scientific progress has an increasingly evident ethical dimension and often presents society with a choice, on which the citizens are increasingly required to pronounce. There are already some interesting initiatives designed to 'bring science into the city.' and to close the gap between the scientific world and that of citizens. In fact, it would seem that a scientific education, encouraging critical and enlightened choices, should form an essential element of authentic education for citizenship for the twenty-first century.
7. **Quantitatively, schooling has progressed.** The number of out-of-school children has indeed gone down, dropping from 127 millions in 1990 to 113 millions in 1998. However, if progress has been marked in some countries and some regions, in others, on the other hand, population growth, together with complex socio-economic and educational factors, has worked against greater access. Above all, as the Dakar Forum reminded us, the principal victims are **girls** and **women.** By way of example, of the 113 million children who do not go to school, two-thirds are girls.
8. **In some countries and regions, progress has been achieved in reducing inequality** (between sexes, in health, among ethnic groups, etc.). But important imbalances still exist, in the first instance, they affect poor and isolated communities or ethnic minorities. Furthermore, 'new inequalities' have appeared, even in countries that are not considered as poor.
9. **On the financial level, countries are investing more in education than in the past,** even if, in some States, the reduction of GNP, combined with other structural or situational factors, and the establishment of other political

priorities, has completely wiped out any efforts to increase the share awarded to education. Several countries have adopted new frameworks for political and legislative action, and have supported them with supplementary financing and resources. Some countries, even poor ones, have made considerable progress by making the best possible use of the financial resources available or by channelling resources arising from debt cancellation towards education. Despite all these efforts, the resources continue to be inadequate in most cases.

10. **Despite progress achieved and the investments agreed to, the matter of educational quality and the relevance of learning remains a matter of concern in all parts of the world.** We have become particularly aware of the fact that alone better access to education without better quality teaching leads to a 'dead end'. School failure and drop-out, a high level of repeating, inadequate methods and structures, too few, ill-trained or untrained teachers working in poorly equipped conditions, the lack of textbook and educational supplies, the absence of or inadequate attempts at serious evaluation of learning outcomes, inefficient management, etc. These represent determining factors in the mediocre quality of education in numerous countries.

Intensifying the dialogue and renewing our approach

To confront these realities and these burning questions for the future of humanity, **education** is directly involved since it **can and must 'make a difference'. It is possible to improve its quality if we tackle in an energetic and rapid manner the true causes of its malfunctions and of its inadequacies.** We are already quite familiar with a certain number of modifications or even changes of course that are required, as well as on the controls that must be activated. **We must reflect further and, above all, take action on the key elements that determine or have an influence upon quality.**

Among these, improving teachers' competence and their working conditions no doubt come first. But this will have no beneficial effect if we do not carry out a thorough reform of the contents, curricula, methods, structures and means of teaching. And if we advance on the level of policy dialogue

towards a better linkage between education and development policies and better teaching, we will also advance step by step towards identifying the necessary resources.

Numerous experiences both successes and failures exist in the world. Let us **collect them, analyse them, discuss them,** in order that they can feed our **reflection** and **action,** and so that they can **renew the content and methods of dialogue,** both at the political level and at the level of schools, teachers and society, this is the **role** and **ambition of UNESCO and the IBE.** Let us **bring them on to the international scene** in order to **share them** and to **take advantage of them:** this is the fundamental **vocation** of the **forty-sixth session of the ICE.** There does indeed exist an **international responsibility** to improve the quality of education in the world.

It is in this way that we expect to respond to the requirements of this new twenty-first century, to the needs expressed by States and to the message of Mr. Koichiro Matsuura, Director-General of UNESCO, following the Dakar Forum: *'Obviously, it is not a message of satisfaction. On the contrary, it is a call to arms and an invitation to act in an urgent and efficient manner.'*

Programming the Conference's Work

1. The official opening of the ICE will take place on Wednesday 5 September at 10 a.m. The Conference's work will follow the agenda, of which a provisional version is included in Annex I.
2. The Conference's work will be organized around **two discussion units** and **two major debates.** The first debate will be devoted to the theme of the contribution of peace to human development in the era of globalization through education, science, culture and communication, and will be **entitled:** *"One world, one future: education and the challenge of globalization"*. The other debate will be devoted to the **theme** of: *"Quality education for all for living together in the twenty-first century: intensifying the international policy dialogue on structures, contents, methods and means of education, and mobilizing the actors and partners."*
3. **Six workshops** will be organized in framework of the two discussion units and will deal with the following themes.

Discussion Unit I: "Quality education for all: living together, democracy and social cohesion".

Workshop 1: Citizenship education: learning at school and in society.

Workshop 2: Social exclusion and violence: education for social cohesion.

Workshop 3: Shared values, cultural diversity and education: when to learn and how?

Discussion Unit II: "Quality education for all: knowledge, technology and the future of the school".

Workshop 4: Language(s) teaching and learning strategies for understanding and communication.

Workshop 5: Scientific progress and science teaching: basic knowledge, interdisciplinarity and ethical issues.

Workshop 6: Narrowing the gap between the information rich and the information-poor: new technologies and the future of the school.

4. Several organizations—international and national, governmental and non-governmental—have already expressed their interest and are ready to collaborate in the organization and/or the financing of workshops.
5. A short document to stimulate discussion will be prepared for each major debate and each workshop. The Conference's main document (reference document) will provide the conceptual foundation for the whole Conference. These documents will be dispatched at least six weeks before the beginning of the meeting.
6. Each major debate and each workshop will be organized in the form of a discussion panel (four to six people) and will bring together a minister, the representative of a co-organizing institution as well as other educational actors and partners (experts, teachers, representatives of social organizations), selected according to the theme of the workshop. The debate will be led by an experienced moderator, a rapporteur will be assigned to each workshop.
7. At all international meetings, ministers regularly express the wish that their conferences could avoid falling into the trap of an often formal, rigid ritual that does not permit debate. As one minister emphasized during the closing ceremony of a recent ICE, they would like "not only to speak

and to listen to each other, but also to be able to reply". During the forty-sixth ICE—between the two major debates, the six workshops and the two summing-up plenary debates—the ministers and delegates will benefit from numerous and varied opportunities to speak. They are invited to select the themes that are of particular interest to them and to envisage short speeches, directly related to the theme being dealt with, so as to be in a position to react to the speeches by their colleagues. If they so wish, they may present to the Secretariat of the Conference longer, more general written texts, which will be distributed during the Conference.

8. In accordance with the decision of the IBE Council, the forty-sixth ICE will not adopt a final document in the form of a formal Declaration or Resolution. During the closing ceremony, a document of "Conclusions and proposals for action to strengthen policy dialogue on the structures, contents and methods for living together in the twenty-first century" will be submitted for the participants's approval. This document, which should fundamentally take into account the Conference's outcomes—in particular the concluding major debate—cannot therefore be written and dispatched in advance.

9. It is highly desirable that the largest possible number of educational partners are involved in the intellectual preparatory activities for the forty-sixth ICE. They may do this, for example, by sharing their principal concerns, by presenting examples of "best practices", of successful (or unsuccessful) experiments, through position documents (theses) on one theme or another, etc.

An Internet forum (English/French/Spanish) has been opened for this purpose at the following address icenetforum@ibe.unesco.org. For information about the Conference, please address your requests to: conference@ibe.unesco.org. You may also contact the IBE by fax: 41.22.917.78.01. Up-to-date information is also available on the IBE's Internet site http://www.ibe.unesco.org.

Other Events on the Fringes of the ICE

10. The **Comenius Medal,** created jointly in 1992 by the Ministry of National Education, Youth and Sport of the

Czech Republic and UNESCO, and intended to recognize innovatory initiatives and achievements in the field of research and educational renewal, will be awarded on Thursday 6 September by the Director-General of UNESCO to the winners selected from individual educators, groups of educators or institutions.

11. Special manifestations will take place during the Conference: exhibitions, presentations of programmes on the website, the video "Expériences éducatives pour apprendre à vivre ensemble", simulation games for preventive education against HIV/AIDS in schools, etc.

A detailed programme of these special manifestations will be distributed at the beginning of the Conference.

Other Meetings During the ICE

12. In parallel with the Conference's work, various meetings could be held on the fringes of the ICE. A detailed programme of them will be established after June 2001.

Organizational Chart of the ICE

13. The provisional organizational chart of the forty-sixth session of the International Conference on Education appears as Annex II. The regular working hours will be from 10 a.m. to 1 p.m. and from 3 p.m. to 6 p.m.

Conference Documents

14. The draft list of Conference documents is given in Annex III.

Working Languages of the Conference

15. The Conference will have six working languages: Arabic, Chinese, English, French, Russian and Spanish for the plenary sessions and debates.

The workshops will have interpretation in English and French, UNESCO's working languages. Interpretation into other languages is possible as long as external funding is provided.

REFERENCES

1. See: 'Preliminary proposals by the Director-General concerning the Draft Medium-Term Strategy for 2002-2007 (31 C/4) and the draft programme and budget for 2002-2003 (31 C/5).' Executive Board, 160th session, October 2000, document 160 Ex/5.

2. See: *The Dakar Framework for Action*. Adopted by the World Education Forum, Dakar, Senmegal, 26-28 April 2000, p. 8, para. 7(vi).

3. *Educate or perish: Africa's Impass[e] and prospects*. Dakar, Senegal, UNESCO Regional Office for Education in Africa; Abidjan, Côte d'Ivoire: UNICEF West and Central Africa Regional Office, 1990.

4. B.H. Haïdara and S.S. Adoveti, Preface o Ki-Zerbo's book.

5. World Forum on Education, *Final Report*, Paris, UNESCO, 2000, p. 32.

6. Susan George, Le rapport Lugano, Paris, Ed. Fayard, 2000, p. 171-72. The quotations in italics are drawn from: Institute for Research of Oslo, *Causes and dynamics of conflict escalation*, Report of a research project, June 1997; see also: *The state of war and peace atlas*, New York; Harmondsworth, Penguin, 1997.

7. World Forum on Education, *Final Report*, Paris, UNESCO, 2000, p. 17.

Conclusions and Proposals for Action Arising from the forty-sixth session of the International Conference on Education (ICE)

PREAMBLE

1. The International Bureau of Education, in its capacity as a UNESCO specialized centre for the contents and methods of education, organized the forty-sixth session of the International Conference on Education in Geneva from 5 to 8 September 2001.
2. More than 600 participants took part in the discussions, of whom eighty were ministers and ten vice-ministers of education, coming from 127 Member States of UNESCO, together with nine representatives of intergovernmental organizations, thirteen non-governmental organizations and three foundations.
3. The objective of intensifying and strengthening dialogue at the level of educational policies on the problems and prospects of solutions with a view to improving the quality of education for *learning to live together* has been largely achieved. These conclusions and the resulting proposals for action present the key features of the debates and preparatory work (Netforum, ministerial messages, national reports, good practices, etc.). The entire collection will be made known through the Final Report, the reports of the workshops, and the other documents to be published after the Conference.

4. These conclusions, adopted on 8 September 2001, have been drawn from the Major Debates, the Plenary sessions and the six workshops that took place during the Conference. They are intended for governments, international intergovernmental and non-governmental organizations, achers and organizations of the teaching profession, the media and all partners in civil society whose efforts improve the quality of education, encourage dialogue and develop the capacity to live together.

A. The challenges

5. Given the enormous complexity of the problems all societies have to face, particularly globalization, and unbearable inequalities between and within countries, *learning to live togehter*, a concept created by the International Commission on Education for the Twenty-first Century, has become a necessity in all regions of the world.
6. One of the major challenges confronting education systems remains that of guaranteeing and respecting the right of education for all. However, the right of children to have free access to schools is far from being respected everywhere in the world and particularly in those countries experiencing situations of war, occupation, violence and intolerance.
7. The plea for education to overcome these challenges facing societies is not a new phenomenon. Yet, today, the expectations have become far more urgent, giving the impression that education can by itself overcome the problems that exist in countries and at the international level.
8. Both formal and non-formal education are essential tools for launching and promoting sustainable processes of constructing peace, democracy and human rights, but they cannot alone provide solutions to the complexity, the tensions and even the contradictions of the present world.
9. It is essential, however, as was stressed in the Jomtien Declaration and the Dakar Framework of Action, that efforts at the national and international levels to develop education be complemented by global strategies to eliminate poverty and to promote participation in political, social and cultural life.

10. Achieving the objective of education for all goes beyond the effort of universal schooling. Within each country, the search for social cohesion, the struggle against inequality, the respect for cultural diversity and access to the knowledge society, which may be facilitated by information and communication technologies, will be achieved through policies that focus on improving the quality of education.
11. These policies must overcome the obstacles posed by inequalities of access and risks of exclusion in the fields of languages, science and technology.
    - As far as languages are concerned, it is possible to note that numerous countries are multilingual even though a single language appears as the official language of communication.
    - Concerning science and technology, particularly those of information and communication, the gulf is growing wider due to inequality in access to the most recent advances.

B. Educational Policies and Practices

12. Throughout the world there is an strong political will on the part of numerous governments and teachers to adapt educational contents, structures and methods in order to respond to the above-mentioned challenges.
13. The experiences of educational policies and practices indicate that it is necessary to consider reforms more as processes than as products. These may arise as much from governmental decisions as from the initiatives of other stakeholders. The way in which they are implemented, involving the mobilization of all actors, is as important as the content.
14. Basic agreements within the international community already exist concerning lines of action for promoting the ability and willingness to live together. Those responsible for education policies at the national level have clearly expressed their will to purse the implementation of these agreements.
15. The evaluation of the outcomes of the reform processes, and particularly "good practices", enables us to highlight

both some conditions unique to each cultural context as well as to pinpoint some common characteristics.

C. Proposals for Action

16. The entire range of teaching and educational practices for living together should be better known, disseminated and exploited with a view to strengthening the endogenous capacities of each country.
17. Training for policy dialogue is essential in order to achieve the major objective of improving the quality of education for all.
18. Reform processes should be continued or undertaken in the following domains:

Contents

- Adapting curricula and updating contents in order to reflect:
  - — economic and social changes set in motion, in particular, by globalization, migration and cultural diversity;
  - — the ethical dimension of scientific and technological progress;
  - — the growing importance of communication, expression and the capacity to listen and dialogue, first of all in the mother-tongue, then in the official language in the country as well as in one or more foreign languages;
  - — the positive contribution that may result from integrating technologies into the learning process.
- Developing not only disciplinary but also interdisciplinary approaches and competencies.
- Supporting and nurturing innovations
- Seeking, in the development of curricula, to ensure relevance at the local, national and international levels at the same time.

Methods

- Promoting active learning methods and teamwork.
- Encouragingly all-round and balanced development and preparing the individual for activity citizenship open to the world.

Teachers

- Facilitating genuine involvement on the part of teachers in decision-making within the school, through training and other means.
- Improving the education of teachers so that they can better develop among pupils behaviour and values of solidarity and tolerance, so as to prepare them to prevent and resolve conflicts peacefully and to respect cultural diversity.
- Changing the relationship between teacher and pupil to respond to the evolution of society.
- Improving the use of information and communication technologies in teacher training and in classroom practices.

Daily life in educational institutions

- Creating within the school a climate of tolerance and respect encouraging the development of a democratic culture.
- Providing a way for the school to function that encourages participation of the pupils in decision-making.
- Proposing a shared definition of projects and learning activities.

Educational research

- Stimulating research that clarifies the concept of *learning to live together* and the implications for policy and practices.
- Promoting research on the development of contents and teaching methods relating to *learning to live together.*
- Stimulating comparative studies in the sub-regional, regional and transregional contexts.

19. Partnerships

- Since education is not the sole answer to *learning to live together,* its improvement requires the contribution not only of the school but also of all concerned actors. It therefore implies the introduction and the strengthening of genuine partisanships with the entire society: teachers, communities, facilities, the economic sector, the media, NGOs, and the intellectual and spiritual authorities.

- Partnerships are also required to expand access to and effective use of new information and communication technologies.

20. *Learning to live together* requires policies for the development of lifelong learning beginning with early childhood education, and paying particular attention to the period of adolescence (12-18 years).

D. International Co-operation

21. The development of international co-operative activities to improve the quality of education for *learning to live together* for all should be based on six main principles.

- Strengthening the function of the IBE as an observatory of trends, as well as its role in the development of easily accessible databanks and information systems.
- Collecting the results of educational research on the development of contents, undertaking comparative studies at the sub-regional and regional levels, and their worldwide dissemination.
- Setting up co-operative networks at the international, regional and sub-regional levels facilitating the exchange of experience and promoting joint projects in order to strengthen endogenous capacities.
- Training educational decision-makers in policy dialogue so as to encourage the definition of common objectives, the search for consensus and the mobilization of partnerships.
- Experimenting with new modalities of technical assistance provided by bi- or multilateral co-operation agencies, in order to emphasize not only North-South but also South-South collaboration.

- Strengthening of partnership between UNESCO and other relevant intergovernmental organizations.

E. The Role of UNESCO and its Specialized Institutes

22. The conclusions of the forty-sixth session of the International Conference on Education are communicated to the General Conference of the Organization in order to be taken into account in the process of reflection and to reinforce, in the short, medium and long terms, the programme of action of UNESCO, the International Bureau of Education and the other specialized institutes with a view to improving the quality of education.

Part—2

International Conference on Education For All For Learning to Live Together

---

* Final Report of the International Conference on Education, 46th Session, UNESCO International Bureau of Education.

Proceedings of the Conference

A. Opening ceremony

1. The 46th session of the International Conference on Education (ICE), convened by the Director-General of UNESCO in accordance with 30 C/Resolution 3 adopted by the General Conference at its 30th session, was held at the International Conference Centre, Geneva, from 5 to 8 September 2001 on the theme "Education for All for Learning to Live Together: contents and learning strategies—problems and solutions".
2. More than 600 participants, including 80 ministers of education and 10 deputy ministers, from 127 Member States of UNESCO, took part in the debates, alongside the representative of nine intergovernmental organizations, 13 non-governmental organizations and three foundations. The list of participants is given in Annex XIX.
3. Following a short video presentation on the education situation in all regions of the world entitled "Living together and building together", the session was opened officially by H.E. Mr Andrés Delich, Minister of Education and Head of Delegation of Argentina, the country which had assumed the presidency of the 45th session. Mr Delich's opening remarks are reproduced in Annex I.
4. The President gave the floor to Mr Koichiro Matsuura, Director-General of UNESCO. The Director-General's address appears in Annex II.
5. The President then called upon Ms Martine Brunschwig Graf, State Counsellor, Head of the Department of Public

Education of the Republic and Canton of Geneva and Head of the Swiss Delegation, to address the Conference. Ms Brunschwig Graf's address is reproduced in Annex III.

6. The President then invited Mr Pieter de Meijer, President of the Council of the International Bureau of Education (IBE), to take the floor. He presented the Council's recommendations concerning the composition of Bureau of the Conference. The Conference accepted those recommendations.

7. Upon the proposal of Electoral Group Va (Africa), the Conference elected by acclamation H.E. Mr. Abraham B Borishade, Minister of Education of Nigeria, as President of the 46th session of the ICE. Mr Borishade's opening address is contained in Annex IV.

8. The President of the IBE Council proposed that Rule 4.1 of the Rules of Procedure of the ICE be suspended for the session in order to raise the number of Vice-Presidents from eight to 10, which would enable an equal number of members from each electoral group to participate in the Bureau of the Conference. The proposal was accepted and the Conference then elected by acclamation the following vice-presidents:
H.E. Mr. Mariana Aylwin Oyarzun (Chile)
H.E. Mr. Radu Damian (Romania)
H.E. Mr. Henry Kosgey (Kenya)
Mr. Pieter de Meijer (Netherlands)
H.E. Mr. Moncer Rouissi (Tunisia)
H.E. Mr. Im Sethy (Cambodia)
H.E. Mr. Burchell Whiteman (Jamaica)
H.E. Mr. Eduard Zeman (Czech Republic)
H.E. Pr. Najib Zerouali Ouariti (Morocco)
H.E. Mr. Xinsheng Zhang (China).

Mr. Philippe Renard (Belgium) was then elected Rapporteur of the Conference by acclamation.

9. The Conference also agreed to the IBE Council's proposal that Mr Pieter de Meijer, President of the Council, should chair the drafting group and recommended to the Bureau of the ICE that the Council's working group set-up to assist the IBE in making preparations for the 46th session of the ICE should constitute the drafting group in cooperation with the Rapporteur and the workshop rapporteurs. In

addition to the President of the Council, the group included one representative from each electoral group, namely: Argentina, Canada, Nigeria, Qatar, Czech Republic and Thailand; Mr. Régnier (France) served in a personal capacity as its Executive Secretary.

10. The President introduced the provisional agenda (ED/BIE/Confinted 46/1), which was adopted. It appears at the beginning of this report. At the invitation of the President, Ms. Cecilia Braslavasky, Director of the IBE, commented on document ED/BIE/Confinted 46/2 "Proposed organization of the work of the Conference", which was adopted.

B. Organization of work—Methodology

11. In response to the wish expressed on many occasions by ministers at earlier sessions of the Conference to enter into a genuine, in-depth policy dialogue, the IBE Council had decided to change the structure and organization in relation to those of previous sessions. Consequently, the proceeding took place as follows:
a major introductory debate;
two discussion units, each consisting of three parallel workshops followed by a plenary summing-up meeting;
a major concluding debate;
a closing meeting.

12. As regards methodology, the two major debates and six workshops were held in the form of discussion panels, with the main speakers representing various education actors (ministers, senior civil servants, researchers, experts and representative of intergovernmental or non-governmental organizations) and the various regions of the world. The list of speakers during the two major debates is provided in Annex XVI and that of speakers during the workshop in Annex XVII. The workshop reports are reproduced in Annex XV.

13. Among the innovations marking this session of the Conference was the substantial use of audio-visual and information and communications technology: an introductory video at the opening and closing meeting ; videos on good practices produced under IBE's BRIDGE

project (young professionals) to introduce each of the six workshops; the recording of a television programme (round table of ministers) with the assistance of the local television station "Léman bleu"; the presentation of some 100 good practices on the Conference's, website; summaries of the proceedings accessible on the Internet the following day, and so on.

14. Other innovations were also introduced in the preparatory phase of the Conference (Netforum, messages of ministers of education, Internet site) For instance, more than 200 people registered on the Netforum and more than 100 messages were sent by the ministers before the Conference. They may be accessed at the Conference's website and will be the subject of a publication. A special edition of Prospects, UNESCO's quarterly journal of comparative education, was devoted to the conference's them. A special edition of Innovation and a poster were also issued in April 2001 to publicize the Conference.

15. The organization of the Conference was made possible by many partnerships in the form of intellectual and/or financial contributions from ministries of education, National Commissions for UNESCO, research and training centres in a number of countries (Argentina, Canada, Cuba, Czech Republic, Denmark, Finland, France, Germany, Japan, Malaysia, Netherlands, Norway, Spain and Switzerland), the UNESCO Dakar Follow-up Unit, the Commonwealth of Learning, the training programme for bilingual intercultural education for the Andean countries (PROEIB-ANDES), the BERUM project (Peru), the University Institute for Development Studies (IUED, Geneva), the City of Science and Industry (Paris) and the Centre for the Study of Violence and Reconciliation (South Africa).

16. The organization, and more particularly the smooth running, of the Conference was also made possible through the active commitment and support of various UNESCO units (central services of the Education Sector, regional offices and other Secretariat services), which co-operated closely during the 46th session of the ICE. The list of members of the Secretariat appears in Annex XX.

C. Special meeting chaired by the Director-General of UNESCO

17. A special meeting, chaired by Mr Koichiro Matsuura, Director-General of UNESCO, was held in the morning of 8 September on the theme of "the involvement of civil society in promoting education for all (EFA)". Mr Matsuura's address at the opening of the meeting is appended in Annex VIII.

18. The special meeting was remarkable in terms of both its symbolic dimension and its substance. Convened by the Director-General of UNESCO, Mr Koichiro Matsuura, it brought 80 ministers and 10 deputy ministers of education and 400 governmental and non-governmental representatives together on the same platform to discuss on the basis of specific examples the manner in which their collaboration is put into practice. The ministers of education of Ghana and Mozambique, the Education Secretary of Nepal and the Deputy Minister of Education of Yemen were joined by representatives of civil society organizations of three of those countries. They gave an account of EFA partnership experiences and identified practical stages for strengthening contributions EFA and for promoting better relations between governments and civil society. The Secretary-General of Education International made an analytical reply, which was followed by a lively debate.

19. The special meeting, which was devoted entirely to the involvement of civil society in EFA, reflects the growing importance attached to the role of non-governmental organizations and civil society in the EFA process and movement. The success of EFA depends on the mobilization of all partners and actors, empowered beforehand to play their role fully in a process that depends first and foremost on a sound democratic base.

20. In Dakar, governments had agreed on their "obligation to ensure that EFA goals and targets are reached and sustained" (paragraph 2 of the Dakar Framework for Action) and that that responsibility "will be most effectively met through broad-based partnerships within countries" (paragraph 2). The main participants at the World Education Forum undertook to "ensure the engagement and participation of civil society in the formulation,

implementation and monitoring of strategies for educational development" (paragraph 8).

21. The special meeting considered in particular the issue of civil society involvement in the process of policy formulation, seen as going much further than the development of specific activities to promote EFA. The meeting also provided an opportunity to pose the key question of how countries can move from a clear recognition of the role of civil society in policy formulation to participation and renewed partnerships. The invited governmental and non-governmental representatives discussed examples, possibilities and preconditions with a view to effective civil society involvement in policy formulation, planning and action, which are linked to the achievement of the Dakar goals.

22. A summary of the panel's statements is provided in Annex IX. A fuller synoptic report will be published separately.

D. Closing ceremony

23. After viewing the video document shown at the opening of the 46th session of the ICE, the participants listened to two songs—on the themes of friendship, tolerance and openness to the world—given a fresh and musical interpretation by the Primary School Choir of Geneva.

24. A Summerhill School pupil (United Kingdom) then read out a message to the Conference on the theme of learning about citizenship. The text is given in Annex X.

25. The President then officially opened the Conference's last meeting, which was devoted to the submission of the general report, the adoption of the "Conclusions and proposals for action" deriving from the 46th session of the ICE, and the closing ceremony proper.

26. The President first called on Mr. Philippe Renard (Belgium) to submit his oral report, which has been transcribed in Part IIA of this report. The Conference adopted the general report by acclamation.

27. The President then requested Mr. Pieter de Meijer, President of the IBE Council and Chairperson of the drafting group, to submit the draft "Conclusions and proposals for action" arising from the 46th session of the

ICE. The President informed the Conference of the suggestion made by the Bureau of the 46th session of the ICE, which had held a joint meeting with the Bureau of the IBE Council, to make a few minor amendments to the draft text. The Conference adopted those amendments and, on the proposal of the President of the IBE Council, seconded by the Head of Delegation of Canada, decided not to make any further amendments. The "Conclusions and proposals for action" were adopted by acclamation. The document is contained in Part II B of this report. The delegations of Iraq[1] and India[2] were invited to submit their remarks in writing to the Director of the IBE, Secretary-General of the Conference, so that they could be included in the final report.

28. Ms. Cecilia Braslavsky, Director of the IBE then addressed the Conference to express her thanks to all those who had contributed to the success of the session. The text of her address is appended in Annex XI.

29. The President invited Mr. Koichiro Matsuura, Director-General is UNESCO, to deliver his closing address. The text of contained in Annex. XII.

30. The President gave the floor to Ms. M. Brunschwig Graf, State Councillor, Head of the Department of Public Education of the Republic and Canton of Geneva and Head of the Swiss Delegation. Ms. Brunschwig Graf's address appears in Annex XIII.

31. After two songs by the Primary School Choir of Geneva, the President made a short address before declaring the 46th session of the ICE closed. Mr. Borishade's address appear in Annex XIV.

E. Award of the Comenius Medal

32. On the evening of Thursday 6 September, the Comenius Medal was awarded by Mr. Eduard Zeman, Minister of Education of the Czech Republic, and Mr. John Daniel, Assistant Director-General for Education, to five educators and three projects selected by the jury chaired by Mr. Pieter de Meijer, President of the IBE Council, whose choices had been endorsed by the Director-General of UNESCO. The statements made by Mr. Daniel, Mr. de Meijer and

Mr. Zeman are reproduced in Annexes V, VI and VII. The Comenius Medal is intended to reward outstanding achievements in the fields of educational research and innovation, which have contributed significantly to the development and renewal of education. The 2001 winners are:

Mr. Abdul Kader Ahmed (Bahrain)
Mr. Thomas A. Bediako (Ghana)
Mr. Yves Brunsvick (France, posthumously)
Mr. Pablo Latapí Sarre (Mexico)
Mr. Sook Jong Lee (Republic of Korea)
The Communidade Solidária Project (Brazil)
The Life Science Project (Namibia)
The Atanas Bourov Vocational School (Bulgaria)

F. Side-meetings

33. The following fringe meetings took place in parallel to the work of the Conference:

(a) Monday 3 and Tuesday 4 September: international research seminar on "La problématique du *vivre ensemble* dans les curricula" organized by the IBE, the University of Geneva (FPSE) and the Educational Research Department (SRED) of the Canton of Geneva;

(b) Tuesday 4 September: Senior Executive Seminar for African Ministers of Education, organized by IICBA, BREDA and UNESCO's Education Sector;

(c) Thursday 6 September: *Demain l'education...*, a television debate programme recorded live and retransmitted of the *Leman bleu TV Geneve* channel;

(d) Friday 7 September: informal consultation on the United Nations Girls' Education initiative, organized by UNESCO's Education sector;

(e) Friday 7 September: working meeting in the IBE's fields of competence with the Ministers of Education of the Gulf States.

34. The Conference also enabled the Director-General of UNESCO, the Assistant Director-General for Education and

the Director of the IBE to hold many bilateral talks and informal discussions with ministers, delegates and representatives of intergovernmental organizations and NGOs.

REFERENCES

1. By correspondence dated 19 September 2001, the Permanent Delegation of Iraq requested the insertion, in the last sentence of paragraph 6, of the world "sanctions".

2. By correspondence dated 12 September 2001, the Head of Delegation of India to the 46th session of the ICE submitted the following remarks: "While the draft conclusions have ably summarized the consensus achieved in the Conference, there are three points which were raised during the Workshops and the major debates which have not been reflected and should find a place in the Final Report. Firstly, that 'learning to live together' is only one aspect of a larger discipline namely 'education in human values'. UNESCO should actively work for evolving a common code of universal values which will be accepted around the globe. Secondly, UNESCO should boldly accept the responsibility of providing philosophical leadership to the world to attempt to harmonize the differences of the participants in the fields of religious faith, economic and political thinking, knowledge systems, living styles and so on. It should effectively promote the right of every human being to chose between different alternatives in an eclectic manner without fear or force: and thirdly, UNESCO should encourage, disseminate and propagate ICT devices such as the SIMPUTER, developed by India, which will enable basic education to be taken to remote locations and to disadvantaged sections of society through education and self-learning, as a part of broader policy of bridging the digital divide and harnessing ICT to the requirements of education in general and EFA in particular".

6

Documents Issued by the Conference

A. General report of the forty-sixth session of the international conference on education (ICE)[3]

SUBMITTED BY MR. PHILIPPE RENARD (BELGIUM), RAPPORTEUR

Mr. President,
Excellencies,
Ministers,
Heads of Delegation,
Mr. Director-General of UNESCO,
Mr. President of the IBE Council,
Madam Director of the IBE,
Mr. Assistant Director-General for Education,
Ladies and Gentlemen,

I shall therefore submit to you the oral report of the 46th session. This report will be included in the final report to be sent to you later.

This is obviously a difficult exercise for, in summarizing 20 hours of often lively and invariably interesting debates in twenty minutes, and in view of the time constraints, I shall inevitably, unlike the children whom we have just heard, create frustrations. Please accept my apologies from the outset.

I think that I should begin this report by referring to the success of this conference. There is nothing self-congratulatory in their statement. I am here as a "notary", and I have therefore genuinely tried—at every moment—to keep a neutral, outsider's eye on this event, in which I am obviously extremely proud to have participated, particularly since, as you know there are more than 600 registered participants, including 80 ministers and 10 deputy ministers of education, nine intergovernmental organizations and thirteen NGOs from UNESCO's 127 Member States. I therefore think that, simply in terms of participation, it has been a real success.

The goal of the conference was to intensify and enrich the educational policy dialogue on problems and prospects of solutions with a view to improving the quality of education for learning to live together. I sincerely believe that the goal has largely been achieved. The method of work that was chosen by the International Bureau of Education and its Council together with the quality of your participation, made by very fertile discussions, which I have to say, are extremely difficult to summarize.

The fact that so many ministers and so many actors in education systems are here in Geneva shows, Madam Minister of Education of the Canton of Geneva, that—apart from your great and widely recognized qualities of hospitality—they attach enormous importance to their political responsibility for improving public education systems and to the need to keep those systems, their content and their curricula on track at a level that is not that of the market but rather that of those whose duty it is to prepare for the future and preserve the common good and equity.

The Director-General of UNESCO, in his introductory address, set out what I regard as pointers for our work, and they will be found later in this report. The first perspective that we were given was that of social cohesion, harmony and non-violence; the second was that of peace, mutual understanding and friendship. I think I can say that all our work and the climate of this session effectively reflected this twin standpoint.

In education systems, these pointers need to be followed-up in practice through improvement of the quality of basic education for all and the effective acquisition of skills, particularly in languages and scientific culture, one key point being the acquisition of skills for living in society: communicating with others, undertaking joint activities; participating and building mutual trust.

In a few words, I will try to summarize the debates in plenary meetings that followed the six workshops on discussion units I and II, namely "Quality education for all: living together, democracy and social cohesion" and "Quality education for all: knowledge, technology and the future of the school". You have already heard the reports of the various rapporteurs, which I shall not repeat—that would be quite pointless—I shall merely try to offer a general synopsis.

GENERAL SYNOPSIS

Quality Education for All: living together, democracy and social cohesion

The context of the coming century is that of globalization. The great political, economic and social upheavals that have marked the last 50 years reflect that trend in our world, of which education is an integral part.

The institutionalization of education in the last century, and in some instances even today unfortunately, was aimed at strengthening national identities and even nationalism of all sorts.

The economic (including the information) empires that dominate the market and widen the gap between the countries of the North and South, which give rise to the brain drain and are sometimes instrumental, through global financial institutions, in lowering the quality of education, are not at all models that we should like to promote.

That is not the type of globalization that we want. The important thing is that human beings, in their individuality, should be educated to "live together", to analyse, to reflect on their uniqueness and become capable of being enriched by diversity. At the same time, the prerequisites for ensuring the minimum results and minimum conditions in the field of education for all must be met with, for example, the assistance of the international organizations concerned with education.

Education, we are all convinced, is a right. That right must be exercised in the context of economic globalization in order to give it a human face. I very much like and readily quote the saying "The world is not a market but a village". And I think that we are all proud to belong to that village.

Acting together to learn to live together, in a context of respect for cultures and languages, that is the role of education in the twenty-first century.

High expectations on the part of participants regarding the linkages between education and citizenship, democratic governance and sustainable development led to extremely open discussions and highlighted conceptual fields that remain to be explored in greater depth:

What is the definition of citizenship?

How can it be put into practice?

How can the challenge of open citizenship education be taken up both locally and regionally and, of course, internationally?

The answer to these questions will doubtless involve the acceptance of "variable geometry" as a method. I personally very much liked the concept of "glo-location" developed by Mr. Benavot, of which you are all now aware. Situations on the ground obviously differ, but a theme that has emerged strongly from the outset has been the call for observance of the values of justice and solidarity among all countries. Even if the school—and by school I do not mean the physical place alone, I mean the institution of education—did not awake early to the reality of a multicultural world, it must ensure quality education for all and further living together through flexible and realistic curricula. There is no one solution at this level that will make dignity accessible to all, in a context of respect for cultural, social or ideological diversities and differences.

LANGUAGE(S) TEACHING AND LEARNING STRATEGIES FOR UNDERSTANDING AND COMMUNICATION

With particular regard to language teaching and learning strategies, it seems to me—and several speakers have also pointed this out—that the sentence that left its mark was in the introductory video, in which the Czech teacher said "the more languages you speak, the more human you are".

The majority of countries in the world are pluri- or multilingual and if language is a communication medium, it is also deeply anchored in the culture of each and everyone.

It is increasingly obvious that the language of instruction at the beginning of one's education, at such a crucial moment for future learning, should be the mother tongue. But there is no unanimity on the issue in all quarters, and it must therefore be studied in greater depth.

Language learning in the context of globalization is a means of facilitating mobility and communication.

Here too, it seems that there are no simple solutions, let alone universal models. On the other hand, everyone is in favour of the exchange of good practices and experience, in particular for teachers undergoing initial and in-service training.

It is clear to everyone that language learning is a key element for living together. However, questions remain as to the measures that need to be put in place, particularly for the least developed countries.

It also seems obvious that the political and economic environment must be such as to permit this education geared to the promotion of languages and living together, with emphasis on understanding and communication.

Scientific progress and Science teaching: basic knowledge, interdisciplinarity and ethical issues

With regard to scientific progress and science education, it seems to me that the discussions have centred on the fact that sciences cannot be taught for their own sake, that they embody universal values and that, in actual teaching situations, they must be contextualized and be oriented towards the real world and life in order to give an ethical dimension to learning and to develop the capacity of "learning how to learn" by oneself and with others. But here too, the lack of infrastructures, resources and teachers obviously poses problems for many countries, and support by the international community is indispensable.

Narrowing the gap between the information rich and the information poor: new technologies and the future of education

On the question of bridging the information technology and information gap between rich countries and poor countries, there can be no doubt that such a gap exists. It would be dishonest not to acknowledge it. The gap exists not only between countries or regions (as understood within the United Nations system), but also within regions in terms of countries and of social groups themselves.

It is obvious that ICTs are potentially a source of innovation and creativity. It is clear that schools equipped with these resources can serve as centres, including community centres and interactive development centres for use in initial training, adult education; etc.

There is a desire for a planned approach at the world level; the development of partnerships, including the media—that is television, books, etc.—could make it possible to narrow the gap, and that is one of the elements in the development of a world citizenship.

Teachers, for their part, must not only have the possibility of acquiring "computer literacy", but they must also be in a position to became creators of educational objects and methods, with the help of the new technologies: this is one of the challenges that will also have to be taken up.

I now turn to the theme of the second major debate and, with your level, I shall read it out in full "Quality education for all for living together in the twenty-first century: intensifying the international policy dialogue on structures, contents, methods and means of education, and mobilizing the actors and partners".

The title of the theme is long. So too were the debates for those persons who stayed until the end, and the last group of people present in the room was roughly the same as the number of speakers at the rostrum. The debates were nonetheless extremely interesting and I have listed a few points that were made.

First of all, the school often remains closed in on itself, a prisoner of its traditions, of its culture and perhaps of its institutionalization. It does not maintain sufficient contacts with society.

And if we push the argument through to its conclusion, we might ask ourselves: "My God, considering how long we have been holding conferences on curricula, learning and school organization and management, how come we are still in this situation?" It is high time—and several delegates said as much—for us to take action. I am thinking here also of the pupil who took the floor before me.

Parents generally feel that the present system pays little attention to them and wonder about the significance of what the school does. Does knowledge alone suffice? On which skills should emphasis be placed?

They are not the only ones who are asking questions. All of us—education specialists as well as political decision-makers—know that educational reforms take a long time and are costly to implement but also that education is undeniably an investment for both the individual and for society. The means must therefore be found to convince the authorities and society as a whole that education for the twenty-first century, education for living together is an investment at the society level—by which I mean, of course, at the global, regional and national levels.

How can we speak of quality education when access to schools is impeded on account of armed conflict or political, not to say psychological, pressures? What meaning does the right to education retain in such circumstances? What quality are we speaking of?

In many countries, the essential resources are lacking: a death of teachers, a lack or semi-lack of textbooks, difficulty in gaining access to information technologies, not to mention methodologies for needs assessment, curriculum design, teaching or results evaluation.

Furthermore, we must ask the following question: of all these criteria can be measured by quantitative indicators, for example—and, it my opinion, this question is crucial—how can we evaluate the quality of human relations and the know-how and commitment required for living together?

Where living together is concerned, it seems clear that the vision of global harmony is a kind of quest for the "inaccessible star"—my appologies here for the reference to a Belgian singer. Conflicts exist, they are unavoidable. What we must do—and I am speaking here of cultural conflicts of course—is to teach young people to manage them, that is to say, to give them the means of preventing and managing these conflicts.

LINES OF APPROACH

There are many lines of approach, and I shall not mention all of them. Here are just a few of them.

The first point—which I think was made again and again throughout this conference—is that there is a strong desire to gain better knowledge of and share experiences and good practices in regard to both the quality of educational and educations reform or practices.

There is deep-seated awareness that the school must build partnerships at all levels of society (local, regional and global), including in the economic sphere, in order to develop human resources and social cohesion. Such partnerships must be understood as a process of appropriation, whereby each person makes the education system his or her own and local energies and resources are mobilized around the school itself of course but also around the various processes that take place in school in the era of planning and, for example, curricula, which are sometimes tricky to deal with. One comment in this connection: this type of partnership should also help, through greater transparency, to eradicate waste in a number of areas and, in some cases, corruption.

Culture, of course, cannot be ranked hierarchically and only education designed to foster empathy will enable conflicts in this sphere to be managed effectively.

I shall conclude by referring to a number of statements concerning the future. We are talking about education in the twenty-first century, it is now 2001, and we therefore have 99 years of the twentieth century ahead of us. Most of us will not be here to see how it ends. Well, I hope that you will—I personally am not over-optimistic—but it is clear that predicting the future, except for those who make a business of it, is a difficult exercise. What knowledge, what skills will tomorrow's youth need to integrate themselves and live in society? What skills will tomorrow's teachers need to teach? Will those who are currently passing through our teacher-training colleges and universities be teaching in the next thirty years? No one can answer that question.

I want to refer here to a very great English educator who said that in 10 years' time 30 per cent of the knowledge that will be taught is as yet unknown today. I therefore believe that we must inevitably come back to skills, to "knowledge in action", or a capacity to translate knowledge into action, to basic skills, to core skills as the English expression has it.

These core skills, seem to have been identified throughout our debates. They are essentially:

1. Learning to learn (which is described in a programme as "lifelong learning" but is basically learning to learn);
2. making relevant and effective use of communication technologies;
3. science education, including mathematics, of course;
4. social skills, for living together, tolerance and empathy.

In conclusion, we may say, indisputably, that the quality of education, having regard to those criteria, is the same as quality of life and that consequently everyone should be guaranteed the possibility of access to such a quality of life. Two remarks before I end,—because I think I have exceeded the time allotted to me. There were many discussions and comments on the status of teachers. I am a teacher, a university teacher, that is to say, not very good from the pedagogical point of view! The higher one rises in the education system, the less one needs to be good from the teaching standpoint. Several delegates stressed that it was high time to review the status of teachers; it is necessary to improve teachers' benefits in practical terms in all countries and review initial and in-service training; it is necessary to place higher value on their work and to support them. I am convinced that society as a whole has a role to play in regard.

We have spoken a great deal about quality, and we have frequently pondered what that could be. I think that several approaches could clearly be adopted, but one approach would involve a combination of commitment and a dual mechanism that is theoretically or conceptually relatively simple but very difficult to put into practice. It is the dual evaluation approach involving both internal and external evaluation. That has not been discussed as such, and I simply wished to make this point of clarification in relation to the discussion that took place. I think that we must necessarily accept that while internal evaluation involves being subject to the scrutiny of others, external evaluation is even harder because the evaluators are persons who are not part of the school community.

I thank you for having listened to me. I hope—as I said at the beginning—that I have not created too many frustrations and that I have provided a more or less faithful account of all the discussions. At all events, I can tell you that I am extremely proud to have taken part in them.

Thank you vary much.

B. Conclusions and proposals for action arising from the 46th session of the ICE

PREAMBLE

1. The International Bureau of Education, in its capacity as a UNESCO specialized centre for the contents, structures and methods of education, organized the 46th session of the International Conference on Education in Geneva from 5 to 8 September 2001.
2. More than 600 participants took part in the discussion, of whom 80 were ministers and 10 vice-ministers of education, coming from 127 Member States of UNESCO, together with nine representatives of intergovernmental orgainzations. 13 non-governmental organizations and three foundations.
3. The objective of intensifying and strengthening dialogue at the level of educational policies on the problems and prospects of solutions with a view to improving the quality of education for *learning to live together* has been largely achieved. These conclusions and the resulting proposals for action present the key features of the debates and preparatory work (Netforum, ministerial messages, national reports, good practices, etc.). The entire collection will be made known through the final report, the reports of the workshops and the other documents to be published after the Conference.
4. These conclusions, adopted on 8 September 2001, have been drawn from the major debates, the plenary sessions and the six workshops that took place during the Conference. They are intended for governments, international intergovernmental and non-governmental organizations, teachers and organizations of the teaching profession, the media and all partners in civil society whose efforts improve the quality of education, encourage dialogue and develop the capacity to live together.

CHALLENGES

5. Given the enormous complexity of the problems all societies have to face, particularly globalization, and

unbearable inequalities between and within countries, *learning to live together*, a concept created by the International Commission on Education for the Twenty-fist Century, has become a necessity in all regions of the world.

6. One of the major challenges confronting education systems remains that of guaranteeing and respecting the right of education for all. However, the rights of children to have free access to schools is far from being respected everywhere in the world and particularly in those countries experiencing situations of war, occupation, violence and intolerance.
7. The plea for education to overcome these challenges facing societies is not a new phenomenon. Yet, today, the expectation have become far more urgent, giving the impression that education can by itself overcome the problems that exist in countries and at the international level.
8. Both formal and non-formal education are essential tools for launching and promoting sustainable processes of constructing peace, democracy and human rights, but they cannot alone provide solutions to the complexity, the tensions and even the contradictions of the present world.
9. It is essential, however, as was stressed in the Jomtien Declaration and the Dakar Framework for Action, that efforts at the national and international levels to develop education be complemented by global strategies to eliminate poverty and to promote participation in political, social and cultural life.
10. Achieving the objective of education for all goes beyond the effort of universal schooling. Within each country, the search for social cohesion, the struggle against inequality, the respect for cultural diversity and access to the knowledge society, which may be facilitated by information and communication technologies, will be achieved through policies that focus on improving the equality of education.
11. These policies must overcome the obstacles posed by inequalities of access and risks of exclusion in the field of languages, science and technology.

- As far as languages are concerned, it is possible to note that numerous countries are multilingual even though a single languages appears as the official language of communication.
- Concerning science and technology, particularly those of information and communication, the gulf is growing wider due to inequality in access to the most recent advances.

EDUCATIONAL POLICIES AND PRACTICES

12. Throughout the world there is a strong political will on the part of numerous governments and teachers to adapt educational contents, structures and methods in order to respond to the above-mentioned challenges.
13. The experiences of educational policies and practices indicate that it is necessary to consider reforms more as processes than as products. These may arise as much from governmental decisions as from the initiatives of other stakeholders. The way in which they are implemented, involving the mobilisation of all actors, is as important as the content.
14. Basic agreements within the international community already exist concerning lines of action for promoting the ability and willingness to live together. Those responsible for education policies at the national level have clearly expressed their will to pursue the implementation of these agreements.
15. The evaluation of the outcomes of the reform processes, and particularly "good practices", enables us to highlight both some conditions unique to each cultural context as well as to pinpoint some common characteristics.

PROPOSALS FOR ACTION

16. The entire range of teaching and educational practices for living together should be better known, disseminated and exploited with a view to strengthening the endogenous capacities of each country.
17. Training for policy dialogue is essential in order to achieve the major objective of improving the quality of education for all.

18. Reform processes should be continued or undertaken in the following domains:

Contents:

- Adapting curricula and updating contents in order to reflect:
  - — economic and social changes set in motion, in particular, by globalization, migration and cultural diversity;
  - — the ethical dimension of scientific and technological progress;
  - — the growing importance of communication, expression and the capacity to listen and dialogue, first of all in the mother tongue, then in the office languages in the country as well as in one or more foreign languages;
  - — the positive contribution that may result from integrating technologies into the learning process.
- Developing not only disciplinary but also interdisciplinary approaches and competencies;
- Supporting and nurturing innovation;
- Seeking, in the development of curricula, to ensure relevance at the local, national and international level at the same time.

Methods

- Promoting active learning methods and teamwork;
- Encouraging all-round and balanced development and preparing the individual for active citizenship open to the world.

Teachers

- Facilitating genuine involvement on the part of teachers in decision-making within the school, through training and other means;
- Improving the education of teachers so that they can better develop among pupils behaviour and values of solidarity and tolerance, so as to prepare them to prevent and resolve conflicts peacefully and to respect cultural diversity;

- Changing the relationship between teacher and pupil to respond to the evolution of society;
- Improving the use of information and communication technologies in teacher training and in classroom practices.

Daily life in educational institutions

- Creating within the school a climate of tolerance and respect encouraging the development of a democratic culture;
- Providing a way for the school to function that encourages participation of the pupils in decision-marking;
- Proposing a definition of projects and learning activities.

Educational research

- Stimulating research that clarifies the concept of learning to live together and the implications for policy and practices;
- Promoting research on the development of contents and teaching methods relating to learning to live together;
- Stimulating comparative studies in the subregional, regional and transregional contexts.

Partnerships

- Since education is not the sole answer to learning to live together, its improvement requires the contribution not only of the school but also of all concerned actors. It therefore implies the introduction and the strengthening of genuine partnerships with the entire society: teachers, communities, families, the economic sector, the media, NGOs and the intellectual and spiritual authorities.
- Partnerships are also required to expand access to and effective use of new information and communication technologies.

20. *Learning to live together* requires politicies for the development of lifelong learning beginning with early childhood

education, and paying particular attention to the period of adolescence (12-18 years).

INTERNATIONAL COOPERATION

21. The development of international co-operative activities to improve the quality of education for learning to live together for all should be based on six main principles:
    - Strengthening the function of the IBE as an observatory of trends, as well as its role in the development of easily accessible data banks and information systems;
    - Collecting the results of educational research on the development of contents, undertaking comparative studies at the subregional and regional levels, and their worldwide dissemination;
    - Setting up cooperative networks at the international regional and subregional levels facilitating the exchange of experience and promoting joint projects in order to strengthen endogenous capacities;
    - Training educational decision-makers in policy dialogue so as to encourage the definition of common objectives, the search for consensus and the mobilization of partnerships;
    - Experimenting with new modalities of technical assistance provided by bi- or multilateral cooperation agencies, in order to emphasize not only North-South but also South-South collaboration;
    - Strengthening of partnerships between UNESCO and other relevant intergovernmental organizations.

THE ROLE OF UNESCO AND ITS SPECIALIZED INSTITUTES

22. The conclusions of the 46th session of the International Conference on Education are communicated to the General Conference of the Organization in order to be taken into account in the process of reflection and to reinforce, in the short, medium and long terms, the programme of action of UNESCO, the International Bureau of Education and the other specialized institutes with a view to improving the quality of education.

ANNEX I

Opening address by Mr. Andrés G. Delich, Minister of Education of Argentina

Ladies and Gentlemen,

Good day to you all. It is a vary great honour for me to preside over the beginning of the opening meeting of the 46th session of the International Conference on Education. I should like to begin by expressing a few thoughts.

Introduction

In recent decades the world has undergone profound and increasingly rapid changes that have affected in irreversible fashion the liver of individuals and countries. As never before in history, the process of economic globalization, the development of communications and population mobility have interlinked the destiny of our societies. This new human condition confronts us with the challenge of reinventing ways whereby all the countries, cultures and inhabitants of the planet are able to live together.

The focus of this 46th session of the International Conference on Education could not be more appropriate and timely. This meeting of education officials from all over the world affords us the opportunity once more to learn with others and to exchange experiences in the context of international cooperation.

We have come together to discuss and agree on how schools and education systems can contribute to the improvement of human coexistence in the twenty-first century. We believe in the transforming power of education. This is why we are here. But it must be said that we are aware of the enormous difficulties and obstacles facing the development of an educational project for coexistence in a world divided by the growing distance between regions and countries.

Inequalities, interdependence and multiculturality

The gaps between rich and poor countries seem to have become unbridgeable gulfs. The average income of the richest countries was 11 times higher than that of the poorest countries in 1913, 35 times higher in 1950, 44 in 1973 and 72 in 1993. The richest 5 per cent of humanity earns 85 per cent of the world income, while the poorest 5 per cent shares 1 per cent. The total wealth of the poorest one thousand million human beings is equal to that of the one hundred richest.

The accelerated transnationalization of economic flows has increased wealth production. It has also caused wealth to be concentrated in a few regions of the world and to be enjoyed only by a small minority of humanity. We have entered the third millennium and millions of people are dying each year from hunger, diseases of social origin or armed conflict among or within countries.

The external debt has become a very difficult obstacle to overcome for many countries with a low or medium level of development. As you know, my country is facing a complex situation arising from the burden of the high interests on its debt and the difficulties experienced in selling its products to countries that strongly protect their markets while exerting pressure for more open trade on politically less powerful and economically less developed nations.

Human development is consensually defined as the process of broadening people's options. But if they do not have those basic opportunities, many other opportunities become unavailable. In countries and continents like mine, which are marked by profound inequalities in life opportunities, education has not yet become a right for everyone. Every boy and girl born today in one of the poor population groups of Latin America, Africa, Asia or other continents has few chances of gaining access to adequate education and is very likely not to find work that would make it possible to live in dignity or dream of a batter future.

Education is a basic tool in building a more just and humane future. But progress in achieving peaceful coexistence will be difficult if the growing inequalities in economic development continue unchanged.

How is it possible to live together peacefully in a world in which inequalities plunge entire nations into despair? In the absence of a more rational pattern of consumption and a fairer distribution of wealth it will be very difficult to educate for living together. If the extreme utopia of freedom that finds expression in the global economy is not counterbalanced by the policies of justice, equity and fraternity, there will be no true coexistence. The fact is that the freedom of action of a minority has been growing at the cost of the right of the majority of humanity to a decent life.

The rapid expansion of communication networks is bringing events that were previously regarded as distant and remote to every corner of the world. These processes are pushing societies in two opposing directions, accentuating simultaneously the trend towards the international standardization of lifestyles and the quest for a community specificity that reinforces local and regional identities and sets itself apart from others, perceived as sources of threat or danger. The disappearance of old lifestyles causes anxiety and a deep sense of loss. Today there is no lack of examples of forms of nationalism that encourage extreme political separatism or incomprehensible genocides in the name of ethnic cleansing. We must work to overcome ethnic and religious fundamentalism, state fundamentalism and market fundamentalism. If we aim to live genuinely together, we must realise that the problems of humanity cannot be solved by closing physical and cultural borders—much less by seclusion or indifferences to the poor or those excluded by the new world order.

It is certainly the case that signs of disquiet and impatience abound. Societies have sensed that a linear projection of current trends does not augur well for a happy or peaceful future.

The role of education

In view of the growing tendency for the social bond to be replaced by individualistic impulses, learning to live together is one of the main tasks of education today.

We must conceive and promote new forms of building the future of societies through education. The challenge facing this Conference is precisely to reflect on the contribution of education to human coexistence at the turn of the twenty-first century. The question that we must consider is whether the schools in each of our countries are helping to prepare the rising generations to live together in the twenty-first century. I should like to make three points in this connection.

1. Educational inclusion policies must be strengthened and transformed, particularly in the developing world

It is clear that there will be no significant advances in human coexistence worldwide if there is not a massive increase in social, economic and educational opportunities for the most disadvantaged population groups in the next few years. Ensuring that all children and young people have access to and remain in basic education should be the first priority of the less developed countries. If people's right to adequate educational opportunities is not guaranteed, it could be a pointless exercise to think about educational strategies for living together in the twenty-first century.

This priority has been identified as a global imperative for more than three decades now. It found expression in the pledges made at the Jomtien Conference, among other fora. But while educational coverage continues to expand, the proposed goals are still very largely unmet: the dark areas on the map of basic education provision coincide with the geography of extreme poverty, economic underdevelopment and social inequity.

At the same time, in recent years, reforms have emphasized the idea that education system must make progress in developing policies to improve quality. This goal, which is necessary to adapt education systems to today's challenge, has in many cases entailed a shift in the focus of attention on the inclusion of the poorest.

Our education systems are faced with a set of highly complex tensions. The priority of catering for those who have the fewest basic education opportunities comes into conflict with other economic, political and social requirements in most developing countries. Our countries need highly qualified staff; they also need to create a body of informed, active and responsible citizens. The demand for resources to finance the universal provision of basic education has to be set against the investment needed for specialized training linked to the world market and to systems of innovation, science and technology.

How can the tension between equity and competitiveness and between social inclusion and the strengthening of sectors with the highest growth potential be resolved? In the first decade of the twenty-first century, education system will have to show flexibility in order find trade-offs and strike balances between these two demands.

Countries with a medium and low level of economic development experience great difficulties in ensuring the universal provision of quality basic education while adopting the same parameters and the same strategies as the main developed countries. The costs are difficult to sustain and, despite the efforts made, the results are not at all encouraging. Efforts to promote educational inclusion must therefore be accompanied by alternatives to traditional schooling, making use of community resources and energies, open and flexible methods and a variety of technologies, methods and materials. A great deal of experience has been gained over the last few decades, but national policies have not acted with sufficient conviction upon the lessons learnt in this domain. It seems clear, however, that the less developed countries' policies to promote inclusion and increase opportunities in basic education should pay closer and more systematic attention to the school system's non-traditional institutional resources and technologies.

2. We must promote systematic human rights education and its reestablishment in each country and culture

Human rights provide a very important normative foundation for education for living together. They constitute the basic reference in the promotion of education in and for human coexistence at the turn of the twenty-first century.

The sphere of influence and normative force of human rights have increased considerably in the last few years. This reflects a change in the sensibility of societies compared with the confrontational styles that prevailed even a few decade ago. However, alongside the victory of these ideas, there is some scepticism or weariness regarding the chances of achieving their effective realization.

We must look at this process in its historical perspective. In the last part of the twentieth century, we have made great strides in building international agreements and consensus about what we consider valuable and what we consider unacceptable for humankind. The human rights tradition is based on the belief that over and above distinctive characteristics, people from different countries and cultures are capable of sharing basic values and of agreeing on a few common commitments.

The universality or specificity of human rights has been much discussed. No one holds the monopoly over the interpretation of cultures and values. We must understand that human rights are one of the traditions that we have devised in order to communicate with each other and debate on a core of ethical issues that affect all human beings. Alongside this tradition in the process of construction, different cultures and ways of seeing the world can coexist and dialogue.

Human rights education should be a priority at all levels of education. Education should promote new ways of understanding and cultivating human rights. While substantial progress has been made, this priority needs to be reflected in curricula and in the training of teachers and educational leaders in every country. One of the goals of the conference should be to conceive clear commitments in this regard.

3. We need to define the outlines of a global education based on knowledge of diversity, dialogue and cultural mixing

We human beings tend to overrate the qualities of the groups and cultures to which we belong, and to nurture prejudice against the others. Will it be possible to design a form of education enabling conflicts to be avoided or resolved in a peaceful manner, by promoting knowledge of others, their culture and spirituality.

The main problem is that the education systems within which education for living together must be provided have historically been based on the glorification of the national culture. They are nearly always based on principles that stem from beliefs that prevailed before the planetary era. In the school systems of many countries, there are still substantial problems regarding the ideas that are taught. Racial prejudice, neo-colonialist visions, one-sided conceptions of science and knowledge continues to be presented to the young generations, impeding awareness of the basic unity of the world around them.

In the last few decades educational policies based on the premise/postulate of a homogeneous national culture have been subjected to critical review, which has given rise to the expression of cultural diversity in schools. However, our schools today are still very limited instruments for promoting the new model of thought that is now required to enable humanity to coexist in peace.

Education in the twenty-first century has a twofold mission: to teach about diversity and the problems of the human species and to help to raise awareness of the similarities and interdependence that exist among all human beings. If the young are taught to adopt other people's point of view, misunderstandings that could lead to hatred and violence in adults can be avoided. But is it merely a question of inculcating feelings of tolerance? Will this be sufficient to overcome the brute force of indifference?

How much time is devoted in schools to learning about and interacting with the realities of other social groups, cultures or countries? Through schools we must cultivate the idea that the peaceful survival of humanity depends on the promotion of global sensibility and knowledge. To educate people to live together, it is necessary to bring about a reform of the way in which schools represent the world and the destiny of the peoples that inhabit the planet.

It is an immense but inescapable task. The development of the peaceful coexistence of humanity demands that we reconstruct the core of moral education. And this core cannot be based only on the cultivation of fine feelings: it must touch upon the structuring of scientific knowledge and the aesthetic, social and philosophical experience that schools promote.

Perhaps the greatest causes for concern is not what is taught but what is not taught. Throughout the world emphasis is being laid once more on the school's role in the development of moral values. But can one value, cooperate and coexist with someone one does not know? If the realities are not known, affections cannot be cultivated. There is no feeling of cooperation or fraternity that can grow when tended by the hand of ignorance.

In the last few decades that need to reflect on cultural diversity has become obvious in a world in which strong manifestations of the tendency to extol the local culture exists alongside one another and are sometimes accompanied by a dangerous rejection of those who think and act differently or possess different cultural values. Peaceful coexistence in tomorrow's world will only be possible if we build shared values founded on the celebration of our differences.

The significance of this conference

The three ideas that I have put forward concerning the role of education for living together in the twenty-first century point to the need to reaffirm the principles and objectives recognized by the international community and at the same time to re-evaluate the strategies and instruments that we use for achieving them.

From the global standpoint, we do not lack the intellectual technical or economic resources for addressing the problems. But only intellectual cooperation, renewed in spirit and endowed with greater resources, will be able to generate the instruments that we need. Sustained and resolute action by the international community, State, non-governmental organizations, groups and individuals all over the world are the means to secure the basic conditions for the full development of harmonious relationships on the part of each human being. Through cooperation we can transform the globalization of problems into a mobilization of educational energies worldwide.

Institutionalized education has a key role to play in building human coexistence. But we should not ourselves. Bringing about the necessary conditions for living together in tomorrow's world does not depend only or mainly on education.

The human species is a large and diverse family. Differences of race and religion, nationality and ideology, gender and sexual preference, economic and social position must be rethought in terms of that fundamental unity. Will we be able to direct our educational efforts along this path?

We share the earth, we share development. The is the basis on which education will be able to make its contribution to living together in the twenty-first century. Today we are being given a new opportunity. Our task is to turn it to account.

Thank you.

ANNEX II

Opening address by Mr. Koïchiro Matsuura, Director-General of UNESCO

Mr. President,
Distinguished Ministers of Education,
Distinguished Heads of Delegations,
Ladies and Gentlemen,
Dear Colleagues and Friends,

It gives me great pleasure to welcome you to the 46th Session of the International Conference on Education (ICE). I would like to immediately express my sincere thanks to you, Mr President, for your opening address, which provided a number of perceptive observations highly relevant to the thematic issues that this Conference will examine. I would also like to thank the Swiss Federal authorities and the authorities of the Republic and Canton of Geneva for the long-standing hospitality they have offered to this Conference and to the International Bureau of Education (IBE). Geneva is truly an international city and it is a pleasure to resume here the great tradition of the ICE after an interval of five years.

I am pleased to see so many ministers and vice-ministers here today. Their presence testifies to the uniqueness of this international forum and to their interest in its thematic concerns and the importance of Education for All. With the greatest respect to the other participants, I would like to emphasize that this is, without question, your conference. Indeed, it is the centrality of your presence, participation and contributions that gives the ICE its distinctive quality compared with other international conferences on education.

However, a vital ingredient of the ICE is the contribution by other participants from the domains of academia, research, international cooperation, and civil society, drawn here by their interest in the Conference's themes and the very nature of the event itself. Your active participation in the Conference is warmly welcomed. Thus, I am pleased to welcome the representatives and observers of non-Members States, United Nations agencies, inter-governmental bodies and non-governmental organizations.

I would also like to express my gratitude to all those who have helped in the preparations for this Conference by providing intellectual and/or financial contributions: the ministries of education, research centres and training institutions of several countries (Argentina, Canada, Cuba, and Czech Republic, Denmark, Finland, France, Germany, Japan, Malaysia, the Netherland, Norway, Spain, Switzerland); the Commonwealth of Learning; the Training Programme for Bilingual Intercultural Education for the Andean Countries; the BERUM Project in Peru; the Graduate Institute for Development Studies in Geneva; the Cité des sciences et de l'industrie in Paris; the NGO Centre for the Study of Violence and Reconciliation in South Africa. Last but not least, I would like to both thank and congratulate the IBE Council for its hard work, education and creativity in designing and preparing this year's Conference; the Council's Chairperson, Mr. Pieter De Meijer, Chairman of the National Commission for UNESCO of the Netherlands, deserves our particular thanks.

The ICE is an event with a rich and interesting tradition. Under the name of 'the International Conference on Public Education', it was first organized in 1934 by the International Bureau of Education at a time when militarism and fascism were on the march. From 1947 onwards, each Conference was organized jointly by the IBE and UNESCO. Since 1969, when the IBE became an integral part of UNESCO, this event has been known as the International Conference on Education. As the only event addressed to all of the world's Ministers of Education, the ICE serves as a unique international forum for high-level dialogue on educational issues and their policy implications.

The International Conference on Education, like the IBE, is an integral part of UNESCO. Notwithstanding the lapse of time since the 45th Session, the ICE is one of the most important events in the Organization's calendar. It is my honour and responsibility to invite the participants. Meanwhile, it is the

General Conference of UNESCO that approves the themes of the ICE in light of proposals submitted by the IBE Council, whose members are chosen by the General Conference. Through the national reports submitted to the ICE and the presentations, discussions and exchanges occurring during the Conference, an abundance of data becomes available to the IBE and to UNESCO more widely. I can assure you that UNESCO greatly values this occasion as a singular opportunity to listen to and interact with many of the world's key decision-makers in the field of education.

As with all the other activities organized by the IBE, the International Conference on Education in embedded within the framework of the UNESCO's Medium-Term Strategy (2002-2007). In fact, the timing of the ICE could not be better, coming as it does just weeks before the Strategy will be submitted to the General Conference for approval. The leitmotif running through the next Medium-Term Strategy is the following: 'Contributing to peace and development in an era of globalization through education, the sciences, culture and communication". For UNESCO, the unifying theme shaping all of its programmes and activities is the challenge of humanizing globalization so that it works for everyone, not just for a privileged few. Central to the process of giving globalization a human face is education, especially in terms of globalizing the right to education so that good quality basic education is available to all.

It is also very timely that the ICE is being held now, when the Dakar follow-up process is gathering much momentum. The meeting of the World Education forum in Dakar, Senegal, in April 2000 was a decisive turning-point for UNESCO. As required by the Dakar Framework for Action, UNESCO has placed the outcomes and priorities of Dakar at the heart of its work. Building upon the reform and structuring that I initiated and completed, UNESCO has refocussed its education programme within the Medium-Term Strategy and is fulfilling its mandated role of co-ordinating EFA partners and maintaining their collaborative momentum. Let there be no mistake: Education for All is UNESCO's highest priority for the period ahead and, thanks to the commitments freely made in Dakar, we are not alone in this endeavour. Without effective partnership, the EFA goals will not be reached. With effective partnership, we have a good chance of achieving something quite remarkable. The true test of partnership will be found at the country level, where the combined efforts of national and international actors must be primarily focused.

Consequently, UNESCO accords great importance to the theme of this year's ICE—"Education for All for learning to live together: contents and learning strategies—problems and solutions". It is most timely and appropriate that the ICE is to address this theme shortly before the 31st session of the General Conference. The outcomes and recommendations of the ICE will be immediately channelled into the deliberations of the General Conference in October and November. I believe that this will serve as a great incentive to make our discussions, debates and decisions in the next few days as relevant and well-conceived as possible.

Ladies and Gentlemen,

The theme of "learning to live together" must be addressed from two main angles: first, from the perspective of social cohesion, harmony and non-violence within our societies, and second, from the perspective of international peace, mutual understanding, and friendship between our societies. These dimensions, of course, are connected: a country at war with itself may also be a threat to its neighbours, and external wars have a habit of generating many internal conflicts and tensions. Concern for the contribution of education to world peace, international understanding social cohesion and non-violence has always been at the heart of the ICE's deliberations. It is precisely for this reason that it has maintained its relevance for almost seventy years. Through the choice of theme for this session, the ICE shows once again how close is the link between the themes of its debates and the priorities of the whole international community.

At this Conference, we have a golden opportunity not only to reinforce the commitments made in Dakar to achieve quality basic education for all by 2015 but also to reflect further upon the meaning and purpose of Education for All. What does quality basic education for all mean? What aims of purposes explain and justify the enormous efforts required to achieve it?

In this regard, it is important to note that the Dakar Framework for Action clearly links the improvement of the quality of basic education to the effective acquisition of literacy, numeracy and essential life-skills. What is literacy today if it does not develop our ability to communicate so that, by opening local, national and global participation to everyone, our personal freedom is enlarged? What is numeracy today if it does not develop our ability to analyse and organize data concerning the many dimensions of our lives and enhance our capacity to participate in the knowledge society? Clearly, literacy and numeracy are not merely technical but are social in character, vitally linked to our capacity for personal freedom and social action.

And what do life-skills mean today if they do not embrace the desire as well as the ability to live together in peace? The term "essential life-skills" must include the abilities to mix with others, cooperate, communicate, undertake joint actions, participate, and build mutual trust as well as self-confidence.

These considerations convince me more than ever that EFA makes good sense for many kinds of reasons but the core of the rationale for EFA is ethical; it concerns the rights of each person to fulfil his or her potential and to live a full human life in society. Living in peace with one another is an integral part of this vision. And learning how to live at peace with others is an indispensable part of all education.

But we still have a long way to go. Since the last session of the ICE, the world has moved into a new century and, indeed, a new millennium but we remain beset by familiar problems. Thus, different groups and entire communities in all he regions of the world continue to suffer from the effects of war, internal conflicts, injustice, poverty, intolerance, racism, marginalization, and different forms of violence. The basic rights of millions remain unfulfilled, including those which go to the heart of personal and group identity such as language and culture. The world remains a place where the conditions for living at peace with one another are fragile and are particularly vulnerable to the resentments arising from injustices and structured social inequalities.

The main educational preoccupation of the past century was to guarantee wider access to educational opportunities but much remains to be done in many countries. The achievement of quantitative educational goals is still important where universal primary education and universal literacy and far from being realized. At the beginning of the twenty-first century, however, the quality of basic education must also be improved so that everyone is well prepared for participation in modern life. Each of us needs the tools, aptitudes and values essential for facing a world of rapid change, increasing complexity, widespread uncertainty, and inter-dependence. Above all, a basic education that fails to equip us to live together peaceably does not deserve to be called an education of genuine quality.

Ladies and Gentlemen,

I have been very impressed by reading a preliminary analysis of the content of the national reports prepared for this Conference. Clearly, much progress has occurred in raising awareness about the need to educate in favour of values, concepts and capacities that help young people to learn how to live peaceably together and, just as important, encourage them to want to live peaceably together.

The analysis contained in the Conference's main working document is very useful. It shows how human rights, the protection of cultural diversity, respect for local languages and mother tongues, the call for peace and the peaceful resolution of conflicts, and the application of scientific procedures and new technologies are being incorporated into the planning of curricula and other aspects of national policy-making.

We also note that Ministries of Education have identified a number of problem areas and related questions. How can learning about peaceful daily life be developed within formal school settings? How can the importance and urgency of this educational issues be matched with available resources? How can learning about peaceful daily life be incorporated into a framework of lifelong learning opportunities for all? Moreover, in many of the preparatory meetings organized by the IBE in various regions of the world, a common refrain has been that violence is a fact of life in many schools. We believe that these critical appraisals arise from an increasingly firm resolve to face these problems squarely: first, by recognizing them; second, by sharing them; and, third, by learning co-operatively to overcome them.

I also applaud the way in which good practices and viable innovations have been collected by the IBE, with the support of UNESCO's Education Sector, the country, cluster and regional offices of UNESCO, national commissions, and numerous non-governmental organizations, especially those NGOs representing teachers involved in education for learning to live together. These lessons from practice show that solutions to existing problems do exist, that such solutions are plentiful and diverse, and that greater knowledge of them can help us to provide fresh responses to the difficulties faced on a daily basis by teachers and pupils alike.

Many ideas and much information will circulate during this Conference, I hope that those responsible for national education will be able, as a result, to make better, more informed decisions. It is important that the duly constituted national authorities do indeed retain the will and capacity for decision-making in education. Some analysts have argued that, given the influence and effects of globalization, the nation-state is losing its validity. I do not agree. On the contrary, I am convinced that the state's guiding role and the legitimate and authoritative character of its policies are more important than ever. On the other hand, we must acknowledge that the definition of the state's role and the performance of its functions are under challenge from a variety of forces: for example, the internationalization of knowledge, the shifting balance between centralization and decentralization and the sheer variety of national and local policy options available.

In addition, quite a number of countries are seeing new actors enter the national education picture. A few of these new actors are international in character, but most are national and local. Some of these actors may not be so 'new' but, due to processes of decentralization, improved communications or democratization, they may be finding their voices or strengthening their presence in the educational domain. UNESCO clearly encourages all states and public authorities to fulfil their core obligations towards education; at the same time, we recognize that the state cannot do everything and need not do some things only by itself. Thus, in regard to certain educational responsibilities, the state may find it useful to build strategic alliances with civil society institutions and the private sector. Within an overall framework of state regulation, monitoring and quality assurance, considerable advantages and benefits may ensure.

In recognition of such trends, and in keeping with the clear massage from Dakar about the need to involve civil society more actively in all aspects of the EFA process, a Special Session will be held on Saturday. This Special Session, which I will chair myself, will be devoted to "the involvement of civil society in promoting education for all". UNESCO is convinced that productive state/civil society relations in the field of education are necessary not only for achieving the quantitative and qualitative goals agreed in Dakar but also for assisting the design and implementation of initiatives for learning to live together. Partnership and cooperation begin at home.

Obviously, the way to promote effective and appropriate education for living together is not the same in all cultures and in all contexts. However, in this globalized world, the intelligent and creative combination of relevant global strategies with a diverse range of local and national solutions offers the greatest promise.

I very much look forward to the outcomes and recommendations of this Conference. I am sure that you will find that the theme of 'learning to live together' intersects with many of your most pressing concerns, ranging from violence in the classroom to the use of information and communication technologies (ICTs), from language teaching to citizenship education within the perspective of lifelong learning. The framing of these issues, problems and concerns within the context of Education for All shows that it is quite wrong to see EFA just in terms of quantitative developments, important though these are. The agenda of EFA must be seen to include the improvement of the quality of basic education. This is our shared challenge.

Thank you,

Annex III

Opening address by Ms. Martine Brunschwig Graf, State Counsellor, Head of the Swiss Delegation

Mr. President,
Excellencies,
Distinguished Ministers and Heads of Delegation,
Mr. Director-General of UNESCO,
Madam Director of the IBE,
Ladies and gentlemen representing teachers, parents, the world of science and civil society as a whole,

Dear friends and conference guests,

On behalf of the Swiss Confederation and the Republic and Canton of Geneva, I have the pleasure to extend warmest greetings to you. We are very proud to host in Geneva a conference that, for the 46th time, has placed education and the future of all the world's young people at the forefront of its concerns. Geneva, the seat of the International Bureau of Education, the centre of activity where Jean Piaget chose to carry out his most important work, is thus honoured and ready once again to fulfil its vocation as host and venue open to all those who are working to improve people's living conditions.

During the next four days we will have the opportunity to get to know each other better and strengthen our ties in the discussion workshops and plenary meetings and on the less formal occasions of the scheduled fringe events. Here and now I have the pleasure of inviting you to the reception to be held by the Swiss delegation this evening at the Hotel Intercontinental.

We can only thank the International Bureau of Education, which organized this conference, for having scheduled the meetings in such a way as to afford opportunities for exchanges of views and socializing so that we can strengthen our ties as education officials from all over the world. We will thus demonstrate that the expression "living together", the common thread running through our work, is not a mere slogan—far from it. We will be able to show that we intend to apply the values and principles that underlie this goal, in particular the respect and willingness to listen that are indispensable to all democratic debates.

International dialogue, exchanges of experience or, to use the terms suggested by UNESCO, "the dissemination and sharing of information and best practices" are the core of the IBE's mission and the goal of the 46th session of the International Conference on Education. In that regard, I wish to stress that we already have an excellent point of departure thanks to the Conference's preparatory work.

I should now like to pay tribute to the Director and staff of the IBE for the quality of the documents submitted to us, which provide valuable considerations for our debates. They encourage us to compare ideas and bring us face to face with our responsibilities.

For example, by showing us that social cohesion and cultural diversity are two of our societies' major challenges in a globalizing world, they remind us that schools play a central role in the training of the world's citizens.

I could hardly say anything else since, being responsible for educational policy in the Republic and Canton of Geneva, I see every day the challenges of communal life in educational institutions attended by students of over 80 nationalities in some instances and with different mother tongues! And what about Switzerland, with its 26 autonomous cantons and school systems, and its 4 national languages? We shall certainly be keenly interested in the topics discussed during the next few days, particularly those concerning the role of languages in people's ability to live together in a climate of respect for each other!

You experience similar problems that are often compounded by very different financial, economic and social conditions. We all know that we must endeavour to combine the need for an identity with the obligation to respect diversity. We all feel that school is a crucial factor, even though we must be brave enough to say that it cannot do everything. Defining its future role and agreeing on innovative and indispensable educational procedures does not mean that we should be silent about the responsibility of all sectors of society.

Blaming schools for all the world's problems is as dangerous as disregarding them and depriving them of all scope for action. We must commit ourselves to quality education for all. We need to be able to rely on the competence and professional commitment of teachers, on educational tools that are suited to the learning processes and on adequate structures and financial resources. But schools cannot live without support from the members of society and the goodwill of all, parents, families and citizens, in applying and transmitting the principles that teachers undertake to develop in educational establishments.

Respect, receptiveness, a feeling for debate and democratic practice are values and principles that schools must apply and develop. But these values and principles must not remain the exclusive preserve of the school or stop at its doors.

We are here to reflect together and to share our successes and our problems. No country, no expert can claim to have miracle solutions in the field of education. We all face the same need to change and adapt education systems to the needs of those who will tomorrow be responsible for our planet's future. That makes us modest and enquiring. I also hope it will encourage us to be willing to listen, to dialogue and to share. That would no doubt be the best guarantee of this conferences' success!

Thank you for your attention.

ANNEX IV

Opening address by Mr. Abraham B. Borishade, Minister of Education of Nigeria and President of the 46th session of the International Conference on Education

Honourable Ministers,
Mr. Director-General,
Your Excellencies,
Madam Director of IBE,
Distinguished Delegates,
Ladies and Gentlemen,

It is with great humility that I rise to thank you all for the confidence you have reposed in me by your unanimous gesture of electing me to guide, with your cooperation, the deliberations of this 46th session of the International Conference on Education, which is taking place at this moment when we are all girding our loins to face the challenges of a new millennium.

Beyond my person, I consider your gesture as an honour to my country, and our President, Chief Olusegun Obasanjo, joins me in thanking you all. The honour is also, of course, being shared by our dear continent of Africa. In that context, I am most grateful to my colleagues from the African continent who kindly proposed my candidature for this position of honour and to all of you from all regions of the world for your generous acceptance of their proposal.

Please allow me at this point to pay due tribute to our outgoing President of the 45th session for her devotion and commitment in guiding our last session to a successful conclusion. Mr. President, please accept our thanks for your exemplary performance and contribution to our corporate work.

It is my determination to uphold the established excellence of our Conferences and with your help and support I am sure our deliberations and their results will live up to the high expectation of us all.

Dear Colleagues,

At its 30th session two years ago, the General Conference, in a forward-looking resolution, recognized the renewed mandate of the International Bureau of Education and the importance of the contribution that it is called upon to make for the achievement of the Education for All Programme of UNESCO. That resolution also bid the IBE to promote policy dialogue between decision-makers, researchers, educators and other partners in the educational process by organizing the 46th session of the International Conference on Education which, taking account of the four pillars of the Delors Report—in particular "Learning to live together"—will focus on ways of ensuring that each learner measters the knowledge, skills and attitudes required for the individual's and the society's intellectual and moral development.

This is the mandate of our gathering and this is the challenge for our deliberations in the next few days; our deliberations which are placed under the label of "Educational content and learning strategies for living together in the twenty-first century; problems and solutions".

Dear Colleagues and Mr. Director-General,

Dialogue and exchanges of ideas have always been essential hallmarks of the functioning of the International Conference on Education. And in the true spirit of dialogue, wide-ranging consultations have taken place in preparation for this Conference, involving Member States and their educational institutions, Ministers of Education, Members of the IBE College of Fellows and several other specialists in the field of education. This preparation has resulted in the rich and varied materials that we have before us, to help our discussions.

The hard reality today in education in many Member States is that in spite of the valiant efforts made in many countries, the achievement of our set goals in education, continue to elude us. It is true that there has been some progress and some achievements, most of them very laudable. But the stark reality is that we are far from achieving our aspiration of providing appropriate relevant and meaningful education for the individuals and for our societies.

So our duty here is, through exchange and dialogue, to fashion our plans for pooling our intellectual resources and sharing our practical experiences in a corporate effort to move our societies forward towards the excellence required for ensuring education for all, quality education for all, and education that is conducive to helping us meet the challenges of this dawning millennium—particularly the challenge of learning to live together.

Dear Colleagues,

You will soon be called upon to examine for approval the plans proposed by the Secretariat and our Bureau for the pursuit of our work at this session. It is a plan full of innovation and crafted out for maximum interaction among the participants and for ensuring the most in-depth examination of the many facets of the value and quality of Education for All. This, I am persuaded, will afford us the opportunities for intensified international dialogues and exchanges of experiences on the contents, the methods and the structures of teaching and education and at every level.

In reviewing the draft programme of work, I would humbly ask you to have firmly in mind the expected results of our deliberations and the proposals and recommendation that we hope will emerge from our work. We should ask ourselves to what extent are these plans suited to the full and thorough examination of the existing situation in education, are they properly geared towards enabling us to determine the "criteria for selection and organization of the contents and methods of our education" and finally, would the proposed format of work help us identify issues of shared concerns by all and the best practices as they exist today?

Dear Colleagues,

If at the end of our deliberation at this session we achieve these goals and we are able to present proposals and recommendations for strengthening national capacities for articulating and implementing innovative and effective educational policies and reforms; if our recommendations are truly geared towards sharply refocusing the Education for All movement and giving new life and meaning to the now established dialogue between our nations, through our Ministers of Education and other stakeholders in the field of education; if our proposals are clearly tailored for contributing to the strengthening of the "links between education, peace and the capacity to live together, then we would have made a meaningful contribution to the progress of the global effort in favour of education, that gathered force in Jomtien, some 11 years ago and which more recently has been reinvigorated in Dakar. And through our success here we would have moved further ahead in our preparation for confronting the educational challenges of the twenty-first century.

Dear Colleagues,

I have no doubt that together we will succeed in reaching our laudable goal.

I wish you "bon courage" and all success at this 46th session of the International Conference of Education on Education. And I thank you for your attention.

ANNEX V

Address by Mr. John Daniel, Assistant Director-General for Education, during the award of the Comenius Medal

Mr. President,

Ladies and Gentlemen,

It is a privilege to address you, on behalf of the Director-General of UNESCO, Mr. Koichiro Matsuura, at this Award Ceremony for the Comenius Medal. The Comenius Medal recognizes educators and researchers, as well as particular initiatives in education, for the excellence and outstanding quality of their work. When UNESCO and the Government of the Czech Republic created this award, we agreed to celebrate all those men and women who, like Comenius, help us build visions for a better future.

Mr. President,

This ceremony takes place at the first international gathering of educational policy-makers since the World Education Forum was held in Dakar, Senegal last year. The Dakar Forum followed a series of important international events, going back at least to the Educational for All conference that was held in Jomtien, Thailand in 1990.

Through these events the international community has been trying to address with what some have called the greatest moral challenge of our time, namely the fact that hundreds of millions of our fellow human beings cannot exercise their right to receive an education.

Let me briefly remind you of the six goals that were agreed in Dakar.

First, to expand and improve comprehensive early childhood care and education, especially for the most vulnerable and disadvantaged children. At present, of the 800 million children in the world who are under six years of age, fewer than one-third benefit from any form of early childhood care and education.

Second, to ensure that by 2015 all children, particularly girls, children in difficult circumstances and those belonging to ethnic minorities, have access to—and complete—free and compulsory primary education of good quality. Progress is being made. The net enrolment rate in primary school, which was under 65 per cent in less developed regions in 1970, had risen to 85 per cent by 2000. However this still leaves 113 million children, 60 per cent of whom are girls, out of school.

It is estimated that there are another 100 million children who start school but are taken out and put to work in homes, factories or armies before they have learned to read, write and use number. Sixty per cent of these uneducated children are in countries in conflict or post-conflict situations—adding to the difficulties.

Third, to ensure that the learning needs of all young people and adults are met through equitable access to appropriate learning and life skills programme.

Fourth, to achieve a 50 per cent improvement in the levels of adult illiteracy by 2015, especially for women, and equitable access to basic and continuing education for all adults. At present one in four of the adult population of our planet, some 800 million people, have their personal lives and the development of their communities blighted by illiteracy.

Fifth, to eliminate gender disparities in primary and secondary education by 2005, and achieve gender equality in education by 2015, with a focus on ensuring girls' full and equal access to—and achievement in—basic education of good quality.

Sixth, and finally, to improve all aspects of the quality of education so that recognized and measurable learning outcomes are achieved by all, especially in literacy, numeracy and essential life skills.

At the World Forum in Dakar the international community charged UNESCO with coordinating the collective effort to progress towards these goals. That is the agenda for Education for All which will be my daily challenge at UNESCO as new Assistant Director-General for Education.

The challenge is so great that we cannot rise to it simply by extending our existing methods and practices. We need innovative approaches to the deployment of media, communications and technologies. We need innovations in the way we train and deploy and respect teachers. We need to develop new and more imaginative ways of cooperating and working together; we need the leadership and commitment of men and women like those we are rewarding today.

Through you, the laureates of the Comenius Medal, I hope that we can achieve greater mobilization and commitment of the academic community and the intellectual community at large, in the collective effort required to meet the challenge of Education for All.

Mr. President,
Ladies and Gentlemen,

My admiration of Comenius is based on a rather general knowledge of his work. I am looking forward to hearing Dr. Sook Jone Lee, who is a Comenius specialist, speak on behalf of the laureates and help all of us to understand better the importance of this visionary educator. However, I do know that Comenius philosophy and educational thought were sometimes considered too grandiose or too general for the mental outlook of the seventeenth century.

Indeed, his "Via Lucis"-the way of light—is as visionary today as it was when he wrote it. Failing to meet the Education for All challenge would send us back to a "way of darkness"; and that would certainly be incompatible with the mental outlook of the twenty-first century.

Ladies and Gentlemen,

Before closing, I should like to thank Mr. Pieter de Meijer who, in his capacity as President of the Council of the International Bureau of Education, chaired the Jury appointed to evaluate and select candidates for the Comenius Medal. The task and the responsibility involved were very difficult in view of the wealth, diversity and quality of proposed candidates. However, when Mr. de Meijer introduces the candidates to you in a few moments, you will be able to ascertain, as I have, that the Jury has made the right and relevant choices.

I am also very grateful to the Ministry of Education, Youth and Sport of the Czech Republic, which not only enabled UNESCO to establish the Medal—as a joint undertaking—but continues to work with us to increase the number of Comenius heirs.

Lastly, I wish to congratulate all the candidates on the exemplary nature of their devotion and competence, to let them know that we are relying on them in the ongoing battle against exclusion, ignorance and poverty entailed in the challenge of

Education for All, and to express to them my admiration and pride in awarding them the Comenius Medal.
Thank you for your attention.

ANNEX VI

Address by Mr. P. de Meijer, President of the IBE Council, during the award of the Comenius Medal

Mr. President,
Excellencies,
Honourable Ministers,
Distinguished Laureates,
Distinguished Delegates, Representatives and Observers,
Ladies and Gentlemen,
Dear Friends,

As President of the Council of the International Bureau of Education it is an honour and a threefold joy to address you tonight.

My first joy, which has nothing chauvinistic about it, is to be doing so as a citizen of the Netherlands, my country, which was home to Jan Amos Komensky, also known as Comenius, for the last fourteen years of his life until his death in November 1670. And it was my home town, Amsterdam, that Comenius also published most of his works, which then spread throughout Europe and beyond.

My second joy is to be doing so at the 46th session of the International Conference on Education, during which ministers and heads of delegation, delegates, representatives and observers are considering together the best ways of achieving progress in Education for All, particularly the quality of education, with a view to "living better together". Comenius would have felt perfectly at ease among us for, to quote Jean Piaget, "the education system proposed by Comenius is universal by its very nature; it is intended for all people irrespective of differences in social or economic status, religion, race or nationality". And Piaget even added that "Comenius would have applauded modern campaigns against illiteracy, viewed as basic education and social reintegration campaigns".

With regard to the 46th session of the ICE, Comenius would have found without any difficulty a key position on some of our panels.

In Workshop No. 1, for example, he would have made the point that moral education (or civics as it is now called) is functional above all and that it emphasizes his preference for real-life practice rather than verbal constraints or lessons. He would also have said no doubt, in Workshop 2 on the subject of violence, that "blows have no power to inspire love of scholastic endeavour, but they are most capable of arousing aversion and hatred".

He would also have felt at ease in Workshop 4 on languages, as the author of the famous "Janua linguarum reserata" (The Gate of Tongues Unlocked), a textbook for teaching Latin which was translated into all the European languages and into Arabic. The book was composed of 100 chapters, which contained a thousand sentences compiled on a particular subject (the universe, animals, human beings, etc.). Opposite the Latin, the text was provided in the vernacular language so that it could be understood immediately. And Comenius did more than this: instead of getting lost in a large number of rules, the child was led, through language practice, in short simple sentences, to discover particular grammatical forms. Comenius also recommended that "instruction should begin in the mother tongue" and, for the purpose of language learning, encouraged people to travel to other countries.

He would also have appreciated Workshop 6 since, in his widely known book "Orbus pictus sensualis" (The Visible World in Pictures), he actually used the most modern technologies of the day to produce the first illustrated children's book. Applying the idea that the child must have direct contact with what it is learning, Comenius linked each sentence of the text to a specific picture and the details in the pictures were numbered and cross-referenced to each of the corresponding words.

Lastly, Comenius would have been fascinated by all the themes of the ICE and by the new line of emphasis of the activities of the IBE as UNESCO's specialized centre for educational content, structures, methods and resources. In his best known work "Didactica magna" (The Great Didactic), he was one of the first to emphasize content and to consider that education should be based on a precise method. He also pointed to the need to lighten curricula and to organize them in such a way as to avoid confusion among pupils, saying that "the art of teaching merely calls for good distribution of time and subjects".

So, the portrait of Comenius that we have before us during this ceremony is not that of a man of the past but of a man "of all times", an educational genius who has even been called at times "the Galileo of education".

My third joy is derived from your presence here as laureates of the 2001 Comenius Medal, the first of the millennium. The Jury, which I had the honour to chair and whose choices have been endorsed by the Director-General of UNESCO, had a very difficult task before it. You have been selected from among more than 40 candidates from all over the world. The Jury would have liked to reward 15 or 20 candidates, but its statutes allow a maximum of only 10 awards. I shall in a moment introduce each of you briefly, but I can already say that you are all worthy spiritual heirs of Comenius and that through your action in very different parts of the world and under very different conditions, you have done outstanding work in advancing the cause of quality education and in building a more human world. I congratulate you and thank you on behalf of all the participants in the 46th session of the ICE and all the teachers and children of the world.

ANNEX VII

Address by Mr. Eduard Zeman, Minister of Education of the Czech Republic, during the award of the Comenius Medal

Mr. Director-General,
Distinguished Colleagues,
Ladies and Gentlemen,

I am personally very glad and honoured to take part again in such an important event, in the ceremony of awarding the Jan Amos Comenius Medal, joint medal of the Director-General of UNESCO and the Minister of Education, Youth and Sport of the Czech Republic, to five most deserving scholars and there pedagogical teams throughout the world, who substantially contributed to current development of pedagogical sciences in the whole world.

We live in a time of rapid and almost unpredictable social changes, which on a global scale necessarily influences the role and status of not only individuals and whole educational system, but also your work as specialists in pedagogical sciences. Indeed, education is an immensely powerfully instrument in the service of society, which could be utilized for the positive formation of the young generation. Nowadays, the mere development of learning skills and the conginitive capacity of individuals no longer suffices. Other qualities and values—spiritual, ethical and aesthetic—need to be acquired and a positive attitude to other people and to society as a whole should be developed. The educated nation, which has a constantly active approach to better and better education, has the only chance to survive on the side of the prosperous nations, in this economically split world. The only way how to cope with such a situation is systematic attention to educating all people, the care of education as such.

Education for partnership, cooperation and solidarity within the globalizing world has become one of the main targets of the National Programme of Development of Education in the Czech Repubuc. We seek to promote a concept of life without conflicts and negative attitudes not only within the national community but also with respect to other nations, linguistic groups, minorities and cultures. We wish to bring up generations of people, who will be able to accept and respect even considerable differences among peoples and cultures of today's interrelated world.

Your predecessor and colleague, Jan Amos Comenius, pedagogue, philosopher and humanist, whose medal you have been awarded today, was born more than 400 years ago on the territory of the contemporary Czech Republic. His importance exceeded the regional framework. His ideas and concepts had a fundamental influence on European as well as world pedagogical thinking and moved the development of education and training in society well ahead. Today, in our turbulent and divided world the ideas of Jan Amos Comenius about the necessity of bringing people close together for a happier life in the future are still appealing to us. Deep contrasts in the development of modern civilization have shaped the world as a place full of violence and misunderstanding. To seek solutions to these problem should be the main task for the generations which have entered the twenty-first century. The motto of the present 46th session of the International Conference on Education-"Learning to Live Together"-is proof that the world community in dealing with education is well aware of such issues and has no intention of ignoring them.

The awarding of the Jan Amos Comenius Medal is an important moment in particular for you, this year's laureates, who are directly involved here and now. The award of the Medal is in a very real sense public recognition, an award, which on the basis of democratic decision has been made by the jury and confirmed by the signatures of the Director-General of UNESCO and the Minister of Education, Youth and Sport of the country which gave birth to one of the greatest teachers of all time—Jan Amos Comenius.

I would like to express my gratitude to all of you who have been presented today with the Comenius Medal for your lifelong commitment to education, for your professional work and for the permanent and devoted effort you have dedicated to raising the level of education as a whole all over the world. I am convinced that you will continue—as you have done hitherto-to bear your share of responsibility in such an irreplaceable activity for the benefit of the human race. I wish you full success in your work and in your personal life as well.

I am glad to use the opportunity of this ceremony to invite you personally, laureates of the Comenius Medal, to visit the Czech Republic and to have an opportunity to learn more about the life and work of Jan Amos Comenius, to get acquainted with the rich history and the pulsing reality of present-day life of country in the heart of Europe. You will have a chance to know more about the Czech Republic and judge for yourselves how far the ideas of its famous citizen—pedagogue, philosopher and humanist Comenius—have come true.

I wish you, distinguished colleagues, as well as the whole world community, to devote your efforts, in cooperation with UNESCO and other international organizations, to safeguarding and strengthening the principal ideas of society—democracy, human rights and respect for man—and to contribute to the positive and dynamic overall development of man, which is primarily based on the level of general education combined with individual creative ability.

I am looking forward to welcoming you, distinguished laureates of the Comenius Medal, within a few days in Prague, the capital of the Czech Republic.

ANNEX VIII

Address by Mr. Koïchiro Matsuura, Director-General of UNESCO at the opening of the special meeting on the involvement of civil society in promoting education for all

Honourable Ministers of Education,
Representatives of civil society,
Ladies and Gentlemen,

It is a great pleasure to be with you today for this Special Session of the International Conference on Education (ICE). It is highly appropriate that this Special Session, on the theme of the involvement of civil society in Education for All (EFA), occurs on a day when citizens around the world, governments, politicians, voluntary associations, grassroots workers, teachers, children and many others are celebrating International Literacy Day. In doing so, they are expressing, directly or indirectly, their commitment to the goals shared by everyone in the global EFA movement.

We all have witnessed the lively discussions here at the 46th Session of the ICE. Major issues have been addressed, such as learning to live together in our conflict-ridden world, the complex relationship between globalization and education, and the urgent need to reinforce the ethos and practice of participation at all levels, not least in regard to EFA processes. Allow me to explain, therefore, why this Special Session has been convened.

Since becoming the Director-General of UNESCO in November 1999, I have made the promotion of dialogue with civil society one of my foremost concerns, especially with reference to EFA. At the meeting of the World Education Forum in Dakar in April 2000, I intervened to ensure the wider participation of civil society in that crucial event. Since then, the encouragement of dialogue with civil society on EFA-related matters has taken place largely at the working level. The significance of this Special Session is two-fold: for the first time, it takes this dialogue to a much higher level, at which civil society representatives interact with a large group of Ministers of Education; in addition, this is the first time that such a Special Session of the ICE has been devoted to the question of civil society.

By bringing together representative from governments and civil society organisations (CSOs) on a single platform, this Special Session has both symbolic and substantive dimensions. It is symbolic by virtue of being a sign of the increasing recognition of the importance of civil society involvement in education, especially basic education. It is also an indication that partnership and collaboration are being pursued seriously and inclusively. I hope that this meeting will serve to symbolize the spirit of openness, dialogue and respect that must shape the relations between all partners in the EFA movement.

Today's meeting also has substantive content. We shall be sharing real experiences of how civil society supports. EFA and how collaboration between governments and civil society is conducted in practice. We shall focus on regions of the world where the EFA challenge is greatest and where, as a result, the international community's priorities must lie in terms of technical and financial assistance. Moreover, our substantive purpose today must be to identify practical steps aimed at enhancing civil society's contribution to EFA and promoting better government/ civil society relations.

I would like next to briefly consider what is meant by "civil society" in regard to EFA. The term "civil society" should be understood as inclusive of all groups and associations involved in EFA that are non-governmental and non-profit in nature. For UNESCO, civil society embraces NGOs and campaign networks, teacher unions and religious organisations, community associations and research networks, parents associations and professional bodies, student organizations and women's groups. I am aware that the definition of civil society is subject to much debate. Should it include political parties? Should it include the private or corporate sector? There is undoubtedly a need for greater clarity regarding who constitutes civil society and why.

Different concepts and contextual experiences influence our understanding, and these call for further thought and analysis on our part. UNESCO will be most attentive to the discussion of such matters. However, in the context of EFA and the efforts to strengthen the EFA movement, I underline the importance of being as inclusive as possible.

Clearly, national situations differ enormously. State/civil society relations vary correspondingly. Some countries have no tradition of partnerships between the state and civil society, and even the concept of civil society may seem alien and inapplicable. By contrast, some countries have benefited immensely from a widening participation of civil society in governance in general and in social development in particular. To reach this point, of course, a prolonged and painful struggle may have been endured but experience suggests that it ultimately bears fruit.

UNESCO believe that EFA will only be achieved if it is rooted in a broad-based societal movement and nourished by viable government/civil society partnerships. Our reasons are based on both principle and realism. The full achievement of the EFA goals requires that the marginalized and excluded are provided with educational opportunities. Civil society organizations are more capable than other EFA partners of reaching the unreached and, especially in the area of non-formal education, they have devised methods and approaches which are more attuned to the needs and life-conditions of the poor.

Moreover, we must acknowledge that, in the majority of developing countries, the public authorities have been unable to satisfy the demand for free and compulsory primary education of good quality for all children. The 113 million school-age children who are out-of-school, high rates of repetition and dropout, and the 875 million adults who are illiterate are evidence of the fact that the size and complexity of the EFA challenge are too great for governments alone to address, even with the best of intentions and effort.

Consequently, there is a need to both reinforce the state's responsibilities and complement its role in order to ensure quality basic education for all, especially for those who have been ill-served by or left out of mainstream education. Therefore we need partnership, drawing on the particular strengths of each partner.

In the tradition of modern democratic nation-states, elected governments are recognised as the legitimate authority to take decisions on national education policy choices, including such key areas as curriculum development, teacher education and system reform. Many states have shown great capacity in establishing national public education systems and ensuring, at least in principle, free education for all children and offering training opportunities for youth and adults. Governments manage the national education budget and, in the case of developing countries, mobilise and negotiate foreign aid. The public authorities, moreover, provide the framework of legislation, regulation, inspection and monitoring.

Civil society organizations cannot replace the state in the areas of its core educational responsibilities and authority. What, then, are the types of roles that CSOs play in regard to education in general and EFA in particular? In considering this question, it is increasingly apparent that the role of CSOs cannot be reduced to that of merely complementing the efforts of the state; moreover, such a narrow conception ill-serves the needs of the EFA movement. I shall now outline the four main roles performed by CSOs in regard to EFA.

In the first place, as suggested above, CSOs often act as alternative service providers where state-provided services are either absent or insufficient. CSOs have organized programmes for literacy, skills training and other forms of learning, thereby helping people to improve their livelihoods and living conditions. In many developing countries, CSOs have shouldered major responsibilities for non-formal education programmes entrusted to them by governments and funding agencies. CSOs have the advantages of being more flexible than the state, closer to the grassroots and local cultures and, in many cases, more innovative in approach. CSOs have emerged as leaders and major actors in the provision of non-formal and alternative education, with experience in linking education to other development sectors and building partnerships at different levels.

CSOs may also perform a second role, within and beyond national boundaries, as innovators, as sources of new thinking and new practices, especially concerning the impact of globalization on education. The EFA vision cannot remain fixed and immutable but must respond to changes and generate new initiatives. As well as the resource gap affecting the achievement of EFA, there is also an 'ideas gap' which CSOs can help to fill in collaboration with other EFA partners.

On the basis of the first two roles, CSOs often perform a third role as informed critics and advocates. The last decade witnesses the emergence of new forms of civil society expression and policy dialogue on a whole range of development issues. In regard to education, collective NGO campaigns were organised and national coalitions built to lobby for free and compulsory education of good quality for all children as well as education programmes for out-of-school youth and adults. Such campaigning has helped to raise important issues and to shape today's international EFA agenda.

Informed criticism and advocacy by CSOs also found expression through the EFA 2000 Assessment. In a path-breaking exercise, some 80 NGOs engaged in a collective evaluation of their own programmes and their role in and contribution to EFA. The evaluation demonstrated the relative strengths of NGOs/CSOs in such areas as community participation and organization, empowerment, literacy, community schools, reproductive health, and early childhood education. Particularly important for reaching the unreached are alternative education programmes for youth and adults (particularly women), nomads, and disabled, people living in isolated locations, and populations affected by armed conflict and displacement.

At the World Education Forum in Dakar, more than 300 NGO representatives came to attend the international NGO Consultation, which was jointly organized by the UNESCO/NGO Liaison Committee and the Collective Consultation of NGOs on EFA, with UNESCO's support. The NGOs drew up a joint communication and made valuable contributions to the drafting of the Dakar Framework for Action. Following a special request from the NGOs, I opened the World Education Forum to all participants who had come to the NGO Consultation, thereby encouraging direct interaction between NGOs, governments and development partners.

It came as no surprise, therefore, that the international community in Dakar agreed to acknowledge and support a new role of civil society in education: as policy partner. Governments, it was agreed, have "an obligation to ensure that EFA goals and targets are reached and sustained" (para 2 of the Dakar Framework for Action) but it was also recognized that this responsibility "will be met most effectively through broad-based partnerships within countries" (para 2). The participants in the World Education Forum pledged themselves to "ensure the engagement and participation of civil society in the formulation, implementation and monitoring of strategies for educational development" (para 8). This pledge highlights the new consensus in acknowledging the role of CSOs not only as implementing agencies and service providers, as innovators, and as informed critics and advocates, but also as policy partners. The key question, of course, is how we can move from this clear recognition of civil society's policy role to genuine participation and partnership at the country level.

National policy dialogue may at times be a cumbersome process, but it is essential for moving the EFA agenda forward. UNESCO is strongly committed to the principle that civil society should participate more fully in the policy process and we very much encourage the development of policy partnership between government and civil society. At the same time, however, we know that different local situations will generate different opportunities, modalities and outcomes. The space for civil society participation may be very limited in some countries today. In such cases, scope must be allowed for circumstances to change and new opportunities to arise so that more democratic and open political processes may develop.

There is no single recipe, no ideal model, and no uniform blueprint to guide our actions regarding the involvement of civil society in EFA. In each country context, we must develop a detailed knowledge of the contributions of civil society to the different EFA themes and goals. Such information is not easily available, so much so, in fact, that there may well be an under-reporting of EFA achievement and progress deriving from the activities of CSOs.

Questions must be raised about how to oragnize meaningful dialogue with a constituency as large and diverse as civil society. Who has the legitimacy to represent the interest and opinion of civil society organisation in dialogue with the government? Who can speak for whom? How does civil society's role fit within or alongside established mechanisms of electoral politics and democratic representation? And what is the real capacity at the level of civil society to negotiate policy choices in substantive areas of EFA? These and other questions need to be seriously addressed within a perspective committed to increasing civil society participation in policy dialogue.

UNESCO is convinced that a new culture of policy dialogue for EFA is needed if we are to connect the international political will for civil society participation with national and local realities. In general terms, the new policy culture should be participatory, democratic, open, transparent and accountable. It should transcend hierarchical and institutional barriers and should focus on issues of direct relevance to people's lives.

I would like now to briefly mention how UNESCO has been actively seeking to foster the participation of CSOs in the policy dialogue within the post-Dakar follow-up process, as today's Special Session bears witness. For example, international civil society networks and NGOs from the different regions were invited to the first meeting last November of the Working Group on EFA. At this meeting, the NGOs drew attention to the importance of decentralisation in national EFA efforts. Joint presentations by government and civil society representatives draw attention to NGO roles in innovative efforts to provides EFA at the community level.

UNESCO also invited NGOs to a consultation on the Global Initiative for mobilizing resources for EFA, held in Paris in March 2001. Both national and international NGOs stressed the need to include civil society in all stages of the planning, formulation and implementation of EFA. The NGOs emphasized how important it is for international agencies to support capacity building that will enable national NGOs and other civil society organizations to play their accorded role in the EFA movement.

In July, UNESCO and the UNESCO/NGO Liaison Committee co-organized the 2001 Annual Meeting of the

Collective Consultation of NGOs on EFA in Bangkok, an event which I consider a milestone in our partnership with civil society. About 100 NGOs from around the world agreed on a new partnership mechanism for EFA that will facilitate and accelerate dialogue, joint reflection, research, and capacity building as well as monitoring and evaluation.

Partnership between governments and civil society at the national level was one of the central themes of the Bangkok meeting. Strategies and activities were proposed that would reinforce the involvement of civil society, including capacity building in policy dialogue and studies of specific country experiences. NGOs also expressed their hope that governments and UNESCO National Commissions would explore various options for creating more space for consultation with civil society. Some NGOs suggested the idea of a protocol to support the dialogue. The meeting also emphasized the need to strengthen civil society coalitions for EFA at the national level; such coalitions will help to build consensus around the priorities and proposals to be brought into the national policy dialogue on education. In addition, international NGOs and NGOs from the different regions agreed to join the co-ordination team which will work with UNESCO to facilitate the implementation of the activities proposed and support the network across the regions.

UNESCO, as the organization mandated to co-ordinate the EFA partners and maintain their collaborative momentum, has a key role to play in nurturing the new culture of policy dialogue. The Dakar follow-up activities just mentioned illustrate the direction UNESCO wishes to take. We would like to play the role of impartial broker, facilitator and catalyst for promoting and furthering the collaboration between governments and civil society. We believe in the desirability of creating, through dialogue and partnership, an enduring national consensus on the goals, strategies and modalities for achieving EFA.

It is vital that the diversity of voices in the EFA movement is heard and, whenever possible, harmonized. At the same time, UNESCO is keen to encourage intellectual exchange and knowledge creation so that the EFA vision can be continuously refreshed. The 'ideas gap' must be addressed through debate and dialogue so that the EFA agenda moves forward but within a shared vision. UNESCO, therefore, will continue to encourage interaction among all EFA partners through the various consultative mechanisms, working groups and fora that exist. The role of informal contacts as well as formal structures is important. UNESCO will encourage governments and National Commissions to talk with civil society and explore how viable mechanisms for consultation on issues related to EFA can be established or strengthened.

We are optimistic because the seeds for the growth of a new culture of EFA policy dialogue do exist in many countries. As stated earlier, there is no single blueprint suitable for all circumstances but there are ideas, experiences and innovations to learn from. Let us listen and learn together.

Thank you.

ANNEX IX

Summary of the panel's statements during the special meeting on the involvement of civil society in promoting education for all

In his opening address, the Director-General of UNESCO spoke of the various roles and responsibilities of governments and civil society organizations in promoting education for all (see Annex VII). He particularly stressed the new role of civil society organizations as policy partners in education and the need to explore how viable mechanisms for consultation on issues related to EFA could be established or strengthened. While recognizing the diversity of country-specific contexts, the Director-General highlighted the way in which UNESCO would continue to promote actively the process of building partnerships and the overall coordination of EFA.

The Minister of Education of Ghana gave a brief account of recent achievements relating to EFA goals and, in particular, to efforts to: (i) integrate early childhood education, which is private for the most part, into the public sector; (ii) raise the provision of compulsory and free universal primary basic education to 83 per cent, with a positive impact on gender disparity under a special programme that began in 1996; (iii) reduce illiteracy rates to 48 per cent; and (iv) improve quality. The Minister then stressed the importance of civil society in this process and explained how Ghana had moved from recognition of the role of civil society as a provider of innovative and complementary services and as an actor in mobilizing communities to its genuine inclusion as a policy-making partner. He gave examples of viable national and local partnership mechanisms.

The representative of Action Aid Ghana also gave examples of viable partnerships with the government, which had led to the recognition and inclusion of new practices in the provision of alternative services. The representative also referred to the Ghana National Education Campaign Coalition, an unprecedented experience in terms of partnership within civil society.

The Minister of Education of Mozambique referred to the establishment of institutionalized mechanisms for consultation with civil society at the national level to provide inputs into the education policy-making process. He also mentioned the responsibility recently entrusted to a new education department (Department for Community Participation) for suggesting possible mechanisms for partnership and participation at the local level.

The Education Secretary of Nepal also gave an account of achievements in respect of EFA goals. The literacy rate had reached 58 per cent and the enrolment rate 72 per cent. Gender disparities and quality issues continued to be sizeable challenges. The representative stressed his government's recognition of civil society's contribution in the establishment of primary schools and other educational services since the 1950s. The establishment of a favourable policy and environment had facilitated the provision of complementary services by more than 30,000 civil society organizations (CSOs) in the country. The representative side that the time had perhaps come to include civil society in policy making and referred to the newly established EFA Forum and the process of drawing up the national EFA plan of action.

The civil society representative of Nepal's Asia Pacific Partnership laid emphasis on the positive correlation between periods of democratization and the extent of civil society's involvement in education. He regretted, however, that the democratization process had not continued and urged the government to involve civil society systematically, not only as a provider of services but also as a political partner.

The Deputy Minister of Education of Yemen stressed the importance of the private schools' role as providers of complementary services in competition with public schools. The Minister gave some examples of the experience of parents' committees and stressed the importance of electing local civil society teams to enable them to participate in the planning and implementation of the national education strategy formulated after the Dakar Forum.

The civil society representative of the teacher' union in Yemen spoke of the recent development of what he called a "diversified and independent education sector". The 1990 democratization process had encouraged the development of individual initiatives in education. The representative drew attention to the need for legislative frameworks to organize the operation of such private initiatives and called for civil society to be represented in decision-making bodies responsible for formulating education society.

The Secretary-General of Education Internation made an analytical response to the various statements and linked them to key issues such as educational funding and the need to ensure quality and equity. He referred to the extraordinary work undertaken by the Global Campaign for Education in raising awareness of the need to enlist public funds to cover the budget shortfall of US $7 billion, which are indispensable, according to the campaign, to ensure EFA at the world level by 2015. The representative examined the dangers of unbridled privatisation to the detriment of free education and the harmful effects of the large-scale employment of too many voluntary teachers on the quality of education. The Secretary-General laid emphasis, in particular, on the importance of the government's responsibility for the overall coordination of EFA efforts at the national level and on the improvement of the status and working conditions of teachers with a view to providing free and compulsory quality education for all.

ANNEX X

Message by a pupil of Summerhill School (UK), during the closing ceremony

Ladies and Gentlemen,

I am a student out of personal choice at Summerhill School, a democratic boarding school in England.

I have come here to speak of democracy in schools and its relevance when learning about citizenship, and more importantly the individual, or should I say the individual child.

At my school, pupils and teachers live together in a democratic community, where we have an equal vote and an equal say. It is an international school, with pupils from Asia, the Middle East, Europe and North America. We all learn tolerance and respect through living together, and accept each other's cultural and ethical backgrounds. Using this, I have been elected as school ombudsmen, that is, the person who is responsible for solving disagreements between all members of the school—teachers and pupils—using peaceful dialogue, patience and understanding. I have been elected every term for three and a half years.

Participating in community democracy has given me: a sense of responsibility for others; the skills needed for peaceful resolutions in disputes; a way of taking part in the creation and use of law and justice; and space to understand who I am and what I am to the world. In this way I am able to participate as a citizen of the world.

As Jacques Delors said in the report, "Learning—The Treasure Within", UNESCO was founded, based upon the hope for a world that is a better place to live in. I share that hope, and like to think that every child will have the opportunity to learn what I am learning, for these values that I hold are evident in the spirit of this conference.

A number of these schools already exist in many countries, such as: New Zealand, Japan, the United States, Thailand, the Republic of Korea, Costa Rica, Portugal, France, Germany, Denmark, Israel and Palestine. It is my hope that such schools will prosper and be successfully founded in other countries as well.

I and many other pupils attending these schools have been lucky in what we have experienced, but why only us?

Despite the fact that Summerhill and schools like it correspond so precisely to what you are recommending here, some of them are facing the threat of closure.

These schools may close and need your support, as the hopes of this conference are in these schools. All that I ask is that these schools are recognized, and have a chance to prosper. In this way you can show the world that using democracy, participation and respect for children's rights, you help form the strong individual citizen, but only if you take action and do not make these simply the worlds appearing in the final report of a conference.

ANNEX XI

Expression of thanks by Ms. Cecilia Braslavsky, Director of the UNESCO International Bureau of Education (IBE)

Distinguished Ministers,
Heads of Delegation,
Mr. Director-General of UNESCO,
Mr. Assistant Director-General for Education,
Madam Counsellor of Sate, Head of the Swiss Delegation,
Representatives of teachers, parents and pupils,
Members of the various intergovernmental and non-governmental organizations,
Dear participants and friends,

On behalf of the Secretariat of the 46th session of the International Conference on Education, and in my capacity as Secretary-General of this Conference, it is with no little emotion that I should like—through you, ladies and gentlemen,—to thank the UNESCO General Conference for the challenge issued to the UNESCO International Bureau of Education in asking us to transform ourselves into a centre specializing in the contents, methods and structures of education and also to organize this 46th session of the International Conference on Education on the theme "learning to live together".

I should also like to thank the Director-General of UNESCO for the opportunity he gave me to become Director of the International Bureau of Education, a specialized institute of

UNESCO. I should similarly like to thank our Council, presided over by Mr. Pieter de Meijer, for its guidance, hard work, professionalism and constant demands for evaluation, which should even become a daily requirement.

Without the commitment of the group responsible for helping in the preparation of the International Conference on Education, which was appointed by the IBE Council before I took up the post of Director and which has worked tremendously hard, sometimes into the early hours of the morning this week, this event would have scarcely been possible. I should like to thank its Chair and all its members, with a particular mention for Jean-Pierre Regnier in personal capacity, while not forgetting that he works in the French National Commission for UNESCO, who has discharged his duties as Executive Secretary with outstanding dedication.

Without the firm support of the Swiss authorities and many Swiss colleagues, among whom I should like to mention Ms Martine Bruschwig Graf, Minister of Education and Counsellor of State in Geneva, Mr. Charles Kleiber, Secretary of State for Science and Research with responsibility for the Federal Office of Education and Science in Berne, and Mr. Francois Nordmann, Ambassador and Head of the Swiss Mission to the United Nations in Geneva, the IBE would not have been able to accomplish in full the mission entrusted to it by the UNESCO General Conference.

I express once again our thanks and gratitude to all the countries and institutions, all the friends and colleagues who—in keeping with the notion of partnership—spared no effort in the preparation of this Conference. My words are addressed to the speakers, organizers, journalists and friends who, in accordance with the programme, all played their part, not hesitating to intervene on occasion to deal with "emergencies", in an admirable spirit of collaboration and dialogue. All these people supported us by virtue of their commitment, their professionalism and their warm presence. There were even "Mariachis" at the cocktail held in honour of the laureates of the Comenius Medal instituted by the Government of the Czech Republic; they were wholly unscheduled, and this was a fine surprise for the laureates and for the Secretariat.

Without the strong commitment of UNESCO's Assistant Director-General of Education, Mr. John Daniel, the integration of this undertaking in the other activities specified in the UNESCO Medium-Term Strategy, the completion of the final stages of the preparatory work and the smooth functioning of this week of work would not have been possible. Many thanks are due to him.

Numerous colleagues in UNESCO's Education Sector and central services, in our Secretariat and in the UNESCO Liaison Office in Geneva have contributed to or helped us in, as the case may be, strengthening bilateral action by organizing additional activities. For instance, they have taken charge of drawing up the list of participants, organizing the distribution of the documents, managing the organization of the rooms, the interpretation services, the press coverage of the events, etc. There has been excellent work—very serious and extremely effective—behind the scenes, all of which has facilitated dialogue on the complex and delicate problems addressed by the Conference. I should like to extend my sincere thanks to all those concerned.

And finally and above all, I should like to thank my colleagues from the UNESCO International Bereau of Education in Geneva. We form a small team, but a team that is increasingly well-knit and enthusiastic. I should have liked to name them one by one, but we do not have the time. On their behalf, I would simply like to single out two silent workers: our Council Secretary and friend, Pierre Luisoni, and also our youngest expert who came as a student, Renato Mariani.

The ICE is drawing to a close. But with all the team that makes up our Organization—and always in a spirit of cooperation and partnership—we are going to pursue the exciting challenge of realizing the objectives of education for all. First formulated in Jomtien and enriched by inputs from various quarters, in particular the reflections of the International Commission on Education for the Twenty-first Century presided over by Jacques Delors and the recommendations of the 45th session of the ICE concerning the teaching profession, these objectives were the subject of a renewed commitment at the Dakar Forum last year. They have also been central to the dialogue at this 46th session of the ICE on "Education for All for learning to live together: Contents and Learning Strategies—problems and solutions".

Once again, many thanks to you all.

ANNEX XII

Closing speech by Mr. Koïchiro Matsuura Director-General of UNESCO

Mr. President,
Distinguished Ministers of Education,
Distinguished Heads of Delegation,
Ladies and Gentlemen,
Dear Colleagues and Friends,

The International Conference on Education, formerly the International Conference on Public Education, has a rich history and tradition. Over the years, it has addressed the leading educational issues of its time, bringing together the leading educational decision-makers of the world to do so. Certain issues and themes have recurred many times, including the dominant theme of this Session: learning to live together. Other words and phrases have sometimes been used: for example, education for international solidarity, education for peace, education for tolerance and mutual understanding, and education for world citizenship. This year's Conference has approached this broad family of educational concerns with a distinctive orientation, namely, education for all. But echoes of earlier conferences have reverberated through our own, reminding us that the ICE is part of the whole world's educational heritage.

We have taken part in four days of hard work; it has been a rich learning experience for all of us. Sometimes we learn things that we want to know; sometimes we learn things that we do not want to know; and sometimes we learn things that we should know. I am sure that this Conference has provided opportunities for all three types of learning. And there is also a fourth type of learning: sometimes we need to learn things over and over again. As we do so, we come to recognize the wisdom and foresight of our predecessors who planted the seeds of a new education. Particularly in the aftermath of World War Two, that new education was based on an agreed perception that education must help us to strengthen our capacity to live together in peace. Fifty years from now, I hope that another generation will look back on our deliberations and admire our wisdom and foresight.

Educational change of various kinds has emerged as a common thread running through this Conference. I would like to draw attention to two important dimensions of educational change. First, changes to the contents and methods of education are long-term in character; they need time to develop and come to fruition. Second, such changes do not have permanent, definitive, once-and-for-all character. In every generation, renewed efforts are necessary so that people may be educated in the values, attitudes and behaviour conducive to living peaceably with one another. Indeed, I have been impressed to learn at this conference of the large numbers of countries that are now embarked upon reforms of their education systems.

At the World Education Forum held in Dakar, Senegal, in April 2000, Ministers of Education, international agencies, bilateral and multilateral development partners, and civil society organizations committed themselves not simply to education for all; they took another step forward, towards quality education for all. At this meeting of the ICE, we have taken another step by looking at how this improved quality might be built and what are the very real problems we face in doing so.

We know that sound educational policies for promoting quality education are indispensable. In view of the complex realities they must address, such policies should be formulated and implemented in close association with civil society, centres of educational research, and, most especially, teachers and parents. In the era of lifelong learning, we must reflect and act as learners ourselves. We cannot encourage children, youth and adults to continue learning while we ourselves remain rooted in outdated or unrealistic assumptions about who are the stakeholders and participants in educational policy-making.

A conference such as this provides an opportunity to learn about the changing world of learning. It is particularly important that educational policies are as well informed as possible, not only in terms of facts and statistics but also in regard to good practices, viable innovations and proven alternatives. We cannot take on new challenges in the emerging knowledge society if we are unaware of the range of policy options available and of the evidence and arguments that support them. We—the decision-makers responsible for fulfilling the commitments made in Dakar—must learn more about the processes of educational change and how they are affected by the realities outside the school gates.

In addressing the theme of International Conference on Learning to Live Together, this conference has been particularly clear about the risk of overloading the school with responsibilities it is not equipped to fulfil. The school obviously cannot solve all of society's problems, nor can it be insulated from those problems. Particularly important are experiences where new educational policies and practices have helped change the lives of people for the good, resulting in a significant decline in violence. We must learn from such experiences wherever they occur and draw out their implications: for example, they point us towards the decentralization of school systems and the embedding of schools in the community.

The Special Session on the involvement of civil society in EFA has allowed us to learn more about very important experiences of cooperation between the state, government institutions and other relevant actors. The new world of education is one where new partners are appearing on the scene, holding different views and pursuing different agendas. But there are always some dimensions of common concern and shared outlook. It is vital that, for a long-term task such as building quality basic education for all and developing viable approaches to learning to live together, the attempt is made to cultivate a sustainable consensus among all educational partners.

This ICE has been a great opportunity for me to learn, and not only from the formal sessions. I have especially benefited from the many bilateral meetings I have held. Such face-to-face meetings are most helpful for reaching a better understanding of your needs and problems. I have been delighted to hear many Ministers comment positively on how the ICE this year is better organized and better structured, and how it has offered more chances for genuine debate. I must say that the new modalities of running the Conference would not have succeeded without your cooperation, for which I thank you all. A number of Ministers have noted that they are addressing the same or very similar problems. This makes the identification and sharing of good practices especially important.

It will be both a duty and a pleasure to report the conclusions and outcomes of this ICE to the forthcoming 31st session of the UNESCO General Conference. The deliberations of this conference will be used to enrich the Organization's Medium-Term Strategy and, in particular, the way we undertake the fulfilment of our commitments made in Dakar. I will be asking the ADG/ED to look at ways of focusing UNESCO's work on such topics as languages, ICTs and school organization so that we may respond more precisely to the wishes you have expressed here.

I have already asked the IBE Council to begin working on the next ICE and the thematic concerns it should address. One possibility is that the next ICE will be devoted to deepening our knowledge and understanding of the education/poverty nexus, particularly in terms of how curriculum design and teaching/learning practices can be related meaningfully to the struggle against poverty in all its forms and dimensions. This agenda could include such questions as the relation between education and migration; the place of preventive education concerning HIV/AIDS in all types and levels of education; education and social exclusion, with particular attention to youth; and the curricular and pedagogical aspects of schooling that serves poor communities. The essential contributions of teachers and civil society will continue to figure centrally in our dialogue. In the time intervening until the next ICE, I am sure that we will have the chance to deepen and extend our knowledge and understanding of the relationship between poverty and education. Such a theme by the way, would stay firmly within the framework of UNESCO's strategic orientation for the period ahead, namely, the humanization of globalization.

Many Ministers have expressed such satisfaction with the Conference that I am encouraged to see it held at more regular intervals. Perhaps the next ICE could be held in three years time, in 2004 or in four years time, in 2005. The ICE is clearly a major event for UNESCO, one which I hope will continue for many years to come.

The 46th Session of the International Conference on Education (ICE) has exceeded our expectations. It has been a great success. I would like to thank all those who have contributed to its preparation and organization, those who have contributed through their active presence, and those who have joined into the process of debate and dialogue with candid and forthright views. I recognize that the speaking opportunities for civil society organizations were quite limited, but I would like to assure you that your presence and involvement in the conferences has been greatly appreciated.

My special thanks go to you, Mr. President, for the way you have fulfilled your duties and tasks with such good-humoured firmness and understanding. I would also like to repeat my thanks to the Swiss Federal authorities and the authorities of the Republic and Canton of Geneva for the welcome and support they have given to this Conference and to the IBE.

The IBE Council, of course, has worked extraordinarily hard and we extend our deep thanks to its members and its Chairperson, Dr. Pieter De Meijer. I would like to thank the professionals of UNESCO from the Education Sector, our regional and country offices, other parts of UNESCO, and the Dakar Follow-up Unit for all their contributions during this week. Further thanks are due to all those non-UNESCO staff who have helped to facilitate and Conference, with special mention to the interpreters.

Last but certainly not least, I would like to specifically thank the staff of the IBE who, under the energetic and capable leadership and their Director, have helped to make this conferences a real success. Your dedication, hard work and sheer professionalism are much appreciated.

Learning how to live at peace with others is an indispensable part of all education. Let us all take this message away with us and apply it conscientiously to our work.

I wish you all a safe journey home.

Thank you.

ANNEX XIII

Closing speech by Ms. Martine Brunschwig Graf, State Counsellor, Head of the Swiss Delegation

Mr. President,
Excellencies,
Distinguished Ministers and Heads of Delegation,
Mr. Director-General of UNESCO,
Madam Direct of the IBE,

Representatives of the teaching profession, parents, the scientific world and civil society as a whole,
Dear friends and guests of the Conference,

The time has passed too quickly, paradoxical as it may be to say so when we are concerned with education. Indeed, what a contrast there is between the urgent need that brings us together, namely improving the quality of our education systems, introducing new technologies and developing citizenship education, and the time required to implement and necessary reforms and measures!

This 46th session of the International Conference on Education has shown once again that everything must be done to ensure that State are able to make available the resources necessary for reform and for the development of the school to which we aspire.

We have taken note, in the course of these days spent together, of so many projects and expectations existing alongside successful experiments, which nonetheless remain too few and isolated.

We have expressed and heard expressed so many hopes in the capacity of the school to make those who attend it free and responsible. We must therefore not let matters remain there. Adopting the conclusions and a plan of action commits us to working not only in our own countries but also to acting with a greater measure of solidarity to further the action of others.

In addition, these are topics that need to be explored in greater depth. It would appear, for example, that we have merely skimmed the surface of the measures that need to be taken to enable young girls to gain readier access to school and especially to pursue scientific subjects. And yet women represent for a world in search of motivated and well-trained teachers a huge potential, which can only be turned to account by a sound basic education.

We have spoken of citizenship education in school, but it remains for us to achieve the practical application of citizenship in society, since we cannot envisage assigning to the pupils we educate the sole responsibility for developing democratic practice and civic commitment in the society in which we live.

The children who have come to sing for you belong to our Geneva state school system. They are from very different backgrounds and living together represents for them, as for us, a challenge that they take-up every day with the help of their teachers, their parents and the entire Geneva community.

They are here to bring us a moment of welcome relaxation through their songs and at the same time to remind us for whom we work, for whom we commit ourselves and for whom we speak, deliberate and negotiate. Let them also be witnesses of our resolve to act!

Shortly, the Council of the International Bureau of Education will carry out an assessment of this 46th session of the ICE. For the moment, I should like to offer my warm thanks to the IBE—particularly Cecilia Braslawsky and Pierre Luisoni but also to all those who have made a contribution to the successful organization of the Conference. I should also like to express our gratitude to the Director-General of UNESCO, Mr. Matsuura, whose support is invaluable and vital for the cause that we defend.

Finally, dear colleagues and friends, members of delegations, experts, parents and teachers, I wish to say how much the people of Geneva have been happy over these last four days to have you among the us in our city. I have only one wish to express by way of conclusion. Come back to Geneva to speak about education! You will be welcomed with open arms!

ANNEX XIV

Closing speech by Mr. A.B. Borishade, Minister of Education of Nigeria and President of the 46th session of the International Conference on Education

Director-General of UNESCO, Mr. Koichiro Matsuura,
Assistant Director-General for Education, Sir John Daniel,
Director of the International Bureau of Education, Mrs. Cecilia Braslavsky,
Honourable Ministers and other Heads of Delegations,
Delegates,
Members of Intergovernmental Organization, Foundations and Non-Governmental Organizations,
Ladies and Gentlemen,

When this conference opened four days ago we were faced with a historic assignment that is to identify problems and proffer solutions to the challenge of living together in a globalizing world.

Today we have listened to the outcome of this Conference, we need to congratulate ourselves for a very fruitful Conference. I feel confident to state that the Conference has fulfilled its essence, which is to examine, more precisely, how to promote the mastery of the knowledge, skills and attitudes necessary for the intellectual and moral development of individuals and our societies so that can live together in peace and harmony.

The outcome of this conference will surely form a major addition to the body of knowledge on human diversity and will become an integral part of strategic prescriptions for the promotion of quality education for all across all activities in which humans are involved, but more importantly on learning to live together.

Distinguished delegates, we should depart from this Conference not only feeling satisfied for being part of a landmark event but also with the full realization that within the assignment of global peace and harmony we are faced with the challenges of human diversity and that global peace is bound intricately with the clear understanding and respect for the mutuality of the diversities of human heritage and identity. The ultimate survival of humanity may, in face, be determined by our individual and collective sensitivity to these challenges.

We should all be grateful to the International Bureau of Education for the choice of the theme of this Conference and for creating this credible platform for us to peer into the future of humanity.

Ladies and Gentlemen, I wish to state that this Conference has also brought to the fore the challenges before UNESCO and its operational units, the need to promote dialogue and to pioneer action towards the building of bridges of understanding based on equity and justice among nations. This is a prerequisite for the surrender of old fears and the promotion of a conducive environment for learning to live together. It is an assignment we must all face by cooperating with UNESCO in our respective dispositions and capacities.

Mr. Director-General, the Assistant Director-General for Education, UNESCO, the Director of the International Bureau of Education and fellow delegates, it has been a wonderful experience for me to guide the 46th session of the ICE. I thank you all for giving me this rare honour and for your cooperation.

I wish to state my profound appreciation of the efficiency, organization and rigorous planning of the conference officials and secretariat staff.

The dedication of the resource persons and conference officials as well as the warmness and cordiality of the secretariat staff remain commendable. I have not been surprised but still I am immensely grateful.

Finally, I want to thank the Swiss Government for the hospitality accorded us in this beautiful city of Geneva even the gods of the city brought us sunshine. This has been wonderful.

Distinguished delegates please bear my love to my members of your family and your love ones and say that we have had a good conference.

Once more, I congratulate all of you for a wonderful conference and I congratulate myself for being part of it all.

Bon voyage.

Thank you.

ANNEX XV

WORKSHOP REPORTS

Workshop 1: "Citizenship education: learning at school and in society"

Workshop No. 1 was dedicated to *citizenship education.* Mr. Sveinn Einarsson, the President of the Icelandic National Commission for UNESCO, was the moderator of the session, with the five panellists being:

- Her Excellency Ms. Mariana Alwyn, Minister of Education Chile;
- Her Excellency Ms. Margrethe Vestager, Minister of Education of Denmark;
- Mr. Benali Benzaghou, Rector of the University of Science and Technology "Houari Boumediene", Algiers, Algeria;
- Mr. Samuel Lee, Director of the Asian-Pacific Centre of Education for International Understanding (Republic of Korea);
- Mr. Cliff Olivier, Co-ordinator of IBIS, Pretoria (South Africa).

A challenging subject, it is currently the centre of debates in all regions and countries of the world. The debates involve not just experts and practitioners but also politicians and decision-makers. For example, citizenship education was the main theme of the Conference of European Ministers of Education help in Crakow, in October 2000.

It is not just politicians and top decision-makers who are interested in citizenship education but also people coming from various business environments, the church, media, politics and civil society. The reason is that the world of education has high *expectations* of citizenship learning. For instance, some of the participants at the worshop mentioned the contribution of citizenship education to social cohesion, social trust and confidence building particularly in area of conflict. For others, citizenship education is the main tool to educate citizens to live in a State governed by the rule of law. For some, citizenship education has to contribute to democratic governance while other contributors put the emphasis on the importance of preparing the student for employment and social participation. Finally, it was a general concern that citizenship is a general factor for sustainable development.

These high expectations could create unrealistic pressures on the school. This is why some other participants called for more pragmatic and feasible approaches, rather than expecting that citizenship education along could solve these societal problems. As stated by one panellist, we have to avoid citizenship education becoming a "semantic illusion" in the way which moral education was traditionally considered as a panacea for all social problems. Similarly, as another panellist stated, we have to overcome the danger of a narrow interpretation of citizenship education related to political or ideological indoctrination often imposed on schools as a ready-made solution.

Beyond these controversies, dilemmas and open questions, the fact is that citizenship education is present in daily life in all countries and regions. This is the result, in some cases, of clear political options, or explicit educational policies, or in other cases, the consequence of initiatives by teachers and parents who find the area of citizenship education a pedagogical space allowing innovation and creativity.

In this framework, most of the contributions focused on four issues. One, the relationship between citizenship education and learning to live together, secondly, the question of how to implement citizenship education in a variety of social and economic contexts, thirdly citizenship education as a challenge for the educational community, and fourthly, education for global citizenship. These four points summarize the direction of the debate which took place.

Message No. 1: Citizenship education in an essential means of learning to live together.

It is important to stress that in this context "together" does not refer uniquely to individuals, but also to institutions, communities and nations which have to cooperate and build partnerships. In this respect, some participants considered that learning to live together is a societal project to which contribute different types of education such as peace education, human rights education, citizenship education and values education. This implies a shift from learning by transmission of knowledge to a social learning perspective and a student centred approach, as well as the incorporation of new forms of learning in the school context. As reported from various national initiatives, this includes contextual learning, activity learning, collaborative learning and particularly, experiential learning. However, the links between citizenship education and learning to live together remain to be explored, at least from certain participants point of view. As pointed out by one panellist, learning to live together is more clear and accessible for all societies than citizenship education for which the content has to be described according to the "variable geometric principle".

This brings us to the second message, namely, *how to implement citizenship education in a variety of contexts*. It was generally accepted that citizenship educations is learning throughout life, in all circumstances and in every form of human activity. As point out in the background paper prepared by the Danish Minister of Education, learning for citizenship makes use of both organized learning (formal and non-formal) as well as of the learning potential to be found in daily circumstances (informal or incidental learning).

Within this lifelong learning system, the school is a major factor of citizenship education. In order to increase the efficiency of citizenship education, participants points out that the school should:

encourage the participation of pupils in internal school decisions and student associations;

create an institutional ethos encouraging dialogue, cooperation and democratic relations;

establish cooperation with families, communities and the social environment;

promote a whole school approach to citizenship education.

Provision is made for citizenship education in the curriculum of all the countries represented at the workshop. In most cases, according to the national reports prepared for the International Conference on Education, citizenship education is a separate subject in the formal curriculum. Other experiences encourage integrated programmes or cross-curricular themes. In addition to the provisions in the formal curriculum, participants stressed the numerous experiences resulting from out-of-school activities such as residential visits, pilot projects or voluntary activities. Finally, the importance of the hidden curriculum was emphasized, namely of natural and spontaneous encounters in daily school life, which often have a greater impact than the formal curriculum.

Message No. 3: Citizenship education creates new challenges for the educational community.

In some cases, citizenship education is the core for reforms and innovations in educational systems. Even though it may not be a subject for formal evaluation and selection to universities, it is an opportunity for alternative approaches, pilot projects and institutional partnerships. In most of the cases, this new pedagogical approach is not possible within the so-called "traditional subjects". As mentioned by one panellist, citizenship education is not a monopoly of one generation, institution or culture, it must be continuously constructed and innovated. In other words, citizenship education is at the same time an opportunity and a challenge for education. In this perspective, participants mentioned the following specific challenges:

- New roles and assignments of teachers. Instead of a unique source of knowledge, teachers must become moderators, learning facilitators, advisors and resource persons.
- Citizenship education, therefore, must not be limited either to a didactic transmission of knowledge or to teaching activity proper. What counts most of all is learner participation and direct practice of citizenship in various educational environments.
- As illustrated by some of the case studies put forward in the workshop, citizenship education involves institutional partnerships, the most common being partnerships between school and family, school and community, or the industrial sector. This would imply a convergence of educational messages and values

between school and societies as a whole, and particularly the media.

- The role of ICTs and Internet for citizenship education has to be elaborated. For example, how to use it constructively and critically, how to provide access and build networks of citizens.

Message No. 4: Education for global citizenship is instrumental to cope with the challenges of globalization.

Although it is not yet properly defined, it is commonly characterized by global awareness, shared values and joint projects. As stressed by a number of participants, global citizenship goes beyond the narrow, national perspective of membership. It implies shared responsibility and the idea of belonging to the same global entity. This is, in fact, the very essence of learning to live together.

Chair/Excellencies/Ladies and Gentlemen,

These messages represent the essentials of the debate held during Workshop No. 1. The question we should ask ourselves now is "How do we make the best use of these messages?" Or, in other words, how can we make these important conclusions produce an impact beyond that of a mere report presented in the ICE plenary?

Without claiming to have covered all possibilities, in our opinion the following means should be taken into account:

1. Obviously, the first possible impact will be to incorporate some of our conclusions in the final report of ICE. This would result in an extended international audience especially within the UNESCO system and among its partners.
2. In the second place, it would be possible to take these recommendations into consideration for the future mid-term programme of UNESCO. Actually, as we observed during the workshop, citizenship education is a major dimension of educational policies in the member countries with high expectations in this field. To meet these expectations, UNESCO must consider citizenship education as a priority among its actions in the field of education and must allot adequate resources.

3. Thirdly, the International Bureau of Education in its capacity of specialized institution could actually implement some of our conclusions. In recent years, IBE has focused its attention on educational contents and learning to live together. IBE could add to its valuable activities an equally important dimension, namely education for global citizenship.
4. In the fourth place, our conclusions could be useful in developing projects at national, regional or international level. These activities should take into account specific contexts and should keep in view the "variable geometry" principle. Ultimately, citizenship education is applied in a concrete cultural and social environment, where priorities and constraints may differ.

Finally, our conclusions might be of particular interest to practitioners in their daily work for citizenship education.

Thank you for your attention.

Workshop 2: "Social exclusion and violence: Education for social cohesion"

Moderator: Mr. Jean-Pierre GONTARD (Graduate Institute of Development Studies, Geneva).

Panelists:

H.E. Mr. Pierre Nzila, Minister of Education, Republic of the Congo;
H.E. Mr. Antanas Mockus, Mayor of Bogota, Colombia;
H.E. Ms Isabel Couso Tapia, Secretary-General, Ministry of Education, Spain;
Professor Ivan IVIC, Faculty of Philosophy, Belgrade, Yugoslavia;
Ms. Pari Zarrabi, Sociologist, Geneva, Switzerland.

The workshop was organized around the question of how formal education relates to processes of social exclusion and to patterns of violence associated with the breakdown of social cohesion. More particularly, the discussion focused on three main questions:

1. What consequences does societal violence have on education?
2. How does formal education relate to wider processes of social exclusion?
3. How can education contribute to strengthening or rebuilding social cohesion?

The following salient points emerged in the course of the discussion:

1. Need for clear definitions and conceptual clarifications

The ideas presented and discussed during the workshop revolved around the relation of education to violence at two distinct levels:

1. schooling and the prevention of violence among youth, and the necessary distinction between school-based violence and wider institutional violence, and
2. the consequences of armed conflict and civil strife on education systems and the possibilities and limits of schooling in restoring social cohesion in post-conflict settings.

The theme of exclusion, whether in terms of poverty, inequality or the denial of fundamental social and political rights, was a common thread that ran through the discussions of violence at both these levels. Although there is clear overlap between the two levels of analysis, the discussions still printed to the need for a distinction between the two, and for clear definitions with regard to patterns of violence.

2. Need to consider schooling with wider environment

It was recalled that formal education, and schooling in particular, must be considered in relation to forms of exclusion that are shaped by wider social, economic, political and historic forces. Any discussion of the relation between education and violence, and of the potential of formal education to contribute to enhancing and restoring social cohesion, must therefore consider these wider societal processes. Moreover, it was pointed out that, at times, schooling also reproduces or even exacerbates forms of discrimination, inequality and exclusion based on gender, socio-economic status, ethic, cultural or political identities.

3. Conditions for education for social cohesion

Protecting fundamental rights

Education for "living together" requires that life, health and human dignity be protected so as to ensure the basic right to education for the poor, girls and women, minority groups, refugees and civilian populations in war-torn areas. Social divisions and exclusion are first and foremost a result of the denial of the right to education for significant proportions of children and young people concentrated mainly, but not exclusively, in the poorest areas of the South.

Ensuring justice

How does one learn to "live together" in the wake of bloody conflicts within divided societies? The notion of "living together" in the aftermath of civil strife and extreme societal violence within divided societies is a problematic and complex endeavour. Many delegations expressed the view that social cohesion presupposes peace, and that peace must be based on justice. And one approach to justice is truth and reconciliation. Education is clearly a complement to such approaches.

4. Limits of educational initiatives

Although schooling may constitute an important vehicle for social reconstruction following periods of internal conflict and weakened if not collapsed state structures, it is important to acknowledge the limits of schooling as a delivery channel for reconciliation and the reconstruction of social cohesion for a number of reasons.

The relative weight of schooling in civic and political socialization

It was noted, for example, that the family, the home and the immediate community have a central place in the informal political socialization initiated from an early age. Also, it can be argued that the media, and (satellite) television in particular, has an increasing weight in the education of young people in an increasingly globalized world. Finally, not only are these processes of socialization multiple, but they are also sometimes in competition or in contradiction. The real impact of peace education through schooling is therefore seriously hampered when it contrasts with surrounding adult role models in the home, the wider community or the media. This points to the need to consider wider initiatives that include adult education and the media.

Transferring values and attitudes from school to wider society

Such observations about the limit of schooling also highlight the lack of conclusive evidence relative to the way in which individual and interpersonal skills and attitudes transmitted through formal or non-formal education transfer to group behaviour, particularly in settings of acute social and political tensions. It is therefore important to acknowledge the limits of educational initiatives in preventing or reducing violence among youth when the causes of such violence lie outside of the education system.

5. Promising combination of strategies

A number of promising experiences relating both to violence prevention among youth and to education in post-conflict settings were shared. These experiences have in common a more holistic approach based on effective context-specific combinations of complementary strategies. These strategies range from curricular enrichment and inclusive participatory school-based processes, to non-formal education and life-long learning perspectives. Examples were also provided of how governing can be creatively made to be a form of citizenship education, developing a civil culture through the awareness of the need for minimal rules to live together, and how this may be a powerful strategy of violence prevention in urban areas. Other examples demonstrated how education can promote social cohesion by preventing and reducing social exclusion. Indeed, measures of positive discrimination have shown how patterns of school failure and drop-out can be reversed thus reducing the probability of exclusion from future welfare. Finally, examples were discussed of how combinations of formal and non-formal approaches (including basic schooling, curricular innovation, adult literacy, alternative accelerated primary education for out-of-school youth, and psycho-social support) have contributed to reconstructing social cohesion in post-conflict settings. It was felt that such experiences deserved to be shared more widely among partners and networks involved in education.

Workshop 3: "Shared values, cultural diversity and education: what and how to learn?"

Moderator: Mr. Luis Enrique Lopez (Proeib-Andes)
Panelists:
H.E. Ms. Lucija Cok, Minister of Education and Sports, Slovenia
Mr. Bodo Richter, Secretary of State, Kultusministerium desd Landes Sachsen-Anhalt, Germany

Mr. Abdeljalil Akkari Sckell, Professor University of Fribourg (Switzerland)

Dr. Geraldine Castleton, Researcher, Griffith University, Brisbane, Australia

Mr. Tesfamichael Gerathu, Director-General, Ministry of Education of Eritrea

The discussions in Workshop No. 3 gave rise to a very strong consensus on the relevance of than question of promoting and developing shared values, cultural diversity and their integration in and by education.

This overall consensus did not necessarily stem from an identity of motives or reasoning.

Cultural diversity and the practice of shared values were recognized as being a functional reality in many societies. Such values, constrained by historical factors such as colonization, had difficulty in endowing their basic postulates with a legal status, official recognition and legitimacy. So it was that these values, despite the fact of their existence, appeared informal, inferior and a source of complex unease. This situation concerned most of the formerly colonized countries of the South. The integration of such practices, values and customs by education was therefore ultimately conditional on their rehabilitation.

Cultural diversity and the importance of sharing the values of other, had only become a requirement for some societies because of the reality globalization, immigration and the mobility of people, ideas and information technologies. For those societies in which "monoculturalism" was the rule, the introduction of interculturalism into education was seen as both a challenge and a need, a necessity that had to be addressed. Some States, even in the West, had committed themselves to work in that direction.

Whatever the case, the introduction of an intercultural and pluralistic perspective by education presupposed:

(a) an epistemological organizational, strategic and ideological shift of focus;

(b) suitable methods;

(c) a revision or adaptation of content;

(d) a keen awareness of the upstream and downstream problems.

METHODS

Taking account of pluralism and cultural diversity at school called for appropriate pedagogical methods such as a renewed approach to teaching, constructivism, "dialogics", interdisciplinarity and active pupil participation, problem solving and conflict resolution, and self-observation and self-evaluation strategies. The aim must be to enable the child to acquire a good grasp of traditional and modern knowledge and, above all, to develop fully as an individual.

Further details on the precise implications of the different methods cited could be supplied by Dr. Lucija Cok, Dr. Geraldine Castelton, Dr. Bodo Richter, Dr. Tesfamichael Gerahtu, Dr. Abdeljali Akkari and Dr. Enrique Lopez and all these who worked in this workshop in their particular areas of concern.

CONTENTS

The contents needed to be taught with a view to taking better account of diversity should first and foremost aim at ensuring:

autonomy with respect to globalization;
transmission of the cultural heritage;
relevance for the community and those most closely involved;
promotion of gender equality.

Mention was made of a number of key value that should be explicit taught. They included love, peace, solidarity, tolerance, learning about differences, etc.

In that connection, while some subjects were mentioned as being best suited to incorporating this teaching, nothing precise seems to have been proposed concerning the methods to be employed for that purpose.

The question that commanded the greatest attention was the teaching of languages, or more precisely use of the mother tongue or minority languages in teaching. Provision was not structured in the same way everywhere. In some cases, the tendency was towards strengthening the rights of minority cultures in relation to their identity without refusing them access to the culture and language of the majority. In other cases, it was a matter of making the whole range of cultural contents of the majority and minorities alike available to all citizens so as to arrive at a common intercultural education for all pupils, thereby providing the basis for constructive coexistence.

An education properly based on cultural diversity should avoid relying on a hierarchy of languages. It should rather be based on the recognition of equal status for all languages. It could also rest on the notion of a complementarily of languages and cultures.

However, well it was organized, education that took account of cultural diversity raised many questions.

For example, it was important to ask whether all the cultural aspects were positive and deserved to be taken up and transmitted? Whether they were all conducive to learning to live together? How shared values could be taught in a context of fear of others, discrimination, etc.?

Were we not asking too much of the school?

How could school alone assume responsibility for problems rooted at different levels (political, economic, historical, etc.)?

Were there institutions in society other than school that could help in the promotion of cultural diversity?

By way of response to these questions, a number of provisions were envisaged:

The first involved work of an epistemological and conceptual nature. The aim here would be:

— to make a distinction between education and school enrolment and to take steps to ensure that, in taking cultural diversity into account, no boundaries were set between formal and non-formal education;

— to carry out systematic research in order to identify the shared values disseminated across cultures;

— to explore in greater depth the concept of globalization;

— to articulate the concept of living together;

— to define bilingualism and multilingualism.

All this presupposed efforts in the political sphere to ensure:

— interdependence between States and regions of the world, within States, between regions, between ethnic and cultural groups, between the efforts of the international community and national educational policies;

— greater involvement of actors and stakeholders in education at all levels: the family, social groups, parents of pupils, target community, pupils, teachers, local, regional and national authorities;

— a high level of cooperation and co-ordination within the school;

— a political choice involving a move from "monolingual" schooling to a multilingual education, geared to imparting life skills and taking into account the learner's socio-cultural context.

These provisions should be accompanied by:

— measures to develop initial and in-service training;

— strengthening of the intercultural dimension of existing curricula, especially in history, geography, civics, social studies, religious studies, ethics, mother tongues and foreign languages;

— the acquisition by students of foreign languages of skills in their mother tongue;

— increased cooperation with other sectors (social sector, youth institutions or those working with young people, institutions engaged in socio-cultural initiatives, local committees);

— the promotion of twinning among schools, pupil exchanges, support for multilateral projects and international school networks such as the UNESCO Associated Schools network;

— the production of textbooks and teaching aids, taking care to ensure that the aspects relating to society and culture were not marginalized or devalued;

— the promotion of foreign language teaching.

By way of an open-ended conclusion, it should be noted that an education that pays due regard to diversity will not simply be aimed at harmonization but rather at "dialogical" coexistence. It is a matter of being aware of the permanence of conflicts and of working through them, not bypassing or displacing them. Intercultural education and education for cultural pluralism needs to be set firmly in a critical perspective.

Workshop 4: "Language teaching and learning strategies for understanding and communication"

Introduction

The conclusion of Workshop 4 of the ICE are drawn from both the outcomes of the preparatory work and discussions that took place on Thursday, 6 September 2001. Workshop 4 was moderated by Mr. Theo van Els, University of Nijmegen, Netherlands.

The panellists were:

H.E. Mr. Jeffrey Lantz, Minister of Education, Prince Edward Island, Canada;

Mr. Abbas Sadri, Consultant to the Minister and Director-General of the Office of Higher Technical-Vocational Schools, Islamic Republic of Iran;

Mr. Gabor Boldizsar, Administrative Councillor, Ministry of Education, Hungary;

Ms. Blanca Estela Colop Alvarado, Coordinator Mayan Education Unit, UNESCO/Promem, Guatemala;

Mr. Abou Diarra, Director-General, National Education Centre, Bamako, Mali

These conclusions taken into consideration and reinforce the guidelines and reflections established at the Jomtien and Dakar Conferences and those appearing in the report of the Delors Commission.

In this sense, language learning and teaching strategies are assumed to be central in learning to live together: Language is a fundamental elements to configure and express personal and group identity. It is also a very important instrument for communicating between each other. Languages teaching and learning develop and improve the capacity of listening, expression, exchange, communication and dialogue.

Dynamic of the debate

The discussion focused on three main themes, including:

1. Linguistic diversity: the different "status" of languages nationally and internationally;
2. The importance of language(s) of instruction;
3. Foreign language(s) instruction.

In the framework of the discussion on the last two themes, participants also made some contributions in a transversal way about (both mother-tongue and other) language learning and teaching strategies.

1. Linguistic diversity: the different "status" of languages nationally and internationally

Many participants recognized that they belong to multilingual countries. In many cases one language is chosen called the national or official language, occasionally two or three. The language chosen it usually spoken by a majority of the population. But, sometimes one "international" language, like English, or another "Lingua Franca" is adopted. This trend has been based on improving the national communication process.

Many delegations and other participants expressed the concern that these unifying trends in the language of exchange bring harm to:

the recognition of other languages that are spoken in the country, and therefore oversimplify the linguistic and cultural diversity;

the non-native speakers of that language, and give an advantage to mother-tongue speakers of the preferred language.

However, the diagnosis is even more complex when faced with the increasingly interdependent world. The languages of many states have no place in the domain of international relations. With regard to this matter, two positions were registered.

First, the moderator tried to de-dramatize the use of "global" languages in international organizations and agencies. On this point, he introduced the concept of the "domain" in which the language is used. In other words, "global" languages are normally used for specific purposes only, and in a restricted number of language-use situations. Moreover, some participants of African countries expressed the opinion that their official languages are not closely related to their cultures and they are only used to "communicate".

Second, however, an important number of delegations and other participants stressed the dangers of granting a preferred status to only one language in international organizations. It would promote and disseminate the idea of teaching and learning only one foreign language, and might thus encourage one unilateral worldview.

Participants emphasized that the importance of the use of languages also taking into account their use in specific domains, such as the international organizations implied not only a way of communicating but also cultural of intercultural aspects.

Unfortunately, due to a lack of time, discussion of this topic could not be continued, but had certainly aroused a great deal of controversy.

2. The importance of language(s) of instruction

A great consensus was registered about the importance of making available, maintaining and reinforcing the teaching and learning of the mother-tongue. The profitability of starting primary education in the mother-tongue was also emphasized, taking into account pedagogical, social and cultural considerations:

- Then access to higher forms of thinking and other languages depends on a good mastery of the mother-tongue. So, receiving instruction in a language other than one's own is a serious handicap for learning. Pupils being instructed in non-native language right from the start of primary school usually fall seriously behind.
- Learning in the mother-tongue re-values the cultural aspects of belonging to the community. This enables the learner to better understand the other members of his/her community and therefore promotes communication and dialogue as a way of conflict resolution in a peaceful way.
- Normally children learn their mother-tongue within their family and community, and they very often learn it in an affective way. Thus, learning of the mother-tongue at school enables learners to deepen and reflect these relationships of affectivity, of personal and community memories, leading to a better understanding of oneself. From a better understanding and appreciation of oneself, it is possible to recognize others, their differences, and become involved with them in a frank and open dialogue leading to an understanding of each other.

Finally, participants agreed that there are neither inferior nor superior languages, that all languages can be useful in transmitting knowledge and to promote dialogue.

3. Foreign language(s) instruction

Participants expressed their support for the inclusion of foreign language(s) learning at school. They gave the following reasons among others:

— the global economy and technology require the learning of foreign languages and promote regional and international communication;

— it facilitates the mobility of students and workers;

— the learning of foreign languages enables a better understand of others and promotes dialogue to understand what is different, for example, in neighbouring countries.

Some participants asked what is the proper age to start learning foreign languages at school. For example, they had no evidence to support the advantages of early learning of foreign languages, and particularly its consequences for the learning of their own language.

Ultimately, then, faced with this complex issue confronting the international educational community and each country in particular, a thorough diagnosis is required. It is recognized that there is no point in putting forward simplistic solutions or easy formulas of universal validity and can be applied in all countries.

A number of other concerns were also expressed, but could not be discussed because of time constraints:

— the immersion method was described, but its teaching strategies were not explained.

— teaching strategies focusing on understanding require the inclusion of actions promoting the qualification of the body of teachers. (Teachers must be properly trained on language-teaching strategies.)

— it was also proposed to reactivate some UNESCO programmes about language-teaching strategies.

Finally, it is necessary to emphasize the importance of maintaining, deepening and, in some cases, extending the political dialogue at all levels, so as to promote the goal of learning and teaching languages as a fundamental key to learning to live together.

Workshop 5: "Scientific progress and science education: basic knowledge, interdisciplinarity and ethical issues"

Conducted by Mr. Jean-Marie Sani, Project Leader at the Cité des Sciences, Workshop 5 gave rise to a fertile discussion, based on an introduction to the topic by the moderator and the five presentations by the panellists, dealing with the following themes:

— scientific progress and science education in Zimbabwe;

— comparisons between science curricula in the developed countries and those in the developing countries;

— reflection on curricular standards against the background of the national standard in Japan;

— individual and social contributions to science education;

— a philosophical perspective on the links between the study of science and ethics.

The speakers were respectively:

— H.E. Dr. Samuel C. Mumbengegwi, Minister of Higher Education and Technology in Zimbabwe;

— Ms. Doris Jorde, Senior Lecturer, Department of Teacher Education and School Development at Oslo University;

— Mr. Shiego Yoshikawa, Department of Curricula at the Ministry of Education in Japan;

— Dr. Jaak Aaviksoo, Professor at Tartu University, Estonia;

— Dr. Pablo Latapi Sarre, Professor, Mexico.

The exchanges during this workshop may be grouped under four main headings:

The first bring, together the idea concerning the link between the theme of the workshop—scientific progress and science education—and the overall theme of the conference, namely learning to live together.

The second relates to the difficulties and problems with which this education was perceived to be confronted.

The third concerns ideas on science teaching, its goals, objective and methods.

The fourth comprises the suggestions and recommendations and emerged from the discussions.

1. Link between scientific progress and science education and the need to learn to live together

Raised by the moderator when launching the workshop, the question of the link between science education and the need to live together gave rise to many observations, which can be summed up as follows:

- The universality of the sciences—not only of their content but also the methods of reasoning they promote, the way of conceiving the world they underpin, and the values of sharing, cooperation and teamwork they foster—is an important dimension of living together. The sciences bring individuals and peoples of different nationalities closer together, often transcending frontiers. They develop intellectual rigour and the need to base results on demonstrations and proof. Science education thereby helps to promote the ability to live with others.
- Science education is a factor of economic growth and development, whose absence can be an impediment to living in community.
- Access to universal scientific knowledge being a right for all, for rich and poor, for boys and girls, regardless of ethnic and religious affiliation, it is accordingly closely linked to democracy and the exercise of citizenship. Life with others can thus be jeopardised by the division in society between the learned and the ignorant.

2. Difficulties affecting the development of science teaching

- Access to scientific knowledge nevertheless remains limited in many countries and the quality of such knowledge is substandard, despite the efforts made and the reforms of science education carried out in many of them. This is due to the difficulties and the problems identified by many speakers, foremost among which is the absence of basic infrastructures, financial and human resources and a favourable cultural environment. These deficiencies are the main cause of the inequalities between the developed countries and the developing countries and between urban and rural districts in this sphere.

- The gap between the developed countries and the poor countries is reflected in the way science is actually viewed in these countries. While the sciences are highly valued by the former, they give rise to suspicion in the latter. This suspicion is rooted in the political spin-off of the sciences, namely the appropriation of the natural and human resources of Third World countries by the industrialized countries, accentuated by the recent advances in the biological sciences. The destructive effects of scientific progress, which are more widely felt in the developing countries, is another reason for this suspicion.
- The nature of scientific teaching in many countries, which remains theoretical and wedded to abstract thinking and obsolete content, is identified as another difficulty responsible for the waning interest of young people in science studies—attested by the decreasing number of students opting for science courses, these are often considered as élitist career paths, an attitude that is reinforced by the tendency of teachers of these subjects themselves to make a mystique of the sciences.
- A further difficulty resides in the shortage of teachers of scientific subjects, a situation which is likely to persist if the status of teachers is not reconsidered by taking into account the difficulty specific to these subjects.

3. What type of science education? Directed to what goals and objectives? What methods should be used for science teaching?

Many speakers placed emphasis on the developing of scientific skills as the objective of science education. Its goal being to train citizens capable of understanding the world and acting upon it, as agents of economic growth and sustainable social development, internalizing the ethical values of citizenship, science education should meet the following conditions:

- Adopt active, application-oriented methods, using the real world as the foundation of the learning process by putting knowledge to the test of reality. These methods are moreover applicable to other disciplines, not to say the apprehension of reality and problems of lived experience, since science teaching must not be aimed solely at the sciences but must be geared to life;
- Foster the development of the critical spirit necessary for intellectual discovery, developing the curiosity that is natural to a child and stimulating interest in the sciences by encouraging a precocious tests for such knowledge while explaining its universal significance;
- Streamline science curricula and adapt them to the learners' capacity to assimilate;
- Adapt scientific curricula to social contexts so as to avoid any discontinuity with reality, bringing them into line with economic change, scientific progress and new scientific and technological discoveries;
- Link science teaching to the social and human context so as to introduce the ethical dimension into such teaching. The ethic in question should be based on the universal foundations and shared values implicit in human rights, responsibility towards others, the environment and future generations;
- Adopt a multidisciplinary and integrated approach as a means to contextualizing knowledge from the social standpoint;
- Develop the capacity to learn how to learn in association with others so as to ensure the continuity of science education;
- Increase the facilities for science education and encourage the links between school and out-of-school education, formal and non-formal learning; .

- Create an environment favourable to science education, which requires among other things a broad-based scientific education fostering the emergence of a scientific and technological culture founded on a culture of innovation, one in which innovation is promoted and society develops its capacity to use the resulting innovations. The media can greatly contribute to the development of such a culture;
- A favourable environment also requires the introduction of the necessary infrastructures, ranging from basic infrastructures to equipment specific to science teaching, including school amenities;
- The new information and communication technologies, whose role was considered by most speakers as crucial to the quality of science teaching at the present time, were nevertheless called into question by some. In one speaker's view, those technologies were not essential to the learning process, which could take place without them and they neither could, nor should, replace learning in and through the real world and practical experiments.

At all events, the need to develop science education was unanimously agreed upon. For, as one speaker explained, the future of humanity depended on such education and not scientific advances alone.

4. Recommendations

The debates gave rise to the following recommendations:

Science education is in need of radical reform in the sense of greater relevance, better adaptation and increased effectiveness. Certain experiments—some fairly original—described during the discussions, including the video presentation of the Cuban experiment on raising awareness of solar energy use through the involvement of learners, could be used as a point of departure.

The technical education model should be extended as a model meeting the citizen's new needs and corresponding to the methods and strategies required for science education and education in general.

The teacher, on whom the quality of science education primarily depends, should receive high-quality, continually updated training and be given improved status.

UNESCO is called upon to play a major role in improving the quality of science education as a dimension of living together, not only by extending successful experiences, by supplying the necessary technical backstopping and expertise and by carrying out the requisite studies and experiments, but also, and above all, by mobilizing partnerships and financial resources to help countries in need to set up the essential infrastructures for high-quality science teaching.

Insofar as science teachers are best equipped to provide education to prevent and combat HIVE/AIDS, the workshop appealed for them to be strongly involved in strategies to combat this scourge.

Workshop 6: Narrowing the gap between the information rich and the information poor: new technologies and the future of education

Chair, Excellencies, Ladies and Gentlemen,

I am pleased to present a summary of Workshop 6 whose central theme was on: "Narrowing the gap between information rich and the information poor: new technologies and the future of education".

The moderator of the session was Mr. Vis Naidoo, Education Specialist, Commonwealth of Learning.

The panellists were:

The Honourable Louis Steven OBEEGADOO, Minister of Education and Scientific Research Mauritius

Dr. Johanna Lasonen, Professor, University of Jyvaskyla

Ms. Heba Ramzy, Director, Kids and Youth Programmes, Regional Information Technology and Software Engineering Centre, Egypt

Professor Alexey Semenov, Rector, Moscow Institute of Teacher Development

Mr. Siva Subramanian, Educational International, Malaysia.

Introduction

The undeniable importance of education within the context of globalization requires an ongoing, in-depth discussion about the role of new technologies. Access to information worldwide today entails having and using ICT. As there in no level playing field from which societies around the world can respond to, and keep up with, the frantic pace of technological change and the effects it brings about, the emerging exclusion of many communities from the benefits of ICT is a growing concern. The imbalance of access fosters inequities among and within countries, localities and workplaces.

The role of new technologies in facilitating access to "education for all" has to be critically examined within the context go globalization. New technologies (ICTs) are often assumed to be a readily available access avenue to quality education in a variety of settings. The impact of ICT, however, may have to be judged on the basis of how effectively it will contribute to the expansion of humanity's knowledge base all over the world.

With these contextual remarks, let's turn our attention to some of the fundamental issues that deserve critical attention as we gauge both the possibilities and the risks intrinsic to the establishment of new technologies as a fixture of the educational landscape.

In doing so, we will examine:

- enduring challenges to be overcome;
- critical ingredients that are deemed essential to start addressing the digital divide; and
- priority action areas for a wide variety of actors.

Fundamental issues and challenges

As part of the reality check at the outset, let's highlight some givens.

Recognize the inequalities in access to technologies, information and knowledge which give rise to the digital divide between the knows and the know-nots, a phenomenon which is not unlike the other divide between the haves and the have-nots.

Evidence shows that the digital divide exists worldwide between the global regions, between countries, and between groups and individuals within countries. Access to ICT is divided along economic, gender, ethnic and linguistic lines.

Notwithstanding the fact that all societies can be said to have a wealth of information and a rich knowledge base, be mindful who structures technologically-transmitted information, who owns it, who decides how it ought to be used and circulated.

Keep in mind that despite improvement, traditional illiteracy remains a reality in many parts of the world and that resources are lacking just to address this reality.

To be aware that access to infrastructures is uneven and once again determined by the availability of economic means.

Opportunities

Notwithstanding these limitations, the benefits of ICT in education cannot be underestimated. With adequate access, the recourse to ICT can:

At an individual level

- maximize the exchange of ideas and creative projects across boundaries.
- unleash the innovative potential of the human mind and put this creativity at the service of problem-solving schemes that can be shared exemplary practices and transferred into a variety of contexts.

At a collective level

- lend itself to the multifaceted networking of users in many places and as such, contribute to the building of communities of learners and problem-solvers across national, cultural, social, and economic boundaries.
- assist in the education of a global citizenry through exposure to the varied and multifaceted perspectives of other communities.

Priority areas

That said, the potential for ICT can be tapped into and if the new technologies are to be successfully integrated into education for all, the following have to be taken into consideration:

At the national level:

- the availability of new technologies has to be organized through policies and programmes which are meant to maximize access to the public in general. This includes:

- strengthening and extending the ICT infrastructures;
- expanding ICT access through public institutions;
- upgrading citizens' and workers' skills;
- making available subsidized ICT access in schools and in other public sites;
- ensuring that ICT is accessible to underprivileged groups through open sites of access.

Resources—software tools—must be put at the disposal of users at no cost so that the support tools that are essential for the training of a technologically and information literate population are available on an equitable basis.

School level

The key learning competencies of learners have to be clearly articulated so that curricular contents can be made more relevant. As well, learning methods have to be updated with a view to making them compatible with the imperatives of e-learning.

Pre-service and in-service education of teachers

Make sure that both incoming teachers and experienced teachers are well prepared so that there can be an effective integration of new technologies into the delivery of education. Newly designed or adapted pedagogical methodologies—including subject—based methodologies—have to be explored, tapped into, and implemented if the education of learners is to occur in an effective way.

Finally, learning materials have to be provided in multi-media formats so that knowledge can be imparted through a variety of modes.

Key messages

Take a planned, holistic approach to policies and strategies to cover not only the integration of technologies in education but also to examine some of the telecommunication issues that need to be addressed.

Build on multi-party partnerships—under the lead role of public institutions and including community-based organizations—to plan, design, and implement key initiatives and sustain them over time.

Invest resources in capacity-building so that a variety of users can become not only technologically proficient but also information literate—that is, be able to put received information under the scrutiny of a lucid and discerning lens.

Proceed with a strategic deployment of resources—based on a carefully designed needs assessment and with focused, complementary actions that are likely to have a systemic impact.

Build on what already exists, including more traditional technologies of learning (i.e. books, radio, audio-visual equipment) so that the potential of technology can be harnessed to expand the learning rather than replace it—beware of tabular as a pseudo-solutions that usually end up eradicating the past and present without any safety net and no transition measures.

Keep in mind that quality of e-learning depends on wide access to ICT and support mechanisms as well as the critical engagement of teachers and learners in the schools and in the classroom.

Education for all is the priority. New technologies should be used to support the established curricular policies and programmes, as well as school management and administration processes. It is therefore imperative that new technologies be customized to the particulars of local contexts.

There is room for an expanded role for UNESCO to assist:

- Countries in the development of their ICT-in-education policies;
- In promoting the integration of new educational technologies on an equitable basis;
- In documenting and disseminating key requirements and competencies for e-learning;
- In evaluating and monitoring the quality of educational software.

Conclusion

In addressing the challenges to narrow the gap between the information rich and the information poor, countries have made substantial progress and undertaken innovative projects.

These examples of successful practices should serve as models on which to draw.

Final remarks

Chair, Excellencies, Ladies and Gentlemen,

This concludes the summary report for Workshop 6 on: "Narrowing the gap between the information-rich and the information poor: new technologies and the future of education". I thank you for your attention.

ANNEX XVI

LIST OF SPEAKERS IN MAJOR DEBATES I AND II MAJOR DEBATE I/GRAND DEBATE I/GRAN DEBATE I

One world, one future: education and the challenge of globalization Un monde, un avenir: l'education et le defi de la mondialisation Un mundo, un futuro: la education y el desafio de la mundializacion

Moderator/Animateur/Moderador: Mr. Pablo Latapi Ortega, Journalist, TV Azteca, Mexico
Key Speakers/Intervenants/Participants:

- H.E. Dr. Mohammed J.K. Al Ghatam, Minister of Education, Bahrain
- H.E. Prof. Abraham Borishade, Minister of Education, Nigeria
- H.E. Mr. Burchell Whiteman, Minister of Education Youth and Culture, Jamaica
- H.E. Dr. Sirikorn Maneerin, Deputy Minister of Education, Thailand
- Mr Aaron Benavot, Professor, Department of Sociology and Anthropology, Hebrew University of Jerusalem Mt Scopus, Israel
- Mr. Alejandro Tiana, Professor, Faculty of Education, UNED, Madrid (Spain)

MAJOR DEBATE II/GRAND DEBAT II/GRAN DEBATE II

Quality education for all for living together in the twenty-first century: intensifying the international policy dialogue on structures, contents, methods and means of education, and mobilizing the actors and partnerships

Éducation de qualité pour tous pour vivre ensemble au XXIe 'siècle: intensifier le dialogue politique international sur les structures, les contenus, les méthodes et les moyens d'enseignement, mobiliser es acteurset les partenariates

Educatión de calidad para todos para vivir juntos en el siglo XXI: intensificar el diálogo politico international sobre las estructuras, los contenidos, los métodos y los medios de enseñanza, y movilizar los actores y los asociados

Moderator/Animateur/Moderador: Ḿ Daniel Bernard, Direceteur, Leman Bleu Télévision, Suisse

Key Speakers/Intervenants/Participantes

- H.E. M. Najib Zerouazli Ouariti, Ministre de l'enseignement supérieur et de la formation des cadres et de la recherche scientifique, Maroc
- Sr. Ricardo Santos, Senador, Brazil
- M. Pierre Thenard, Conseiller technique au Cabinet du Ministre-délégué à la Cooperation et à la Francophonie France
- M. Thomas Bediako, Chef Coordinateur pour la région Afrique, Education International, Ghana
- M. Moncef Guitouni, Président de la Fédération international pour l'éducation des parents, Montreal (Canada)
- Mrs. Michèle Riboud, Manager, Human Development Division; World Bank, Washington DC
- Mr Kazimier Korab, Director, Department of Strategy and development, Ministry of Education, Poland
- Dr. Ella Yulaelawati, Head, Curriculum Division of Primary School, Ministry of Primary School, Ministry of Education, Indonesia

ANNEX XVII

LIST OF SPEAKERS IN THE WORKSHOPS
WORKSHOP 1/ATELIER 1/TALLER 1

Citizenship education: learning at school and in society
L'éducation à la citoyenneté: les apprentissages scolaires et sociaux
La educatión para la ciudadanía: aprendizajes escolares y sociales

Elaboration of Discusson Paper Elaboration document de débat Autor del documento de debate	Danish Research and Development Center for Adult Education Copenhagen
Co-organization and financing Coorganización y financiatión Co-organisation et financement	Danish Ministry of Education

Moderator/Animateur/Moderador: Mr. Sveinn EINARSSON, Counsellor of Culture, Iceland

Rapporteur/Rapporteur/Relator: Mr. Cesar BIRZEA, Directeur, Institut des Sciences de I'Éducation, Roumanie

Key Speakers/Intervenants/Participantes:

- H.E. Ms. Mariana AYLWIN OYARZÚN, Minister of Education, Chile
- H.E. Ms. Margrethe VESTAGER, Minister of Education, Denmark
- Mr. Benali BENZAGHOU, Recteur de l'Université des Sciences et de Technologe, Alger
- Mr. Samuel LEE, Director, Asian-Pacific Centre of Education for International Understanding, Seoul (Republic of Korea)
- Mr. Cliff OLIVIER, Co-ordinator, The Life Science Project, Namibia

Introductory Video	: Citizenship practics: school and social learning (Geneva)
Vidéo d'introduction	: Pratiques de la citoyenneté: l'école et l'apprentissage social (Genève)
Videocinta de presentación	: Prácticas de la ciudadania: aprendizaje escolar y social (Ginebra)

WORKSHOP 2/ATELIER 2/TALLER 2

Social exclusion and violence: Education for social cohesion
Exclusion sociale et violences: L'éducation pour la cohésion sociale
Exclusión social y violencia: la educatión para la cohesión social

Elaboration of Discussion Paper / Elaboration document de debat / Autor del documento de debate — Mr. Sobhi TAWIL (IUED)

Co-organisation / Co-organisation / Co-organisation — Institut Universitaire d'Etudes du Développement (IUED), Suisse

Financing / Financement / Financiacion — Ministerio de Education de Argentina

Moderator/Animateur/Moderador : M. Jean-Pierre GONTARD, Sécrétaire Général (IUED)

Rapporteur/Rapporteur/Relator : Mr. Joo-Seok KIM, Minister, Deputy Permanent Delegate to UNESCO, Republic of Korea

Key Speakers/Intervenants/Participants:

- S.E. M. Pierre NZILA, Ministre de l'enseignement primaire, secondaire et supérieur de la Rep. Du Congo
- Sr. Antanas MOCKUS, Alcalde d Bogotá (Colombia)
- Excma, Sra, Isabel COUSO TAPIA, Secretaria General de Educación y Formación Profesional, Ministerio de Educación, España
- M. Ivan IVIC, Professeur Universitaire, Filozofski fakulter, Belgrade (Yougoslavie)
- Mme Pari ZARRABI, Sociologue, Genève

Introductory Video : Forty School Project (South Africa)
Vidéo d'introduction : Projet des 40 Ecoles (Afrique du Sud)
Videocinta de presentatión : Proyecto de las cuarenta escuelas (Sudáfrica)

WORKSHOP 3/ATELIER 3/TALLER 3

Common values, cultural diversity and education: what and how to teach Valeurs communes, diversité culturelle et éducation: qu' apprendre et comment apprendre?
Valores comunes, diversidad cultural y educatión: ¿qué y cómo aprender?

Elaboration of Discussion Paper Elaboration document de débat Autor del documento de debate	Sr. Luis Enrique LÓPEZ (PROIEB-ANDES)
Co-organization Co-organisation Coorganizacion	Programa de Formación en Educación Intercultural Bilingüe para los Países Andinos (PROIEB-ANDES)
Co-financing Cofinancement Cofinanciation	German National Commission for UNESCO
Moderator/Animateur/Moderador :	Sr. Luis Enrique LÓPEZ (PROEIB-ANDES)
Rapporteur/Rapporteur/Relator :	M. Mohamadou Aly SALL, Directeur de l'Enseignement élémentaire, Dakar (Sénégal)

Key Speakers/Intervenants/Participantes:

- H.E. Ms. Lucija COK, Minister of Education & Sport Slovenia
- Mr. Bodo RICHTERR, Secretary of State, Kultusministerium des Landes Sachsen-anhalt, Magdeburg (Germany)
- M. Abdeljalil AKKARI SCKELL, Professeur, Université de Fribourg (Suisse)
- Dr Geraldine CASTLETON, Research Fellow, Griffith University, Brisbane (Australia)
- Mr. Tesfamichael GERAHTU, Director-General, Department of Education, Ministry of Education, Erit

Introductory Video : A new meaning for the education system (Nunavut, Canada)

Vidéo d'introduction : Une nouvelle orientation pour le systéme éducatif (Nunavut, Canada)

Videocinta de presentación: Nuevo sentido para el sistema educativo (Nunavut, Canadá)

WORKSHOP 4/ATELIER 4/TALLER 4

Language(s) teaching and learning strategies for understanding and communication Les stratégies d'enseignement et d'apprentissage des langues pour la compréhension et la communication
Estrategia de ensenanza y de aprendizaje de los idiomas para la comprensión y la communicación

Elaboration of Discussion Paper Elaboration document de débat Autor del documento de debate	Prof. Dr. Theo J.M. VANELS, Professor Emeritus, University of Nijmegen, The Netherlands
Co-organization and financing Co-organization et financement Coorganizacion y financiación	Ministry of Education, The Netherlands

Moderator/Animateur/Moderator : Prof. Dr. Theo J.M. VAN ELS

Rapporteur/Rapporteur/Relator : Prof. Antonio GUERRA CARABALLO, Uruguay

Key Speakers/Intervenants/Participants:

- H.E. Mr. Jeff LANTZ, Minister of Education, Prince Edward Island (Canada)
- Mr. Abbas Sadri, Consultant to the Minister and Director General for the Office of Higher Technical-Vocational Schools, Islamic Republic of Iran
- M. Gabor Boldiszar, Conseiller général d'administration, Ministére de l'Education, Hongrie
- Mrs. Blanca Estela COLOP ALVARADO, Co-ordinator, Mayan Education Unit, UNESCO/PROMEM, Guatemala
- M. Abou DIARRA, Directeur général, Centre national de l'Education, Bamako (Mali)

Introductory Video : Language Education (Czech Republic)

Vidéo d'introduction : L' enseignement des langues (République Tchèque)

Videocinta de presentación : Ensenanza de idiomas (República Checa)

WORKSHOP 5/ATELIER 5/TALLER 5

Scientific progress and science teaching: basic knowledge, interdisciplinarity and ethical problems
Progrés scientifique et enseignement des sciences: connaissances de base, interdisciplinarité et problèmes éthiques
Progreso císentifico y ensenanza de la cieñcia: conocimientos básicos, interdisciplinaridad y problemas éticos

Elaboration of Discussion Paper
Elaboration document de débat
Autor del documento de debate — M. Jean-Marie SANI, Cité des sciences et de l'industrie, La Villette, Paris

Co-organization
Co-organisation
Coorganización — Cité des sciences et de l'industrie, La Villette, Paris

Financing
Financement
Financiacion — Norway and Finland (from the Dakar Follow-up Special Account)

Moderator/Animateur/Moderator: M. Jean-Marie SANI, Cité des sciences et de l'industrie, La Villette, Paris

Rapporteur/Rapporteur/Relator: Mme Naïma TABET, Secrétaire générale, Commission nationale marocaine pour l'UNESCO

Key Speakers/Intervenants/Participantes:

- H.E. Dr. S.C. MUMBENGEGWI, Minister for Higher Education and Technology, Zimbabwe
- Prof. Jaak AAVIKSOO, Rector, Professor, University of Tartu (Estonia)
- Dr. Pablo LATAPI SARRE, Profesor, Universidad Naciónal Autonoma de México D.F. (México)

- Mr. Shigeo YOSHIKAWA, Senior Curriculum Specialist, Ministry of Education, Japan
- Mme Doris JORDE, Senior Lecturer, Oslo University, (Norway)

Introductory Video : Awareness of solar energy and renewable energy (Cuba)

Vidéo d'introductión : Sensibilisation á l' énergie solaire et aux énergies renouvelables (Cuba)

Videocinta de presentación : Sensibilización a la energía solar y las energías renovables (Cuba)

WORKSHOP 6/ATELIER 6/TALLER 6

Narowing the gap between the information rich and the information poor: new technologies and the future of education

Réduire le fossé entre ceux qui sont riches et ceux qui sont pauvres en termes d'accés à l'information: Les nouvelles technologies et l'avenir de l'education

Reducir la brecha entre ricos y probres en información: las nuevas tecnologías y el futuro de la escuela

Elaboration of Discussion Paper / Elaboration document de débat / Autor del documento de débate : Mr. Vis NAIDOO, Commonwealth of Learning, Vancouver (Canada)

Co-organization / Co-organisation / Coorganizacion : The Commonwealth of Learning (COL)

Financing / Financement / Financiación : Norway and Finland (from the Dakar Follow-up Special Account)

Moderator/Animateur/Moderador : M. Vis. NAIDOO, The Commonwealth of Learning

Rapporteur/Rapporteur/Relator : Mme Marie-Lison FOUGÉRE, Directorate, Direction des politiques et des programmes, Ministére de l'Éducation de l'Ontario, Canada

Key Speakers/Intervenants/Participantes:

- H.E. Mr. Louis Steven OBEEGADOO, Minister of Education and Scientific Research, Mauritius
- Dr. Johanna LASONEN, Professor, Institute for Educational Research, University of Jyvaskyla (Finland)
- Mrs. Heba RAMZY, Director, Regional Information Technology & Software Engineering Centre (RITSEC), Cairo (Egypt)
- Prof. Alexey SEMENOV, Rector, Moscow Institute of Teacher Development, Moscow (Russian Federation)
- M. Siva SUBRAMANIAN, Secrétaire Général de NUTP, Education Internationale, Kuala Lumpur (Indonesia)

Introductory Video	:	Internet Mobile Unit (Malaysia)
Vidéo d' introduction	:	L' Unité Mobile Internet (Malaisie)
Videocinta de presentación	:	Unidad Móvil Internet (Malasia)

ANNEX XVIII

LIST OF DOCUMENTS DISTRIBUTED DURING THE SESSION

Working documents

ED/BIE/Confinted 46/1	Provisional agenda
ED/BIE/Confinted 46/2	Proposed organization of the work of the Conference
ED/BIE/Confinted 46/3	Reference document on: "Education for all for learning to live together": contents and learning strategies—problems and solutions.
ED/BIE/Confinted 46/4	Documents to assist the discussions during the six workshops
ED/BIE/Confinted 46/5	General overview of the 46th session of the ICE
ED/BIE/Confinted 46/6	Draft "Conclusions and proposals for action" arising from the 46th session of the ICE"

Information documents

"Messages of ministers of education", a delegate's guide, a provisional list of participants and a conference evaluation questionnaire were distributed to the participants. Many delegates' statements were also made available at their authors' request.

National reports submitted to the 46th session of the ICE

A total of 99 national reports were submitted by the following Member States: Algeria; Angola; Argentina; Australia; Austria; Azerbajjan; Bahrain; Barbados; Belarus; Belgium (Flemish community and French community); Benin; Bolivia; Botswana; Brazil; Bulgaria; Cambodia; Cameroon; Canada; Central African Republic; Chad; China; Colombia; Congo; Congo, People's Democratic Republic; Costa Rica; Côte d'Ivoire; Croatia; Cuba; Cyprus; Czech Republic; Denmark; Egypt; Estonia; Ethiopia; Federal Republic of Yugoslavia; Finland; France; Germany; Ghana; Guinea; Honduras; Hungary; India; Indonesia; Iran, Islamic Republic of; Iraq; Ireland; Italy; Japan; Jordan; Kazakhstan; Kenya; Korea, Democratic People's Republic; Korea, Republic of; Kuwait; Kyrgyzstan; Latvia; Lebanon; Libyan Arab Jamahiriya; Madagascar; Malaysia; Mali; Mauritius; Mexico; Moldova; Mozambique; Namibia; Nigeria; Norway; Oman; Pakistan; Peru; Poland; Portugal; Qatar; Romania; Russian Federation; Rwanda; Saudi Arabia; Senegal; Slovakia; Slovenia; Spain; Sudan; Swaziland; Sweden; Switzerland; Syrian Arab Republic; Thailand; The Former Yugoslav Republic of Macedonia; Tunisia; Turkey, Uganda; Ukraine; United Arab Emirates; United Republic of Tanzania; Zambia; Zimbabwe.

Other documents available during the Conference

(a) World Data on Education, fourth edition of the CD-ROM produced by the IBE and containing data on 158 education systems.

(b) Education for citizenship, a CD-ROM produced by the Education Sector of UNESCO

(c) Prospects, special issue of UNESCO's quarterly review prepared by the IBE on the theme "learning to live together".

(*d*) Video-cassette on the BRIDGE project (introductory documents for the six workshops).

(*e*) "Demain l'education ..." recording of the debate programme produced by Leman bleTV Geneva

(*f*) 100 and 1 terms for human rights education: a glossary prepared by Ramdane Babadji for the World Association for the School as an Instrument of Peace (EIP), in collaboration with the IBE.

ANNEX XIX

Liste des participants/List of participants/Lista de participantes
Etats Membres/Member States/Estados Miembros

Albanie/Albania

M. Fation PENI
Secrétaire géneral de la Commission nationale pour l'UNESCO

Mr. Artan CANAJ
Director of Foreign Relations

Mrs. Mira SCHNEIDER
Second Secretary
Albanian Permanent Mission, Geneva

Algérie/Algeria/Argelia

S.E.M. Boubeker Benbouzid
Ministre de l'éducation nationale
Président de la Commission nationale algérienne pour l'UNESCO/ALECSO/ISESCO
(Chef de délégation)

S.E. M. Mohamed-Salah DEMBRI
Ambassadeur, Représentant permanent de l'Algerie auprés de l'Office des Nations Unies a Genéve

Mme Kheira OUIGUINI
Déléguée Permanente adjointe de l'Algérié auprés' de l'UNESCO

M. Tahar BERCHICHE
Secrétaire général de la Commission nationale algérienne pour l'UNESCO/ALECSO/ISESCO

M. Hocine SAHRAOUI
Ministre Conseiller auprés de la Mission permanente d' Algérie á Genéve

M. Baghdad LAKHDAR
Conseiller

M. Nourreddine TOUALBI
Conseiller

M. Brahim MAHFOUD
Conseiller

M. Nor-Eddine BENFREHA
Conseiller auprés de la Mission permanente d' Algérie á Genéve

Allemagne/Germany/Alemania

H.E. Dr. Bodo RICHTER
State Secretary, Ministry of Education and Cultural Affairs of Land Saxony-Anhalt
(Head of Delegation)

Mr. Klaus METSCHER
Deputy Permanent Representative
Permanent Mission of German to the Office of the United Nations Geneva

Mr. Frank BURBACH

Adviser on Multilateral Cultural Activities
Federal Foreign Office, Berlin

Dr. Hans HAENISCH
Institute of the Land North-Rhine/ Westphalia for School and Further Education

Prof. Dr. Klaus HUFNER
President
German Commission for UNESCO, Bonn

Dr. Traugott SCHOEFTHALER
Secretary General
German Commission for UNESCO, Bonn

Dr. Birgitta RYBERG
Director, International Department
KMK

Mrs. Christine M. MERKEL
Officer for Education
German Commission for UNESCO, Bonn

Prof. Heribert HINZEN
Director
Institut for International Cooperation
German Adult Education Association (DVV-IIZ)

Angola

S.E. M. Antonio B.S. NETO
Ministre de l'éducation et de la culture (Chef de délégation)

M. David Leonardo CHIVELA
Directeur général
Institut national d'investigation et développement éducation (INIDE)

M. Francisco DOMINGOS
Directeur général
Institut national éducation des adultes

M. Eduardo Domingos MULENDE
Directeur
Institut national de l'enseignement général

M. Emilio LEONCIO
Directeur
Institut national de l'enseignement moyen et technique

M. Antonio Campos NETO
Attaché de presse
Ministere de l'éducation et de la culture

Mme Francisca MARTINS
Chef
Department de l'enseignement général de l'INIDE

M. Eduardo ANDRE
Chef des relations publiques et protocole auprés du Ministére de l'éducation et de la culture

Mme Sofia Silvério PEGADO
Conseiller

Arabie saoudite/Saudi Arabia/ Arabia Saudi

H.E. Dr. Mohamed Ahmed RASHEED
Minister of Education
(Head of Delegation)

Mr. Ibrahim AL-AWAD
Deputy Minister for Education Development

Dr. Fida AL ADEL
Permanent Delegate of the Kingdom of Saudi Arabia to UNESCO

Mr. Abdallah Al HOWIMAL
Director General for Education
Holz Mekkah Region

Mr. Ibrahim AL-WADI
Chief of Protocol and Relations Unit Minister's Office

Argentine/Argentina

S.E. Lic. Andrés Guillermo DELICH
Ministro de Educacion
Presidente de la Comision Nacional Argentina de Cooperacion con la UNESCO
(Jefe de delegacion)

Sr. Sergio PALACIO
Secretario General
Consejo Federal de Cultura y Educacion

Sra. Alicia Beatriz DE HOZ
Ministro
Misión Permanente en Ginebra

Lic Silvia Graciela FINOCCHIO
Coordinadora
Programa Nacional de Gestión Curricular y Capacitación

Sra. Silvia MONTOYA
Directora Ejecutiva
Instituto para el Desarrollo de la Calidad Educativa (IDECE)

Australie/Australia

Mr. Paul Bernard COWAN
Deputy Permanent Delegate (Education) to UNESCO
(Head of Delegation)

Mr. Geoff SPRING
Chief Executive of the Department of Education, Training and Employment in South Australia

Mr. Patrick MARKWICK-SMITH
Director
International Education Services

Ms. Joy DELEO
Vice President (Programmes)
UNESCO Asia Pacific Network for International Education and Values Education
Director, Office of Multicultural Affairs

Mrs. Anne SIWICKI
Policy Officer
Australian Permanent Delegation to UNESCO

Autriche/Austria

H.E. Mr. Reinhard NOBAUER
Ministry of Education, Science and Culture (Head of Delegation)

Mrs. Ruth Mitschka
Expert

Azerbaïdjan/Azerbaijan/ Azerbaiyán

M. Elmar GASYMOV
Ministre-adjoint de l'éducation de la République azerbaïdjanaise
(Head of Delegation)

M. Azad AKHUNDOV
Expert en chef du Ministere de l'éducation de la République azerbaïdjanaise

Bahreïn/Bahrain/Bahrein

H.E. Dr. Mohammed J.K. ALGHATAM
Minister of Education
(Head of Delegation)

Dr. Yousif ABDEL WAHID
Advisor to H.E. The Minister
Ministry of Education

Mrs. Lulwa Khalifa ALKHALIFA
Director of Curricula
Ministry of Education

Mr. Badriya ALAHMED
Acting Secretary General
Bahrain National Commission for UNESCO
Ministry of Education

Mr. Ahmed ALHAMMADI
Senior System Analyst
Information and Documentation Centre, Ministry of Education

Mr. Ebrahim AL-SULTAN
Specialist
Public Relations
Ministry of Education

Dr. Emad A. TAQI
Vice President for Planning and Community Services
University of Bahrain

Dr. Mohmmed H. AL-MUTAWA
Head of Psychology Department
University of Bahrain

Dr. Mahmoud SALEH
Director of the Counselling Centre
University of Bahrain

Dr. Sajida TABBARA
Director of English Language Centre, University of Bahrain

Bélarus/Belarus/Belarús

Mr. Boris IVANOV
First Deputy Minister of Education
(Head of Delegation)

Ms. Katsiaryna YERMILINA
Secretary General
National Commission for UNESCO

M. Evgeny YUSHKEVICH
Mission du Bélarus auprés de l'Office de l'ONU a Genéve

Mrs. Irina EGOROVA
First Secretary
Permanent Mission of the Republic Belarus

Belgique/Belgium/Bélgica

S.E. Mme Francoise DUPUIS
Ministre de l'enseignement supérieur, de l'enseignement de promotion sociale et de la recherche scientifique
(Chef de délégation)

Mme Catherine Antonacchio
Collaboratrice de Monsieur le Ministre-Président du Gouvernement de la Communauté française de Belgique

Mme Jeanine VAN DE VELDE
Collaboratrice de Monsieur le Ministre-Président du Gouvernment de la Communauté française de Belgique

M. Christophe KELECOM
Collaborateur de Madame la Ministre F. Dupuis

Mme Suzie DELMEZ
Attachee au départment éducation du Cabinet de Monsieur Jean-Marc Nollet Ministre de l'enfance, Chargé de I'enseignement fondamental

Mme Anne HICTER
Collaboratrice au Cabinet de Monsieur Pierre Hazette, Ministre de l'enseignement secondaire et de l'enseignement spécial

M. Dominique BARTHELEMY
Directeur des Relations internationales au Secrétariat général
du Ministère de la Communauté française de Belgique

M. Philippe NAYER
Délégué de la Communauté française de Belgique à Genève

Mme Christine CACOUAULT
Collaboratrice à la Délégation de la Communauté française de Belgique à Genève

M. Philippe RENARD
Expert
Cabinet du Ministre de l'enseignement
(Rapporteur général de la CIE)

M. Marc THUNUS
Délégué permanent adjoint de Belgique auprès de l'UNESCO
Chargé d'affaires a.i.

Mme Ruth Lamotte
Adjointe au Directeur
Département Enseignement
Communaute flamande de
Belgique

Bénin/Benin

S.E. M. Jean Bio CHABI OROU
Ministre des enseignements
primaire et secondaire
(Chef de délégation)

S.E. M. Olabiyi B.J. YAÏ
Ambassador, Délégué permanent
du Bénin auprès de
l'UNESCO

M. Toussaint TCHITCHI
Professeur
Ancien Ministre de l'information et
de la communication
Directeur de l'Institut national
pour la formation et la
recherche en éducation (INFRE,
Porto-Novo, Benin).

Bhoutan/Bhutan/Bhutan

H.E. Mr. Bap KESANG
Ambassador and Permanent
Representative
Permanent Mission of Bhutan,
Geneva
(Head of Delegation)

Mr. Sherab TENZIN
First Secretary
Permanent Mission of Bhutan
Geneva

Mr. Sonam TOBGAY
Second Secretary
Permanent Mission of Bhutan
Geneva

Bosnie-Herzégovine/Bosnia and Herzegovina/Bosnia y Herzegovina

Mrs. Dragana ANDELIC
First Secretary
Permanent Mission of Bosnia and
Herzegovina to the
UN Office at Geneva

Botswana

H.E. Mr. Kgeledi GEORGE
KGOROBA
Minister of Education
Ministry of Education
(Head of Delegation)

Mr. Philemon Themba RAMATSUI
Permanent Secretary
Ministry of Education

Mr. Lucky Tebalebo MOAHI
Director
Curriculum Development and
Evaluation

Ms Bontle Pauline MOLEFE
Principal Education Officer

Mr. Raymond CHARAKUPA
Senior Lecture
University of Botswana

Ms. Violet ESSILFIE
Programme Officer
Botswana National Commission
for UNESCO

Brésil/Brazil/Brasil

Sra. Maria Helena CASTRO
Cheffe da Delegaçao
Presidente do Instituto Nacional de
Estudos e Pesquisas
Educacionais—INEP e Secretária
de Educaçáo Superior

Sra. Raquel TEIXEIRA
Presidente do Conselho Nacional
de Secretários de Educacao
CONSED e Secretária de Estado da
Educação de Goiás

Sr. Adeum Hilario SAUER
Presidente da Uniao Nacional de
Dirigentes Municipais de
Educacão
UNDIME e Secretária de Estado da
Educação de Itabuna

Mª Claudia P.C. BAENA SOARES
Assessora da Assessoria
International do Gabinete do
Ministro
AI/GM

Sra. Elisabeth VARGAS
Coordenadora Nacional do Programa Universidade Solidária/Comunidade Solidária

Sra. Juçara Maria Dutra VIEIRA
Vice-presidente da Confederação Nacional de Trabalhadores em Educação

Sr. Ricardo SANTOS
Presidente da Comissao de Educacao do Senado Federal

Bulgarie/Bulgaria

Mr. Yulian NAKOV
Deputy Minister of Education and Science
Leader of the delegation
(Head of Delegation)

Ms. Lubov DRAGANOVA
State Expert in "International Activities"
Directorate, Ministry of Education and Science

Ms. Aneta HRISTOVA
Headmaster of Vocational School "Atanas Bourv"
SPTUM, Russe

Assoc. Prof. Diana ANTONOVA
Representative of "Bistra and Galina" Foundation

Ms. Zdravka BARDAROVA
Representative of "Bistra and Galina" Foundation

Mr. Stoyan RALEV
Secretary General of the Bulgarian National Commission for UNESCO

Burkina Faso

M. Louis Honoré OUEDRAOGO
Conseiller technique du Ministre de l'enseignement de base
(Chef de délégation)

M. Julien DABOUE
Directeur des études et de la planification (enseignements secondaire et supérieur)

M.D. Bernard YONLI
Secrétaire général
Commission nationale pour l'UNESCO

M. Sibiri Laurent KABORE
Directeur des études et de la Planification de l'enseignement de base

Burundi

S.E. M. Prosper MPAWENAYO
Ministre de l'éducation nationale
(Chef de delegation)

S.E. M. Adolphe NAHAYO
Ambassadeu, Représentant permanent du Burundi á Genéve

M. Cyrille NZOHABONAYO
Directeur du Bureau de coordination et de suivi des Organismes personnalisés

Mme Justine BIHOTORI
Premier Conseiller

Cambodge/Cambodia/Camboya

H.E. Mr. Sethy IM
Secretary of State
(Head of Delegation)

H.E. Mr. Nay Leang KOEU
Director General of Education
Ministry of Education, Youth and Sports

Cameroun/Cameroon/Camerun

S.E. Prof. Joseph OWONA
Ministre de l'éducation nationale
(Chef de délégation)

S.E. M. Pascal BILOA TANG
Ambassador Délégue Permanent du Cameroun auprès de l'UNESCO

M. Barthélémy MVONDO NYINA
Secrétaire général de la
Commission nationale pour
l'UNESCO

M. Richard WILLAYI
Conseiller Technique n°2
Ministere de léducation nationale

M. Yaya YAKOUBA
Directeur de l'Enseignement
primaire, maternel et normal
Ministère de l'éducation nationale

M. Alphonse NKOME
Chef de service de
l'Alphabétisation et de la post
alphabétisation, Ministere de
l'éducation nationale

Mme Berthe AFFANA
Sous-Directeur de la Prospective
Ministére de l'éducation nationale

M. Antoine WONGO AHANDA
Conseiller Culturel a l'Ambassade
du Cameroun a Paris

M. Charles ASSAMBA ONGODO
Deuxiéme Secrétaire chargé du
suivi permanent des dossiers
de l'UNESCO

Canada/Canadá

The Hon. Jeff LANTZ
Minister of Education
Prince Edward Island
(Head of Delegation)

H.E. Mr. Louis HAMEL
Permanent Delegation of Canada
to the UNESCO (PESCO)

Mme Marie-Lison FOUGÉRE
Directrice
Direction des politiques et des
programmes
Ministère de l'éducation
Ontario

Dr. Paul CAPPON
Director General
Council of Ministers of Education,
Canada (CMEC)

Mr. Richard MARTIN
Senior Program Manager
International Academic Relations
Division
Department of Foreign Affairs and
International Trade

Mrs. Eva EGRON-POLAK
Chairperson of the Sectoral
Commission on Education
Canadian Commission for
UNESCO

Mr. Doug WILLARD
President
Canadian Teachers' Federation

M. Jean-Claude TARDIF
Conseiller
Centrale des Syndicate du Quebec

Mme Diane LABERGE
Chargee de programme
(Education)
Commission canadienne pour
l'UNESCO

Mr. Donald R. MACPHEE
Councellor
Permanent Mission of Canada

Chili/Chile

S.E. Sr. Mariana AYLWIN
OYARZUN
Ministra de Educacion
(Jefe de delegacion)

Sra. Paz PORTALES GRADO
Oficina de Relaciones
Internacionales Mineduc
Secretaria Adjunta Comision
Nacional Chilena de
Cooperation con UNESCO

Sr. Cristian COX
MECE
Ministerio de Educacion Chile

Chine/China

H.E. Mr. Xinsheng ZHANG
Vice Minister of Education
Chairman
Chinese National Commission for
UNESCO
(Head of Delegation)

H.E. Mr. Xuezhong ZHANG
Ambassador, Permanent Delegate of China to UNESCO

Ms. Xiaoya CHEN
Director General
Department of Policies and Regulations
Ministry of Education

Mr. Jianguo WANG
Deputy Director General
Department of Basic Education
Ministry of Education

Mr. Yue DU
Director of Division
Chinese National Commission for UNESCO

Mr. Jianjum ZHAI
First Secretary
Chinese Permanent Delegation to UNESCO

Mr. Dezheng LIU
Chinese National Commission for UNESCO

Ms. Yunying CHEN
Researcher
China National Institute of Education Research

Ms. Xiangming CHEN
Professor
Beijing University

Ms. Aijun YUAN
Principal
Experimental Middle School attached to Beijing Normal University

Chypre/Cyprus/Chipre

H.E. Mr. Uranios IOANNIDES
Minister of Education and Culture
(Head of Delegation)

Mr. George ZACHARIADES
Director
Pedagogical Institute

Colombie/Colombia

S.E. Sr. Margarita Peña Borrero
Viceministra de Educación Nacional
(Jefe de delegación)

Sr. Maria Elvira POSADA-CORRALES
Segundo Secretario
Misión Permanente de Colombia
Ginebra

Sr. Antanas MOCKUS
Alcalde de Bogotá

Sra. Alicia Eugenia SILVA
Secretario Privado
Alcalde de Bogotá

Comores/Comoros/El Comoro

S.E. M. Cheikh Soilihi SAID ABDALLAH
Ministre de l'Education nationale, de la Formation Professionnelle et des Droits de l'Homme
(Chef de délégation)

Dr. Boina ABOUBAKARI
Secretaire général
Commission nationale des Comores pour l'UNESCO

Congo

S.E. M. Pierre NZILA
Ministre de l'enseignement primaire, secondaire et superieur
Chargé de la recherche scientifique
(Chef de délégation)

M. Justin BIABAROH-IBORO
Ministre Conseiller
Mission permanente du Congo á Genéve

Mme Delphine BIKOUTA
Premier conseiller
Mission permanente du Congo á Genéve

M. Gabriel NGUENGUE-MONTSE
Conseiller économique
Mission permanente du Congo á Genéve

M. Francois NGUIE
Conseiller
Mission permanente du Congo á L'UNESCO

M. Marie-Joseph MALLALI-YOUGA
Fonctionnaire
Ministére de l'enseignement primaire, secondaire et supérieur

M. Alphonse DONGO
Fonctionnaire
Ministére de l'enseignement primaire, secondaire et supérieur

M. Serge BORET BOKWANGO
Attaché chargé du Protocole
Mission permanente du Congo á Genéve

Côte d'Ivoire

S.E. M. Michel Amani N'GUESSAN
Ministre de l'éducation nationale
(Chef de délégation)

S.E. M. Claude BEKE
Ambassadeur, Représentant permanent
Mission permanente, Genéve

Mme Yao-Yao Akissi KAN
Secretaire general
Commission nationale ivoirienne pour l'UNESCO

M. Kipré NEA
Membre du Synares

M. Jerome Klôh WEYA
Premier Conseiller
Mission Cote d'Ivoire, Genéve

Croatie/Croatia/Croacia

H.E. Mr. Vladimir STRUGAR, Ph.D.
Minister
Ministry of Education and Sports
(Head of Delegation)

Mr. Tomislav STOJAK
Head of Minister Office

Mr. Niksa Nikola SOLJAN Ph.D.
Member of the Croatian National Commission for UNESCO

H.E. Mr. Neda RITZ
Ambassador Extraordinary and Plenipotentiary to UNESCO

Cuba

S.E. Dr. Luis Ignacio GÓMEZ GUTIÉRREZ
Ministro de Educatión
(Jefe de delegación)

S.E. Sr. Carlos AMAT FORES
Embajador, Representante Permanente de la República de Cauba ante la Ofician de la ONU y las Organizaciones Internacionales en Ginebra

Lic, Carlos ALFARO ALFARO
Director de Relaciones Internacionales del Ministerio de Educación de Cuba

Sr. Anayansi RODRÍGUEZ CAMEJO
Segunda Secretaria
Misión Permanente de Cuba en Ginebra

Sr. Alejandro CASTILLO-SANTANA
Tercer Secretario
Mision Permanente de Cuba en Ginebra

Danemark/Denmark/Dinamarca

H.E. Ms. Margrethe VESTAGER
Minister of Education
(Head of Delegation)

Mr. Torben Kornbech RASMUSEEN
Director
Ministry of Education
(Alternate Head of Delegation)

Ms. Bodil RASMUSSEN
Secretary to the Minister
Ministry of Education

Mr. Erik NEXELMANN
Head of Division
Ministry of Education

Mrs. Kirsten DANIELSEN
Chief Adviser
Ministry of Education

Mrs. Hjordis DALSGAARD
Deputy Permanent Delegate
The Danish UNESCO Delegation
Paris

Mr. Nils-Georg LUNDBERG
Rector of Hjoerring Teacher
Training College
The Danish UNESCO National
Commission

Mrs. Birgitte SIMONSEN
Professor, Director
The Board of the International
Academy on Education and
Democracy

Mr. Erik PRINDS
Senior upper secondary school
teacher
Danish Teacher Trade Unions—
International

Mrs. Anne Slej KRISTENSEN
Head of Documentation
The Danish Research and
Development Centre for
Adult Education

Egypt/Egypt/Egipto

M. Mohamed TAWFIK
Chargé d'Affairs a.i.
Mission d'Egypt, Geneve

Mr. Ahmed ABDEL LATIF
Third Secretary
Mssion of Egypt, Geneva

Emirates arabes unios/United Arab Emirates/Emiratos Arabes Unidos

H.E. Dr. Jamal Mohamed
AL-MEHERI
Under Secretary of Education
Chairman
(Head of Delegation)

H.E. Dr. Ahmed Saad AL-SHARIF
Ass. Under Secretary

H.E. Dr. Hussein Obaid
GHOBASH
Permanent Representative to
UNESCO

Dr. Obaid Ben Ali Ben Butti
AL-MOHAIRI
Director
Center for Development of
Educational Methods

Mr. Awad Ali SALEH
Secretary General
U.A.E. National Commission

Mr. Youssef Mohammed
AL-NAJJAR
Director of General Education

Mr. Fahd Abdalla AL-JASSEMI
Director
Under-Secretary's Office

Mr. Mohamed Belhassen BEN
AMARA
UAE Permanent Mission
Geneva

L'Erythrée/Eritrea/El Eritrea

H.E. M. Osman SALEH
Minister of Education
Ministry of Education

Espagne/Spain/España

Ilma. Sr. Doña, Isabel COUSO
Secretaria General de Education y
Formaciòn Professional
(Jefe de delegaciòn)

Ilma. Sra. Doña. Pilar MARTÍN-LABORDA
Directora de Comité de la Secretaría General de Educatión y Formación Professional

Ilmo. Sr. Don Francisco LÓPEZ RUPÉREZ
Consejero de Educacion de la Embajada de Espana ante la UNESCO

Ilmo. Sr. Don Jaime CISNEROS
Subdirector General de Administraciones Territoriales

Sra. Doña. Maria-Mireia MONTANÉ
Directora del Proyecto Educativo del Foro Universal de las Culturas
Barcelona 2004

Ilmo. Sr. Don Juan Angel ESPAÑA
Director General de Cooperacion Territorial y
Alta Inspeccion de este Ministerio

Doña Maria Victoria REYZÁBAL RODRÍGUEZ
Coordinadora de Area de la Direccion General de Promocion Educativa de la Comunidad de Madrid

Sr. Don Pedro ORTEGA GARCÍA
Coordinator de Area de la Dirección General de Ordenación Academica, igualmente de la Comunidad de Madrid

Estonie/Estonia

H.E. Mr. Tonis LUKAS
Minister
(Head of Delegation)

Mrs. Epp REBANE
Adviser on Education Policy

Mr. Andres KOPPEL
Head of the Policy Department

Ethiopie/Ethiopia/Etiopia

Mr. Hiruy AMANUEL
Permanent Delegate of Ethiopia to UNESCO

Mr. Girma ASFAW
Deputy Permanent Delegate of Ethiopia to UNESCO

Federation de Russie/Russian Fédération/Federacion de Rusia

H.E. Mr. Vladimir FILIPPOV
Minister of Education
(Head of Delegation)

Mr. Nikolai DUITRIEV
Head of the Department for International Cooperation
Ministry of Education

Mr. Vladimir SOKOLOV
Head of Section
Ministry of Foreign Affairs

Ms. Tatiana GUREEVA
Counsellor
Permanent Delegation of the Russian Federation to UNESCO

Finlande/Finland/Finlandia

Mr. Petri POHJONEN
Director of Planning Division
National Board of Education
(Head of Delegation)

Mrs. Armi MIKKOLA
Counsellor of Education
University Division
Ministry of Education

Mr. Heikki KOKKALA
Counsellor
Department for International Development Cooperation
Ministry for Foreign Affairs

Ms. Matti Sakari SUUTARINEN
Senior Researcher
Normaalikoulu/ylaaste
University of Jyväskyla

Mrs. Satu HEIKKINEN
Special Adviser
International Relations, Finish National Commission for UNESCO
Ministry of Education

France/Francia

Mme Suzy HALIMI
Professeur des universites
Présidente du Comité éducation et formation de la
Commission nationale française pour l' UNESCO
(Chef de délégation)

Mme Sylviane LEGRAND
Deuxiéme secrétaire á la Délégation permanente de la France
auprés de l' UNESCO

M. Renaud RHIM
Adjoint an Délégué aux relations internationales et á la coopération (DRIC)
Ministére de l'éducation nationale

M. Jean-Pierre BOYER
Secrétaire général de la CNFU

M. Patrick DEBUT
Chef de bureau des institutions multilatérales et de la francophonie (DRIC)
Ministére de l'éducation nationel

Mme Colette GUILLOPÉ
Professor des universités
Présidente de l'Association francaise "Femmes et mathematiques"

M. Alain MICHEL
Inspecteur général de l'éducation nationale

M. Francis GOULLIER
Inspecteur général de l'éducation nationale

M. Andre GUYETANT
Adjoint au chef du bureau DRIC

Mme Marie-Josee De FORNEL
Chargée de mission pour l' UNESCO
á la DRIC

M. Jean-Pierre REGNIER
Secrétaire général adjoint de la CNFU

M. Gilles BRAUN
Chargé de mission á la direction de la technologie

M. Francois SAINT-PAUL
Représentant permanent adjoint de la France auprés des
Nations Unies

Gabon/Gabón

M. Jean-Marie BOUYOU
Secrétaire général
Commission nationale pour l' UNESCO

Gambie/Gambia

Mr. Joseph Paul JASSEY
Deputy Permanent Secretary
Department of State for Education
(Head of Delegation)

Mr. Momodou K. TOURAY
Principal Education Officer
Regional Education Office
Department of State for Education

Géorgie/Georgia

Mr. Tamaz TATISHVILI
Deputy Minister of Education
National Coordinator "Education for All" Progam
(Head of Delegation)

Dr. Petre METREVELI
Secretary-General
Georgian Commission for UNESCO

Ghana

H.E. Prof. C. AMEYAW-AKUMFI
Minister of Education
(Head of Delegation)

H.E. Mr. Konina WUDU
Ambassador and Permanent Representative
Ghana Permanent Mission
Geneva

Mr. F.A. BEN-EGHAN
Ag. Chief Director
Ministry of Education

Prof. J. ANAMUA-MENSAH
Principal
University College of Education of Winneba

Mr. J. KUSI-ACHAMPONG
Secretary General
Ghana National Commission for UNESCO

Mrs. Georgina QUAISIE
Basic Education
Co-ordiantor Action-Aid
Ghana

Mr. William AWINADOR-KANYIRIGE
Deputy Permanent Delegate
Ghana Permanent Delegation, Paris

Ms. Victoria TETTEGAH
First Secretary
Ghana Permanent Mission, Geneva

Gréce/Greece/Grecia

Mr. Georges MAVROIDIS
Vice President of the Pedagogical Institute

Guatemala

S.E. Sr. Mario TORRES MARROQUIN
Ministro de Educación
(Jefe de delegación)

Sra. Lorena ARAGON DE ARGUETA
Subdirectora de Profesionalización del Sistema Nacional de Mejoramiento de los Recursos Humanos
(SIMAC)

Sra. Blanca Estela COLOP ALVARADO
Coordinadora de la Unidad Técnica de Educacion Maya y Bilingue Intercultural de Unesco/Promem

Sr. Iván Espinoza FARFAN
Primer Secretario

Srta. Araceli PHEFUNCHAL ARRIAZA
Primer Secretario

Srta. Sulmi BARRIOS MONZON
Primer Secrétario

Sr. Pablo ARENALES
Premier secretaire
Ambassade du Guatemala á Paris

Srta. Stephanie HOCHSTETTER Skinner-Klee
Segundo Secretario

Sr. Carlos ARROYAVE PRERA
Tercer Secretario

Guinée/Guinea

S.E. M. Germain DOUALAMOU
Ministre de l'enseignement Pré-Universitaire et de l'éducation civique
(Chef de délégation)

M. Saidou SOUARE
N. Conseiller
Coordonnateur national du PASE

M. Ibrahima MAGASSOUBA
Secrétaire général
Commission nationale guinéenne pour l'UNESCO

M. Alpha Mahmoudou DIALLO
Directeur national
Enseignement elémentaire

M. Laye Aboubacar KONATE
Fédération syndicale
professionnelle de l'éducation

Honduras

S.E. Sra. Olmeda RIVERA
Embajadora
Representante Permanente de Honduras ante la Ofician de las Naciones Unidas y demás Organismos Internacionales con sede en Ginebra
(Jefe de delegación)

Sra. Gracibel BU
Consejero
Mision Permanente de Honduras

Sr. César Enrique LOPEZ
Primer Secretario
Misión Permanente de Honduras

Sra. Karen P. CIS ROSALES
Segunda Secretario
Misión Permanente de Honduras

Hongrie/Hungary/Hungría

Mr. Gábor NĂRAY-SZABO
Deputy State Secretary
Ministry of Education
(Head of Delegation)

Mr. Peter GRESICZKI
Secretary General
Hungarian National Commission for UNESCO

India

Mr. Maharaj Krishen KAW
Secretary, Secondary and Higher Education
Central Government
(Head of Delegation)

Mr. C. BALAKRISHNAN
Joint Secretary
Government of India
Ministry of Human Resource Development

Mr. PURAN CHAND
Professor
NCERT India

Indonésie/Indonesia

H.E. Prof. Dr. Bambang SOEHENDRO
Ambassador, Permanent Delegate of Indonesia to UNESCO
(Head of Delegation)

Prof. Dr. W.P. NAPITUPULU
Executive Chairman
Indonesian National Commission for UNESCO

Mr. Ade Padmo SARWONO
Second Secretary
Permanent Mission of the Republic of Indonesia
Geneva

Irak/Iraq

H.E. Dr. Ali ALMASHAT
Ambassador, Permanent Delegate of Iraq to UNESCO
(Head of Delegation)

Mr. Raad MAHMOUD
Second Secretary

Iran (République islamique d')/ Iran (Islamic Republic of)/Irán (República Islámica del)

Mr. Seyed Farhad EFTERKHARZADEH
Director General
Bureau of International, Scientific Cooperation
(Head of Delegation)

Dr. Abbas SADRI
Counsultant to the Minister
Director General
Office of Higher Technical Vocational Schools

Dr. Jafar TOFIGHI
Deputy Minister for Education
Ministry of Science, Research and Technology

Mr. Ali ZARAFSHAN
Consultant to the Minister

H.E. Mr. Ahmad JALALI
Ambassador and Permanent Delegate of the Islamic Republic of Iran to UNESCO

H.E. Mr. Ali A. MOJTAHED SHABESTARI
Ambassador and Permanent Delegate
Permanent Mission
Geneva

Mr. Shahabeddin GHANDALI
Director General
Education Department of Townships of Tehran

Mr. Javad AMIN-MANSOUR
Counsellor of the Mission

Irlande/Ireland/Irlanda

Miss Anne O'MAHONY
Assistant Principal Officer
International Section
Department of Education and Science
(Head of Delegation)

Ms. Liz HIGGINS
Senior Education Advisor
Development Cooperation Division
Department of Foreign Affairs

Islande/Iceland/Islandia

Mr Sveinn EINARSSON
President
Icelandic National Commission for UNESCO

Israël/Israel

S.E. M. Yitzhak ELDAN
Ambassador
Délégue Permanent d'Israël auprés de l'UNESCO

M. Daniel BAR-ELLI
Secrétaire général
Commission nationale d'Israël pour l'UNESCO

Italie/Italy/Italia

Mme Valentina APREA
Sous-secrétaire d'état
Ministére de l'éducation, de l'université et de la recherche scientifique
(Chef de délégation)

M. Antonio DE GASPERIS
Ministere de l'éducation, de l'universite et de la recherche scientifique

Mme DEA PELLEGRINI
Ministére de l'éducation, de l'université et de la recherche scientifique

Mme Ester GANINI GAMALERI
Ministere de l'education, de l'université et de la recherche scientifique

M. Luigi CLAVARINO
Ministére de l'éducation, de l'université et de la recherche scientifique

Mme Sandra CIGNI
Ministere de l'éducation, de l'université et de la recherche scientifique

Mme Maria Letizia MELINA
Ministere de l'éducation, de l'université et de la recherche scientifique

M. Giovanni PUGLISI
Secretaire général
Commission nationale Italienne pour l' UNESCO

M. Paolo OREFICE
Commission nationale Italienne pour l' UNESCO

Mme Margherita SABATINI
Ministere des Affaires étrangère

M. Luigi DE CHIARA
Première Secretaire
Mission Permanent de l'Italie

M. Giuseppe MARUCCI
Ministére de l'éducation et de la recherche scientifique

Jamahiriya arabe libyenne populaire et socialiste/Socialist People's Libyan Arab Jamahiriya/Jamahiriya Arabe Libia Popular y Socialista

M. Abdalla ZARRUGH
Secrétaire général de la Commission nationale
(Chef de délégation)

M. Abdalla ABUJAFER
Professeur á l'Université Al Fatih

M. Abdalla TAGURI
Directeur des programmes
Centre national de planification de l'enseignement et de l'apprentissage

M. Asad ELMASOUDI
Secretaire de l'unite UNESCO
Commission nationale

M. Mahmud Deghdagh
Expert en Programmes
Commission nationale

Jamaique/Jamaica

H.E. Mr. Burchell WHITEMAN
Minister of Education and Culture
(Head of Delegation)

H.E. Mr. Ransford SMITH
Ambassador/Permanent Representative
Permanent Mission of Jamaica
Geneva

Ms. Symone BETTON
First Secretary
Permanent Mission of Jamaica
Geneva

Japon/Japan/Japón

Mr. Yasushi MITARAI
Deputy Minister of Education, Culture, Sports, Science and Technology
(Head of Delegation)

Mr. Yuzuru IMAZATO
Director
Office of Planning and Coordination
International Affairs Division
Ministry of Education, Culture, Sports, Science and Technology

Mr. Hiroshi KATSUHIRA
Senior Specialist for Cooperation with UNESCO Office of Director-General for International Affairs, Ministry of Education, Culture, Sports, Science and Technology

Mr. Akiyoshi YONEZAWA
Associate Professor
Research Institute for Higher Education, Hiroshima University

Mr. Toshikazu ISHINO
Minister-Counsellor
Permanent Delegation of Japan to UNESCO, Paris

Mr Toru SATO
First Secretary
Permanent Mission of Japan to the International Organizations in Geneva

Jordanie/Jordan/Jordania

Mr. Hisham AL-ATRASH
Director General of Education and Information Technology
(Head of Delegation)

Mrs. Muna Mu'taman HA'UBSHA
Director of Educational Publications

Mr. Waleed O'BEEDAT
Second Secretary
Permanent Jordanian Delegation for UNO/Geneva

Kazakhstan

H.E. Mr. Nurali S. BEKTURGANOV
Minister of Education and Science
(Head of Delegation)

S.E. M. Nurlian DANENOV
Ambassadeur, Representant permanent de la République de Kazakhstan auprés de l'Office des Nations Unies a Genéve

M. Murat TASHIBAYEV
Mission permanente de la Republique du Kazakhstan aupres de l'Office des Nations Unies a Genéve

Kenya

H.E. Mr. Henry KOSGEY
Minister for Education
Chairman of the Kenya National Commission for UNESCO
(Head of Delegation)

Mrs. Naomy WANGAI
Director of Education

Mr. Benjamin Kapkiai SOGOMO
Secretary
Teachers Service Commission

Prof. Justin IRINA
Secretary
Commission for Higher Education

Mr. Ephraim Waweru NGARE
Chargé d'Affairs a.i.
Permanent Mission of Kenya
Geneva

Miss Tabu IRINA
First Secretary
Permanent Mission of Kenya
Geneva

Mr. M.L. EMURUGAT
Third Secretary
Permanent Mission of Kenya
Geneva

Mrs. Elizabeth K. WAFULA
Director, Adult Education
Ministry of Labour and Human Resource Development

Mr. Elmanus A. VODOTI
Secretary General
Kenya National Commission for UNESCO

Mr. Josiah Obuog OKUMU
Senior Deputy Director of Education

Mrs. Ruth CHERUIYOT
Assistant Secretary General
Kenya National Commission for UNESCO

Mr. Francis NG'AN'GA
Secretary General
Kenya National Union of Teachers

Koweit/Kuwait

H.E. Dr. Musaed Rashed AL-HAROUN
Minister of Education and Higher Education (Head of Delegation)

H.E. Mr. Dharar A.R. RAZZOQI
Ambassador, Permanent Representative
Permanent Mission of the State of Kuwait, Geneva

Dr. Jafan AL-ARYAN
Secretary-Geneva
Kuwait National Commission for UNESCO

Mr. Taleb AL-BAGHLI
Acting Permanent Delegate of the State of Kuwait UNESCO

Dr. Jasem AL-KANDARY
Dean of the Faulty of Education
Kuwait University

Dr. Abdullah AL-KANDARY
Dean of the Faculty of Basic Education
Public Authority for Applied Education and Training (PAAET)

Dr. Abdulmohsen AL-AKHORAFY
Public Authority for Applied Education and Training (Paaet)

Mr. Najeeb AL-BADER
Second Secretary
Permanent Mission of the State of Kuwait, Geneva

Mr. Abdullah AL-KANDARY
Chairman of the Kuwait Society for Teachers

Mr. Faisal Suliman AL-SAJARY
Headmaster

Mrs. Khadeeja Salem AL-ABDULHADI
Headmistress
Mrs. Entisar Al-Roomy
Kuwait National Commission for UNESCO

Mr. Mohsen AL-OTIABI
Ministers Office

L'Ex-Republique yougoslave de Macédoine/The Former Yugoslav Republic of Macedonia/La ex República Yugoslava de Macedonia

H.E. Mr. Nenad NOVKOVSKI
Minister of Education
(Head of Delegation)

Mrs. Dragica ZAFIROVSKA
Charge d'Affaires

Mr. Nazif DZAFERI
Second Secretary
Permanent Mission

Lesotho

H.E. Mr. Lesao LEHOHLA
Minister of Education
(Head of Delegation)

Mr. Chabana MOSHAPANE
Principal Secretary for Education

Lettonie/Latvia/Letonia

Mr. Nils SAKSS
Director
Department of European Integration and Technical Assistance Programme Co-ordiantion, Minister of Education and Science
(Head of Delegation)

Mr. Maris KRASTINS
Head, Centre for Curriculum Development and Examination

Ms. Dace NEIBURGA
Secretary-General
Latvian National Commission for UNESCO

Prof. Tatjana KOKE
Director Institute of Pedagogics and Psychology
University of Latvia
Educational Adviser of the Latvian National Commission for UNESCO

Liban/Lebanon/Líbano

Dr. Metanios HALABI
Directeur général de l'éducation
(Chef de délégation)

Dr. Nemer FREIHA
Président du CNRDP

Lituanie/Lithuania/Lituania

H.E. Ms. Vaiva VEBRAITE
Vice-Minister of Education and Science

Madagascar

S.E. M. Jacquit Nivoson SIMON
Ministre de l'enseignement secondaire et de l'éducation de base
(Chef de délégation)

S.E. M. Boniface LEVELO
Ministre de l'enseignement technique et de la formation professionnelle

M. le Professeur Rakotomanantsoa RABENANTOANDRO
Secrétaire général du Ministère de l'enseignment supérieur de Madagascar

Ministére de l'enseignement supérieur de Madagascar

M. Biclair ANDRIANANTOANDRO
Chargé'd' affairs a.i.
Représentation permanente de Madagascar Genéve

M. Albert RAFALIMANANA
Directeur de la Planification de l'éducation du Mineseb

Mme Cécile MANOROHANTA
Recteur de l'Université d' Antsiranana
Ministére de l'enseignement supérieur de Madagascar

Mme Yolande PASEA
Conseiller
Représentation permanente de Madagascar Genève

M. Koraiche ALLAOUIDINE
Secrétair d'Ambassade
Représentation permanente de Madagascar, Genève

Malaisie/Malaysia/Malasia

H.E. Mr. D.A. Rafie MAHAT
Director General of Education
(Head of Delegation)

Mr. Rashdi RAMLAN
Deputy Director General of Education

Ms. Sharifah Maimuah Syed Zain
Director of Curriculum Development Centre

Mr. Ahmad SHAZALI
Assistant Secretary
International Relations Division
Ministry of Education

Mr. Hamzah HASNUDIN
Deputy Permanent Representative
Geneva

Malawi

Mr. B. MUNTHALI
Principal Secretary
Ministry of Education, Science and Technology

Mr. C. GUNSARU
Director of Higher Education
Ministry of Education, Science and Technology

Mr. David MULERA
Senior Programme Officer (Education)
Malawi National Commission for UNESCO

Mr. Charles CHOKA
Ministerial Assistant
Ministry of Education, Science and Technology

Mali/Malí

M. Abou DIARRA
Directeur
Centre National d' Education
(Head of Delegation)

Mme Aminata SALL
Secrétaire général
Commission nationale Malienne pour l' UNESCO

Malte/Malta

Prof. Kenneth WAIN
Adviser to the Minister of Education
Professor, Faculty of Education
University of Malta
(Head of Delegation)

Mr. Carmel BUSUTTIL
Senior Vice-President
Malta Union of Teachers

Maroc/Morocco/Marruecos

S.E. Pr. Najib ZEROUALI OUARITI
Ministre de l'enseignement supérieur et de la recherche scientifique
Président de la Commission nationale Marocaine pour l' UNESCO
(Chef de délégation)

S.E. M. Nacer BENJELLOUN TOUIMI
Ambassadeur, représentant permanent du Maroc à Genève

Pr. Ali Ben BACHIR
Conseiller du Premier Ministre pour l'éducation

M. Aziz HASBI
Président de l'Université Hassan II-Ain Chock

M. Ahmed LAMARINI
Secrétaire général du Ministére de l'éducation nationale

M. Annis BIRROU
Chef du cabinet du Ministre de l'enseignement superieur, de la formation des cadres et de la recherche scientifique

M. Abderrazzak KHALED
Directeur des Etudes juridiques et de la promotion des droits de'l homme, Ministère des droits de l'homme

M. Jamal KHALLAF
Directeur des études et des stratégies éducatives
Ministère de l'éducation nationale

M. Mohamed BENMAIZA
Chef du Service des programmes de formation des cadres
Ministère de l'éducation nationale

Mme Naïma TABET
Secrétaire général de la Commission nationale marocaine pour
l' UNESCO

Mme Zakia EL MIDAOUI
Ministre Plénipotentiaire auprés de la Mission permanente du Royaume du Maroc à Genève

Maurice/Mauritius/Isla Mauricio

H.E. Mr. Steven OBEEGADOO
Minister of Education
(Head of Delegation)
Mr. Shaffick Osman
Communication Adviser
Ministry of Education and Scientific Research

Dr. Arjoon SUDHOO
Executive Director
Mauritius Research Council

Mrs. Usha DWARKA-CANABADY
Minister Counsellor
Permanent Mission of Mauritius to the UN

Mr. Bipin Kumar RUDHEE
First Secretary
Permanent Mission of Mauritius to the UN

Mr. Ravindranath SWAMY
Second Secretary
Permanent Mission of Mauritius to the UN

Miss. Martine YOUNG KIMFAT
Second Secretary
Permanent Mission of Mauritius to the UN

Mr. Haman Kumar BHUNJOO
Attaché
Permanent Mission of Mauritius to the UN

Mauritanie/Mauritania

M. Ould Moulaye Ahmed SALEH
Conseiller
Ministère de l'éducation nationale
(Chef de délégation)

M. Youba Abdallahi OULD KHALIFA
Premier conseiller
Représentation de Mauritanie auprés de l' UNESCO

Mexique/Mexico/México

Dr. Reyes TAMEZ GUERRA
Secretario de Educación Pública
Presidente de la Comisiòn Mexicana de Cooperacion con la UNESCO (Conalmex)
(Jefe de delegación)

Prof Lorenzo GÒMEZ MORIN, M. ed C. Subsecretario de Educación Básica y Normal
Secretaría de Educatión Pública

Dr. Daniel GONZÁLEZ SPENCER
Director General de Relaciones Internacionales
Secretario General de la CONALMEX
Secretaría de Educación Pública

Lic. Isabel Farha Valenzuela
Directora de Relaciones Multilaterales y Secretaria General Adjunta de la Conalmex
Secretaria de Educación Pública

Sra. Lourdes Sosa MARQUEZ
Segunda Secretaria
Misión Permanente de México en Ginebra

Mozambique

H.E. Mr. Alcido Eduardo NGUENHA
Minister of Education
(Head of Delegation)

Mrs. Sarifa FAGILDE
National Director of Secondary Education

Mrs. Paula MENDONCA
EFA Coordinator

Mrs. Maria Teresa Miguel ANSELMO
Pedagogical Technician

Mr. Antonio TUZINE
Pedagogical Technician

Ms. Paula MENDOZA
EFA Co-ordinator

M. Manuel CARLOS
Troisième Secrétaire
Mission du Mozambique a Genéve

Myanmar

Mr. Tin Maung AYE
Deputy Permanent Representative
Permanent Mission of Myanmar Geneva
(Head of Delegation)

Mrs. Aye Aye MU
Counsellor
Permanent Mission of Myanmar Geneva

Mrs. Ei Ei TIN
Second Secretary
Permanent Mission of Myanmar Geneva

Namibie/Namibia

H.E. Mr. James Ebrahim W. WENTWORTH
Deputy Minister of Higher Education, Training and Employment Creation
Chairperson
Namibia National Commission for UNESCO
(Head of Delegation)

Dr. Patti SWARTS
Director
Namibia Institute for Educational Development
NIED

Népal/Nepal

Mr. Lava Kumar DEVACOTA
Secretary
Ministry of Education and Sports
(Head of Delegation)

Mr. Chuman Singh BASNYAT
Director General
Department of Education

Mr. Nabin Bdr SHRESTHA
Minister Counsellor
Permanent Mission of the Kingdom of Nepal to the UN
Geneva

Nicaragua

S.E. Lic. Fernando ROBLETO LANG
Ministro de Educación, Cultura y Deportes
(Jefe de delegación)

Sra Ximena FLORES
Embajada de Nicaragua ante Francia

Sr. Alcides MONTIEL
Ministro Consejero
Representate Permanente Alterno

Lic. Emilio PORTA
Asesor de la Dirección Superior de este Ministerio

Sr. Santiago URBINA
Primer Secretario

Nigéria/Nigeria

H.E. Prof. Babalola BORISHADE
Honourable Minister of Education
Federal Ministry of Education
(Head of Delegation)

H.E. Prof. Michael OMOLEWA
Ambassador and Permanent Delegate
Permanent Delegation of Nigeria to UNESCO

Dr. Samuel A.B. ATOLAGBE
Director, Education Support Services
Federal Ministry of Education

Prof. Mrs. Ebele MADUEWESI
Executive Secretary
Nigerian Educational Research and Development Council

Mr. Tunji OLAOPA
Deputy Director (Policy)
Federal Ministry of Education

Mr. Unubi Joseph IDACHABA
Deputy Director forAdministration
Federal Ministry of Education

Eng. Julius Adebayo AYENI
Secretary General
Nigerian National Commission for UNESCO
Federal Ministry of Education

Mrs. Ireti BORISHADE
Federal Ministry of Education
Federal Secretariat

Mrs. Fatma OTHMAN
Delegation's Counsellor
Permanent Delegation of Nigeria to UNESCO

Mr. A. JAJI
Specialist in Education
Federal Ministry of Education

Mr. Michael Udofia
Media Assistant
Nigerian Permanent Delegation to UNESCO

Mr. Isaac AFFRAM
Special Assistant
Nigerian Permanent Delegation to UNESCO

Mrs. Hauwa YUSUF
Electronic Media Journalist

Mr. Adamu HASSAN
Minister Counsellor
Nigerian Mission
Geneva

Norvège/Norway/Noruega

H.E. Ms. Nina Tangnaes GRONVOLD
State Secretary
Ministry of Education, Research and Church Affairs
(Head of Delegation)

Mr. Dankert VEDELER
Deputy Director General
Department of Policy Analysis and International Affairs
Ministry of Education, Research and Church Affairs

Ms. Tove BREKKE
Deputy Director General
Department for Education and Training
Ministry of Education, Research and Church Affairs

Ms. Ellen LANGE
Adviser
Department of Policy Analysis and International Affairs
Ministry of Education, Research and Church Affairs

Mr. Tor E. GJERDE
Adviser
Multilateral Department
The Ministry of Foreign Affairs

Ms. Monica DALEN
Vice President of the National Commission
Chair of Sub-Committee for Education
The Norwegian National Commission for UNESCO

Ms. Tone ABRAHAMSEN
Senior Executive Officer
The Norwegian National Commission for UNESCO

Mr. Jens Petter BERG
Board Member
The Norwegian Union of Teachers

Mr. Roar GROTTVIK
Head of Department
The Teachers' Union

Ms. Sigrid MELKERAAEN
Vice President
Norwegian School Student Union

Ms. Doris JORDE
Associate Professor
University of Oslo

Mr. Lars ULSNES
Adviser
Permanent Delegation of Norway to UNESCO

Nouvelle Zélande/New Zeland/ Nueva Zélandia

Mr. Alyn WARE
Consultant
P.O. Box 23-257 Cable Car Lane
Wellington

Oman/Omán

H.E. Mr. Sayyid Hamoud BIN FAISAL AL BUSAIDI
Minister, Secretary General of the Cabinet
(Head of Delegation)

H.E. Mr. Mohammed ALTOBI
Under-Secretary
Ministry of Education, Educational Planning and Projects

H.E. Dr. Moosa J. HASSAN
Ambassador, Permanent Representative of Oman to UNESCO

Mr. Mohammed AL YAGOUBI
Deputy Secretary
National Commission on Education, Culture and Sciences

Mr. Rashid ALMAZROI
Vice-President
Office of H.E. the Secretary General of the Cabinet of Ministers

Mr. Idris AL-KHANJARI
Chargé d'affaires and first secretary

Mr. Ali AL-QASSIMI
First Secretary

Mr. Zakarya AL-SA'DI
First Secretary

Ouganda/Uganda

H.E. Mrs. Geraldine Namirembe BITAMAZIRE
Minister of State for Primary Education
(Head of Delegation)

Ms. Florence Malinga
Commissioner
Education Planning
Ministry of Education and Sports

Ms. Anastasia NAKKAZI
Secretary General
Uganda National Commission for UNESCO

Mr. Nathan NDOBOLI
First Secretary
Permanent Mission of Uganda to Switzerland

Pakistan/Pakistán

Mr. Tariq FAROOK
Secretary Education
Government of Pakistan
(Head of Delegation)

Dr. Mohammad Saleem RAJA
Assistant Educational Adviser
Ministry of Education

Dr. Rukhasana ZIA
Deputy Permanent Delegate
Permanent Delegation of Pakistan to UNESCO

Paraguay

S.E. Sr. Darío ZÁRATE ARELLANO
Ministro de Educación y Cultura
(Jefe de delegación)

S.E. Sra. Blanca OVERLAR DE DUARTE
Viceministra de Educación

Pays-Bas/Netherlands/Paises Bajos

Mr. Fons VAN WIERINGEN
Member
National UNESCO Commission
Chairman of Working Group on Education
(Head of Delegation)

Mr. Pieter DE MEIJER
Chairman
Council of the Bureau of Education

Mr. Henricus J. SMEETS
General Secretary
National UNESCO Commission

Mr. Dirk LAGEWEG
Vice-General Secretary
National UNESCO Commission

Mr. Jan OOIJENS
Member
National UNESCO Commission working group on education

Mr. Herald VOORNEVELD
Deputy Permanent Delegate
Permanent Delegation of the Netherlands to UNESCO

Pérou/Peru/Perú

S.E. Sr. Manuel IGUIÑIZ E.
Vice Ministro de Gestión Institucional
Ministerio de Educación

Philippines/Filipinas

Hon. Raul S. ROCO
Secretary of Education
(Head of Delegation)

Mrs. Ester Garcia
Chairperson
Commission on Higher Education

Mrs. Monina Estrella CALLANGAN-RUECA
First Secretary
Permanent Mission of the Philippines to the United Nations Office in Geneva

Pologne/Poland/Polonia

H.E. Prof. Edmund WITTBRODT
Minister of National Education
(Head of Delegation)

Mrr. Jerzy ZDRADA
Under-Secretary of State
Deputy Minister of National Education

Mr. Tomasz KNOTHE
Plenipotentiary Minister
Permanent Mission of the Republic of Poland to the UN
Office and other International Organizations at Geneva

Mr. Wojciech FALKOWSKI
Secretary General
Polish National Committee for UNESCO

Mr. Kazimierz KORAB
Director
Department of Strategy and Development
Ministry of National Education

Mrs. Magdalena MAZINSKA
Director
Department of European Integration and International Cooperation
Ministry of National Education

Prof. Alfred Andrzej Janowski
Expert

Ms. Krystyna ZUREK
Counsellor
Permanent Mission of the Republic of Poland to the UN
Office and Other International Organizations at Geneva

Portugal

S.E. le Professeur Julio PEDROSA LUZJESUS
Ministre de l'éducation
(Chef de délégation)

Mme Maria Eduarda BOAL
Directrice du Cabinet des affaires européennes et des relations internationales
Ministère de l'éducation

Mme Isabel ANTUNES
Directrice adjointe du Départment de l'enseignement de base
Ministère de l'education

Qatar

H.E. Dr. Alhmad K. ALMANSORI
Minister of Education
(Head of Delegation)

Dr. Abdul Aziz AL-HORR
Assistant Deputy Minister for Educational Planning and Curricula

Dr. Nawal Alshekh
Assistant Manager of Educational Curricula

Mr. Abdul Aziz F. ALANSARI
Secretary General of Qatar National Commission for Education, Culture and Science

Mr. Kalid ALKAWARI
Director of Minister of Education Office

République arabe syrienne/ Syrian Arab Republic/República Arabe Siria

S.E. Dr. Mahmoud AL-SAIED
Ministre de l'éducation
(Chef de délégation)

M. Karim HANNA
Chef de la section de la traduction

M. Mohammad Wassim Al Ghazi
Directeur de l'Education Primaire

République de Corée/Republic of Korea/República de Corea

H.E. Mr. Jae Gil LEE
Ambassador
Deputy Permanent Representative
Permanent Mission of the Republic of Korea at Geneva
(Head of Delegation)

H.E. Mr. Joo-Seok KIM
Minister
Embassy of the Republic of Korea to the French Republic

Mr. Younsoo LEE
Counsellor
Permanent Mission of the Republic of Korea at Geneva

Mr. Jong Goo YEO
Education Attaché
Permanent Mission of the Republic of Korea at Geneva

Mr. Minsik HONG
Deputy Director
Ministry of Education and Human Resources Development

Mr. Yersu KIM
Secretary General
Korean National Commission for UNESCO

Miss Soon-Ho Choi
Programme Specialist, Education Unit
Korean National Commission for UNESCO

Mr. Samuel LEE
Director
Asia-Pacific Centre of Education for International Understanding

Mr. In-Jong Park
Director, Office of Educational Credit Bank System
Korean Educational Development Institute

Mr. Sook Jong Lee
Professor
Kangnam University

République Démocratique du Congo/Democratic Repúblic of the Congo/República democrática del Congo

S.E. M. Omer KUTUMISA
Ministre de l'Education National
Président de la Commission nationale de la République Démocratique du Congo pour l' UNESCO
(Chef de délégation)

M. Bolaluete NSAMBI
Secrétaire général
Commission nationale de la République démocratique du Congo pour l' UNESCO

M. Giovanni N'KWATAATA Kwetwkadila
Secrétaire particulier du Ministre de l'éducation nationale

République dominicaine/Dominican Republic/República Dominicana

Dr. Angel HERNÁNDEZ
Subsecretario de Estado de Educación
(Jefe de delegación)

Sr. Rafael Espinal
Subsecretario de Estado de Educatión

S.E. Dr. Federico CUELLO CAMILO
Embajador Permanente ante la Oficina de las Naciones Unidas en Ginebra

Dr. Magaly BELLO DE KEMPER
Consejero en la Misión Permanente, Ginebra

République populaire démocratique de Corée/Democratic People's Republic of Korea/República Popular Democrática de Corea

M. Se Pyong SO
Représentant permanent adjoint de la Mission
(Chef de délégation)

M. Tong Hwan KIM
2e Secretaire de la Mission

République tchéque/Czech Repúblic/Republica Checa

H.E. Mr. Eduard ZEMAN
Minister of Education, Youth and Sport
(Head of Delegation)

H.E. Mr. Milan HOVORKA
Ambassador, Chargé d'affairs
Permanent Mission of the Czech Republic in Geneva
Alternate

Mr. Jan SOKOL
Adviser of the Minister of Education, Youth and Sport

Mr. Pavel CINK
Director
Department of Foreign Relations and the European Integration
Ministry of Education, Youth and Sport

Mrs. Jaroslava TLÁSKALOVÁ
Department of Foreign Relations and the European Integration
Ministry of Education, Youth and Sport

Mr. Ivan PINTÉR
Counsellor
Permanent Mission of the Czech Republic in Geneva

République-unie de Tanzanie/ United Republic of Tanzania/ Republica Unida de Tanzania

H.E. Hon. Joseph J. MUNGAI
Minister for Education and Culure
(Head of Delegation)

Hon. Sultan M. MUGHEIR
Deputy Minister
Ministry of Education, Culture and Sports
Zanzibar

Prof. Mohammed S. SHEYA
Deputy Permanent Delegate
Tanzania Permanent Delegation to UNESCO

Mr. Alexander S. NDEKI
Commissioner for Education

Mrs. Mwanaidi S. ABDALLA
Commissioner for Policy, Planning and Administration
Zanzibar

Dr. Nesta SEKWAO
Assistant to the Commissoner for Education

Mr. Gordian Joseph Mukiza
Education Programme Officer
UNESCO National Commission of Tanzania

Roumanie/Romania/Rumania

M. Radu Mircea DAMIAN
Secrétaire d'état pour l'enseignement supérieur
(Chef de délégation)

Mr. Catalin CROITORU
President of National Education Federation (FEN)

Mme Veronica FUSELOVA
Chef du service Programmes et institutions internationales

Rwanda

Dr. Jean Damascène NTAWUKURIRYAYO
Secrétaire d'état á l'éducation chargé de l'enseignement supérieur et de la recherche scientifique
(Chef de délégation)

M. Gratien MUREKUMBANZE
Responsible de la sous commission éducation á la Commission national ruandaise pour l' UNESCO

M. Johnson NTAGARANBA F
Chef de division enseignement secondaire au Centre national de dévelopment des programmes au Ministère de l'éducation

Saint-Christophe et Nevis/Saint Kitts and Nevis/Saint Kitts y Nevis

H.E. Mr. Timothy HARRIS
Minister of Education
Ministry of Education—St. Kitts and Nevis
Basseterre

Sénégal/Senegal

M. Diégane Samb THIOUNE
Chargé d'affaires a.i.
Mission du Sénégal

M. Elhadj Tamsir MBAYE
Conseiller technique de Madame le Premier Ministre

M. Mbaye Ndoumbé GUEYE
Directeur de la planification et de la reforme de l'education

M. Mohamadou Aly SALL
Directeur de l'enseignement élémentaire

Seychelles

Mrs. Jeanne SIMEON
Director-General for Schools
Chairperson of the Seychelles Education for All Forum
(Head of Delegation)

Mrs. Marie-Therese PURVIS
Director
National Institute of Education

Sierra Leone/Sierra Leona

Mr. Abass M. COLLIER
Deputy Minister of Youths, Education and Sports
(Head of Delegation)

Dr. Albert C.T. DUPIGNY
National EFA Coordinator

Dr. Thomas YORMAH
Senior Lecturer
Fourah Bay College
University of Sierra Leone

Slovaquie/Slovakia/Eslovaquia

H.E. Mr. Milan FTÁCNIK
Minister of Education
(Head of Delegation)

Mrs. Mária HRABINSKÁ
Head of the NARID
Institute of Information and Prognosis of Education

Mrs. Jana BARTOSIEWICZOVÁ
Counsellor
Permanent Mission of Slovakia
Geneva

Slovénie/Slovenia/Eslovenia

H.E. Mrs. Lucija COK, Ph.D.
Minister of Education, Science and Sport
(Head of Delegation)

Mr. Darko ŠTRAJN, Ph.D.
President
Slovenian National Commission for UNESCO

Mrs. Andreja BARLE LAKOTA, Ph.D. Director of the Educational Development Unit
Ministry of Education, Science and Sport

Mrs. Zofija KLEMEN-KREK
Secretary General, Slovenian National Commission for UNESCO

Mrs. Tatjana JURKOVIČ
Councillor to the Minister

Soudan/Sudan/Sudán

H.E. Mr. Ali TAMIM FARTAK
Minister of Education
(Head of Delegation)

Dr. Adil Ahmed M. KARDAWI
Secretary General
Sudanese National Commission for UNESCO

Mr. Ibrahim Suliman EL-DASIS
Director
Education Planning

Mr. M.Y.A. MOHAMED
Diplomat

Mr. Christopher Leonardo JADA
Second Secretary
Permanent Mission to U.N. Office
Geneva

Suéde/Sweden/Suecia

Mr. Carl LINDBERG
Deputy State Secretary
Ministry of Education and Science
(Head of Delegation)

Mr. Torgny DANIELSSON
Member of the Swedish Riksdag
Member of the Swedish National Commission to UNESCO

Mrs. Ulla-Stina RYKING
Senior Administrative Officer
Ministry of Education and Science

Mrs. Gunilla ZACKARI
Special Advisor
Ministry of Education and Science

Ms. Ann-Katrin WIRÉN
Senior Administrative Officer
Ministry of Education and Science

Suisse/Switzerland/Suiza

S.E. Mme Martine BRUNSCHWIG GRAF
Ministre de l'éducation de la République et canton de Genève
Vice-présidente de la Conférence suisse des Directeurs cantonaux de l'instruction publique, Genéve
(Chef de délégation)

S.E. M. Denis FELDMEYER
Délégué permanent de la Suisse auprès de l'UNESCO
Paris

M. Bernard WICHT
Chef des Affaires internationales
Conference suisse des Directeurs cantonaux de l'instruction publique
Berne

M. Marino OSTINI
Adjoint scientifique
Office fédéral de l'éducation et de la science
DFI
Berne

M. Bernard THEURILLAT
Secrétaire général
Commission nationale suisse pour l' UNESCO
DFAE
Berne

Mme Christine KÜBLER
Expert
Conférence suisse des Directeurs cantonaux de l'instruction publique
Berne

M. Ahlin BYLL-CATARIA
Direction du dévelopment et de la coopération
DFAE, Berne

M. Jean-Etienne BERSET
Chef des "Affaires Internationales"
Office fédéral de la formation professionannelle et de la technologie (OFFT)
Berne

Mr. Marios VASSILIOU
Secondary School Inspector

Swaziland/Swazilandia

H.E. Mr. John P. CARMICHAEL
Ministry of Education
(Head of Delegation)

Mr. Sibusiso Samuel MKHONTA
Acting Principal Secretary

Mr. Bethuel S. NDLOVU
Chief Inspector Secondary

Mrs. Dorothy LITTLER
Secretary General
Swaziland National Commission for UNESCO

Thaïlandé/Thailand/Tailandia

Dr. Sirikorn MANEERIN
Deputy Minister of Education
(Head of Delegation)

Dr. Panom PONGPAIBOOL
Permanent Secretary
Ministry of Education
Deputy Head of Delegation

Dr. Prapatpong SENARITH
Director-General
Department of Curriculum and Institute Development

Dr. Nongram SETAPANICH
Senior Advisor on Educational Policy and Plan
Office of the National Education Commission

Mrs. Weeranus POLNIKORN
Expert
Department of Fine Arts

Ms. Duriya AMATAVIVAT
External Relations Division
Ministry of Education

Mrs. Asha DVITIYANANDA
Charge d'affaires
Permanent Mission of Thailand to the United Nations in Geneva

Mr. Nikordey BALANKURA
Second Secretary
Permanent Mission of Thailand to the United Nations in Geneva

Mrs. Pornnipha LIMPAPHAYOM
Deputy Permanent Secretary
Ministry of Education

Togo

S.E. M. Kodzo Senanu NOGLO
Ministre Pleinpotentaire, Délégue du Togo a l'UNESCO

Trinité-et-Tobago/Trinidad and Tobago/Trinidad y Tobago

Senator Hon. Roy AUGUSTUS
Minister
Ministry of Education

Tunisie/Tunisia/Túnez

S.E. M. Moncer ROUISSI
Ministre de l'Education
Président de la Commission nationale tunisienne pour l' UNESCO
(Chef de délégation)

M. Salem EL MEKKI
Coordinateur Général du programme nationale d'enseignement pour adultes
(Secrétaire d'état)

Mme Fatma TARHOUNI
Secrétaire général
Commission nationale tunisienne pour l'UNESCO

M. Omrane BOUKHARI
Directeur des programmes et des livres scolaires
(Ministère de l'éducation)

M. Nejib AYED
Directeur de l'Institut national des sciences de l'éducation
(Ministère de l'éducation)

M. Adel GAALOUL
Directeur général de l'Institut national de bureautique et de Micro-informatique
(Ministère de l'éducation)

M. Farouk KRIAA
Responsable du bureau de la recherche, de la planification et de la programmation
(Ministère de l'enseignement supérieur)

M. Ahmed MEDIMAGH
Directeur général de la normalisation et de l'évaluation
(Ministére de la formation technique et professionnelle)

M.M. Samir KOUBAA
Conseiller des affaires etrangères auprès de la Mission

Mlle Samia Ilhem AMMAR
Conseiller des affaires entrangères auprès de la Mission

Turquie/Turkey/Turquía

Mr. Ahmet MUTLUOGLU
Education Counsellor

Ukraine/Ucrania

H.E. Mr. Vasyl KREMEN
Minister of Education and Science
(Head of Delegation)

Mr. Petro BEKH
Head of Department of International Relations
Kyiv National University

Uruguay

Sr. Carlos SGARBI
Ministro Consejero
Encargado de Negocios a.i.
(Jefe de délégation)

Sra. Alejandra De Bellis
Segunda Secretaria

Venezuela

S.E. Sr. Héctor NAVARRO
Ministro de Educación, Cultura y Deportes
(Jefe de delegación)

Sr. Madai HERNÁNDEZ
Consejero
Misión de Venezuela
Ginebra

Viet Nam

S.E. M. Snah Chau PHAM
Ambassadeur, Délégué permanent à l' UNESCO
Représentant personnel du Président du Vietnam à la Francophonie
(Chef de délégation)

M. Huu Anh HOANG
Attaché de la Délégation due Vietnam auprés de l'UNESCO

Yémen/Yemen

S.E. Dr. Fadel ABOU GHANEM
Ministre de l'éducation et de l'enseignement
Président de la Commission nationale
(Chef de délégation)

S.E. Dr. Abdullah EL ZINE
Ambassadeur Délégué permanent auprés de l'UNESCO

M. Mageed A. GHANEM
Deputy Minister of Curricula
Education Inspection Sector

M. Rushdi AL-KUSHAB
Directeur du Cabinet du Mnistre de l'éducation et de l'enseignement

M. Ali ALAMIR
Secrétaire de la Commission nationale

Yougoslavie/Yougoslavia

H.E. Mr Gaso KNEZEVIC
Minister of Education and Sports
Republic of Serbia
(Head of Delegation)

H.E. Mr. Predrag IANOVIC
Minister of Education and Sciences
Republic of Montenegro
(Head of Delegation)

Mrs. Srbijanka TURAJLIC
Deputy Minister of Higher Education
Ministry of Education
Republic of Serbia

Mrs. Tinde KOVAC-CEROVIC
Deputy-Minister
Sector for Development and International Educational Relations
Republic of Serbia

Miss Natasa ZIVKOVIC
Advisor to the Minister of Education and Science
Republic of Montenegro

Mr. Dragan BOGOJEVIC
Advisor to the Minister of Education and Science
Republic of Montenegro

Mrs. Mirjana RADIC
Minister Counsellor
Charge d'affaires a.i.
Permanent Mission of the FR of Yugoslavia, Geneva

Mr. Aleksandar RADOVANOVIC
Counsellor
Permanent Mission of the FR of Yugoslavia
Geneva

Zambie/Zambia

H.E. Mr. Reuben MUSAKABANTU
Minister of Education
(Head of Delegation)

Ms Irene FUNDAFUNDA
Counsellor
Charge d'affaires a.i.

Mrs. Hilda MUSUMSA
Assistant Secretary
Ministry of Education

Zimbabwe

H.E. Dr. Samuel C. MUMBENGEGWI
Minister of Higher Education and Technology
(Head of Delegation)

Dr. Michael MAMBO
Permanent Secretary
Ministry of Higher Education and Technology

Mr. Brighton MUGARISANWA
Diplomat
Zimbabwe Permanent Mission

Mr. Josiah MHLANGA
Deputy Permanent Delegate
Zimbabwe Permanent Delegation to UNESCO

Mr. Elias K. MATIMATI
Civil Servant
Ministry of Education

Etats membres associés/Associate Member States/Estados Miembros Asociados

Macao, China

Ms Kit SAM
Adviser of the Secretary for Social Affairs and Culture

Mr Chio Fai SOU
Deputy Director
Education and Youth Affairs Department

Etats non members/Non-member States/Estados no miembros Observateurs/Observers/ Observadores

Etats-Unis d'Amérique/United States of America/Estatos Unidos de América

Mr. Richard T. La POINTE
Counsellor to the Deputy Secretary of Education
Department of Education
(Printed Observer)

Mrs. Stephanie MULOT
Office of the United States Observer to the United Nations
United States Embassy
Paris

Saint-Siège/Holy See/Santa Sede

Mgr. Lorenzo FRANA
Observateur Permanent du Saint-Siège après de l' UNESCO
(Principal Observer)

Mgr. Edgar PEÑA PARRA
Conseiller
Mission Permanent du Saint-Siège
à Genève

Abbé Dr Jean-Pierre Schaller

Palestine (Observateur)

H.E. Dr. Naim ABU HOMOS
Minister of Education

H.E. Mr. Ahmad ABDELRAZEK
Ambassador
Permanent Observer

Invités/Invites

Prof. Jaak AAVIKSOO
Rector
Professor
University of Tartu
Estonia

Prof. Dr. Christel ADICK
Lehrstuhl Vergleichend
Erziehungswissenschaft
Institut fuer Paedagogik
Bochum
Allemagne

Prof. Mohamed Abd Elkader
AHMED
Professor, Bahrain University
Bahrain

M. Abdeljalil AKKARI
Professeur
Université de Fribourg
Suisse

Mr. Shigeru AOYAGI
Director
Literacy Promotion Division
Asia/Pacific Cultural Centre for
UNESCO

M. Francois AUDIGIER
Professor
Fapse
Université de Genève
Suisse

Mr Bal Gopal BAIDYA
Executive Member
Executive Committee
South Asia Partnership
Nepal

Mr. Aaron BENAVOT
Professor
Department of Sociology and
Anthropology
Hebrew University of Jerusalem
Israel

M. Benali BENZAGHOU
Recteur de l'Université des
Sciences et de Technologie
Alger
Algérie

M. Daniel BERNARD
Directeur
Leman Bleu Télévision
Genève
Suisse

M. Cesar BIRZEA
Directeur
Institut des Sciences de l'Education
Roumanie

M. Gabor BOLDIZSAR
Conseiller général d'administration
Ministère de l'Education
Hongrie

M. Norberto BOTTANI
Directeur du Sred
Genève
Suisse

M. Alain BRUNSVICK
France

Dr. Geraldine CASTLETON
Research Fellow
Center for Literacy & Language
Education Research
Griffith University
Brisbane
Australia

M. Gustavo COSSE
Argentina

Mr. Erik DE CORTE
University Professor
University of Leuven
Belgium

M. Cheikhe DEM
Président
Gretaf International
(Groupe d'Etudes sur l'Education en Afrique)
France

M. Abou DIARRA
Directeur général
Centre national de l'Education
Bamako
Mali

Mr. Sveinn EINARSSON
Senior Advisor to the Minister
Chairman, Icelandic National Commission for UNESCO
Ministry of Education, Science and Culture
Iceland

Mme Laura FUMAGALLI
IIEP
Buenos Aires
Argentine

Mr. Tesfamicael GERAHTU
Director-General
Department of General Education
Ministry of Education
Eritrea

Mr. Abdullah GHAITHY
Yemen

M. Jean-Pierre GONTARD
Director Adjoint
IUED
Genève

Prof. Antonio GUERRA CARABALLO
Uruguay

M. Guy HAUG
Expert
France

M. Ivan IVIC
Professeur Universitaire
Filozofski fakultet
Belgrade
Yougoslavie

Mr. Jonathan JANSEN
Dean of Education at the University of Pretoria
South Africa

Mr. Samir JARRAR
Director
Arab Resource Collective—ARC
Beirut
Lebanon

Mrs. Maria Lourdes A. KHAN
Secretary General
Asian South Pacific Bureau of Adult Education
(ASPBAE)

Dr. Johannan (Lahja) LASONEN
Professor
Institute for Educational Research
University of Jyvaskyla
Finland

Mr. Pablo LATAPI ORTEGA
Journalist
TV Azteca
Mexico

Dr. Pablo LATAPI SARRE
Professor
Universidad National Autónoma de México D.F.
Mexico

Sr. Luis Enrique LÓPEZ
Proieb-Andes
Cochabamba
Bolivia

Sr. Antanas MOCKUS
Alcalde de Bogotá
Colombia

M. Vis NAIDOO
Education Specialist
The Commonwealth of Learning
Vancouver
Canada

Mr. Nicholas C.C. OLIVIER
Chief Technical Advisor
Pretoria
South Africa

Miss Heba RAMZY
Director
Kids & Youth Programmes
Regional Information Technology and Software Engineering Center (RITSEC)
Cairo
Egypt

M. Jean-Marie SANI
Cité des sciences et de l'industrie
La Villette
Paris
France

Prof. Alexei SEMENOV
Rector
Moscow Institute of Teacher Development
Moscow
Russian Federation

Mr. Gorgui SOW
Lead Moderator
Africa Network Campaign on Education for All (ANCEFA)
Senegal

Mr. Sobhi TAWIL
Research Associate
Graduate Institute of Development Studies
Geneva

M. Pierre THENARD
Conseiller au Cabinet du Ministre Délégué à la coopération et á la Francophonie
Paris
France

Sr. Alejandro TIANA
Facultad de Education UNED
Madrid
Espagne

Mme Judith TORNEY PURTA
Department of Human Development
College of Education
University of Maryland
USA

M. Uri Peter TRIER
Université de Neuchâtel
Suisse

Prof. Dr. Theo J.M. VAN ELS
Professor Emeritus
Université de Nijmegen
Nijmegen
The Netherlands

Mr. Daniel WAGNER
Director
International Literacy Institute
Philadelphia PA
USA

Mr. Herb WALBERG
Editor
Chicago, IL 60611
USA

Mr. Shigeo YOSHIKAWA
Senior Curriculum Specialist
Ministry of Education
Japan

Dr. Ella YULAELAWATI
Head of Curriculum Division of Early and Primary Education
National Office of Research and Development
Ministry of National Education
Indonesia

Mme Pari ZARRABI
Sociologue
Genève

Ms. Madeline ZUÑIGA
Board Member
Ceaal (Transitory Coordinating Group-CCNGOs/
EFA and Foro Educativo
Peru

Représentants d'Organisations du système des Nations Unies/ Representatives of Organization of the United Nations System/ Representantes de Organizaciones del sistema de las Naciones Unidas

Conférence des Nations Unies sur le Commerce et le Dévelopment (CNUCED)/United Nations Conference of Trade and Development (UNCTAD)

Mr. Lev KOMLEV
Senior Economic Affairs Officer
Office of the Special Coordinator for Least Developed
Landlocked and Island Developing Countries

Office de secours et de travaux des Nations Unis pour les réfugiées de Palestine dans le Proche-Orient (UNRWA)/The United Nations Relief and Works Agency for Palestine Refugees in the Near East (UNRWA)

M. Rene AQUARONE
Chief Liaison Office
Geneva

Organisation internationale du travail (OIT)/International Labour Office (ILO)

Mr. William Ratteree
Senior Technical Specialist
Education Sector

Programme d'Alimentation Mondiale/World Food Programme/

Ms Katrin VON DER MOSEL
Programme Adviser
School Feeding Suport Unit

L'Université des Nations Unies/ United Nations Univesity/ Universidad de Naciones Unidas

Prof. Marco Antonio DIAS
Advisor to the Rector of UNU

OBSERVATEURS/ OBSERVERS/OBSERV ADORES

Organisations du système des Nations Unies/Organizations of the United Nations System/ Organizaciones del Sistema de las Naciones Unidas

Banque Mondiale/World Bank

Mme Michelle RIBOUD
Manager/Directrice
Groupedu Development Humain
Institut de la Banque Mondiale

Corps Commun d'Inspection/ Joint Inspection Unit

Dr. Doris Bertrand
Inspector

Organisations intergouvernementales/ Intergovernmental Organizations/ Organizaciones intergubernamentales

Agence Intergouvernementale de la Francophonie (AIF)

M. Roger DEHAYBE
Administrateur général

M. Hamidou, A. SIDIKOU
Directeur de l'éducation et de la formation technique et professionnelle

Mme Myriam SENGHOR-BA
Relations Publiques

M. Ousouf DIAGOLA
Animateur-Redacteur
Canal EF/DEFTP

Mme Murielle GAUTIER
Documentaliste

Bureau arabe de l'éducation pour les Etats du Golfe (ABEGS)/ Arab Bureau of Education for the Gulf States (ABEGS)

Dr. Saeed M. AL-MULLAIS
Director General
Saudi Arabia

Mr. Abdulrahman M. AL-SHERAIMY
D.G. Office Manager
Saudi Arabia

Dr. Rasheed ALHAMAD
Director
Arab Center for Educational Research for the Gulf States (GASERC)
Kuwait

Conférence des Ministres de l'éducation des pays ayant le francais en partage (CONFEMEN)/Conference of Ministers of Education of French-speaking Countries (CONFEMEN)

M. Bougouma NGOM
Secrétaire Général
Sénégal

Conseil de l'Europe/Council of Europe

Ms. Michela CECCHINI
Chef
Division de l'éducation à la citoyennetè dèmocratique et aux droits de l'homme

M. Jean-Pierre TITZ
Secrétaire le la Conférence permanente des ministres européens de l'Education

M. Josep VARELA I SERRA
Membre
Commission de la Culture, de la Science et de l'Education de l'Assemblée parlementaire du Conseil de l'Europe

Fédération arabe pour l'enseignement technique (FAET)/Arab Federation for Technical Education (AFTE)

Dr. Sharaf Eddin MOHAMAD
Secretary General

Ligue des Etats arabes/League of Arab States

H.E. Mr. Saad ALFARARGI
Ambassador
Permanent Observer
Permanent Delegation of the League of Arab States

Mr. Mohamed MOUAKI
Counsellor
Permanent Delegation of the League of Arab States

Mr. Salah AEID
Member
Permanent Delegation of the League of Arab States

Organisation arabe pour l'éducation, la culture et la science (ALECSO)/Arab League Educational, Cultural and Scientific Organisation (ALECSO)

M. Mongi BOUSNINA
Directeur Général

M. Ahmed GABSI
Membre du Cabinet du D.G. de l'organisation

Organisation des Etats ibéro-américains pour l'éducation, la science et la culture (OEI)/ Organization of Ibero-American States for Education, Science and Culture

Sr. Francisco PIÑÓN
Secretario General

Sr. Roberto MARTÍNEZ
Asesor del Secretario General

Sr. Francisco DE LUCA
Asistente del Secretario General

Organisation Islamique pour l'Education, les Sciences et la Culture (ISESCO)/Islamic Educational, Scientific and Cultural Organisation (ISESCO)

Dr. Abdulaziz ALTWAIJRI
Director General

Mr. Mohamed RIFFI
Responsible of Public Relations Division

Mme Asmaa ABDALLA
Specialist in charge of Cooperation with International Organizations

Organisations internationales non gouvernementales
International non governmental organizations
Organizaciones internacionales no gubernamentales

Association internationale des professeurs et maîtres de conférences des universités (IAUPL)/International Association of University Professors and Lecturers (IAUPL)

Prof. Louis-Philippe LAPRÉVOTE
Vice-président
Chargé des relations avec l' UNESCO

Association mondiale pour l'Ecole instrument de paix (EIP)/ World Association for the School as an Instrument of Peace (EIP)

Mme Monique PRINDEZIS

M. Ramdane BABADJI

Mme Gisella CELLINA

Mme Suzanne GALL

Mme Verdiana GROSSI

M. Yves LADOR

M. Edouard MANCINI

Mme Lucie N'KAKE

M. Michel VUILLE

Association des universités européennes/European University Association (EUA)

Mrs. Andree SURSOCK
Programme Manager
10 rue Conseil General
1204 Geneva
Switzerland

Caritas Internationalis

M. Michel DEYGLUN
Représentant Permanent auprès de l' UNESCO

Confédération internationale des syndicats libres (CISL)/ International Confederation of Free Trade Unions (ICFTU)

Ms. Marie-Thèrèse BELLAMY
Assistant

Conseil international des femes (CIF)/International Council of Women

Mme Brigitte LEGOUIS
Représentate accréditée du CIF à l' UNESCO

Mme Brigitte POLONOVSKI
Vice-présidente
Représentante accréditée du CIF auprès de Nations Unies de Genève

Conseil international des médias éducatifs (CIME)/International Council for Educational Media (ICEM)

Mr. Maurice BETTEX
Membre du Comitè exécutif

Conseil internationa de la préparation à l'enseignement/ International Council on Education for Teaching (ICET)

Mr. Darrell BLOOM
Executive Director

Confédération syndicale mondiale de l'enseignement (CSME)/World Confederation of Teachers (WCT)

M. Gaston DE LA HAYE
Secrètaire general

M. Herman BRINKHOFF
Consultant auprès du Secrétaire généra UNESCO et Enseignement supérieur

Mr. Tinti E. RABOTAPI
National Professional Teachers' Organization of South Africa (NAPTOSA)

Mr. Siphosethu NGCOBO
National Professional Teachers' Organisation of South Africa (NAPTOSA)

M. Claudio CORRIES
Vice-President
CSME
Argentina

Fédération Africaine des associations des parents d'élèves et d'étudiants (FAPE)

M. Martin ITOUA
President
BP 1113
Brazzaville
Congo

Fédération internationale pour l'éducation des parents (FIEP)/ International Federation for Parents Education (IFPE)

M. Moncef GUITOUNI
Président

M. Luc DUPONT
Président de la région Amerique du Nord

Fédération internationale des femmes diplômées des universités (FIFDU)/ International Federation of University Women (IFUW)

Ms. Conchita PONCINI
Representation to the UN/ILO
President NGO Status of Women Committee

Ms. Murielle JOYE
Secretary General

Mlle Marise PASCHOUD
Représentante auprès du l'ONU

Internationale de l'éducation (IE)/Education International (IE)

Mme Mary FUTRELL
Présidente

M. Elie JOUEN
Secrètaire Général Adjoint

M. Thomas Amgo BEDIAKO
Chef Coordinateur pour la région Afrique

Mme Monique FOUILHOUX
Coordinateur Education

M. Ulf FREDRIKSSON
Coordinateur Education

M. Siva SIVA SUBRAMANIAM
Secrétaire Général
NUTP (Malaisie)

M. Yves BAUNAY
Consultant de l'IE

Ms Ranka MANDIC
Directeur d'école
Bosnie-Herzègovine

Mr Jakov JUKIC
Directeur d'école
Bosnie-Herzegovine

Mr. Mehmed ALIBEGOVIC
Directeur d'école
Bosnie-Herzégovine

M. Hans LAUGESEN
Secrétaire International GL
Danemark

M. Jean-Marc BOUCHET
Secrétaire International de la
Fnec.p-Fo
France

M. Jean-Pierre RULIE
UNSA
France

Mme Anna GALETTI
Membre
SNS-CGIL

Mme Florence TRAUSCHT
Assistante Professionnelle à l'Ie

Mouvement international ATD Quart Monde/International Movement ATD Fouth World

M. Gérard BUREAU
Chargé de Mission

Organisation internationale pour le développement de la liberté d'enseignement (OIDEL)/International Organization for Development of Freedom of Education (OIDEL)

Mme Scarlet FLOHR

Office international de l'enseignement catholique (OIEC)/Catholic International Education Office

P. Gilbert ACCAMBRAY
Représentant de l'OIEC a Genève
Chef de delegation

Fr. André VERNHES
Enseignant Retraite

Chan, Xavier BURIN

M. Fulgence KONE
Repésentation Permanente auprès
l' UNESCO

Organisation du Baccalaureat International (OBI)/ International Baccalaureate Organization (IBO)

Prof. George WALKER
Director General

Mr. Ian HILL
Deputy Director General

Mrs. Nélida ANTUÑA
BARAGAÑO
Regional Director for Africa,
Europe and Middle East

M. Philip THOMAS
Représentant de l'OBI

Organisation Mondiale du Mouvement Scout (OMMS)/ World Organization of the Scout Movement

Mme Jacqueline COLLIER
Deputy Director
Youth Programme

M. Kjeld JESPERSEN
Deputy Director
European Scout Office

Fondations/Foundations/ Fundaciones

Centre UNESCO de Catalunya

Mme Carme ROMIA
Présidente du groupe l'Université de Barcelone

M. Enric MASLLORENS
Président
Centre UNESCO de la Catalogne

M. Miquel Martí
Secrétaire du groupe
Coordinateur des Écoles Associées

Mme Araceli VILARRASA
Institut d'Education de Barcelone

Mlle Nicole DENAYROLLES
Ingenieur-Project Educatif
Forum Universel des Cultures

Mme Josefina CAMBRA
Doyenne du Corps des Licenciés de la Catalogne

Mme Anna PIGUILLEM
Association des enseignants "Rosa Sensat"

Fondation Marangopoulos pour les Droits de l'Homme (FMDH)

Mme Alice MARANGOPOULOS
Présidente de la FMDH

M. Thomas Ganiatsos
Représentant permenant á Genève

Mme le Prof. Elly SIALIANOU
Présidente de l'Université Ionienne
Athènes

Observateurs Divers/Other Observers/Otros Observadores

Sr. Manuel CARDENAS MUÑOZ
South America Region Learning Advisor
Plan International—Oficina Regional Sud América

M. Michel Celi VEGAS
President
Peru-Interandes

Sra. Susana FINOCCHIETTI
Consultora Temporal
UNESCO Lima

M. Klevor FLORES
Export Rural Development
Peru-Interandes

Dr. Michel LOOTS
Human Info Ngo
Belgium

M. José MARIN
Assistant Anthropolog Matters
Peru-Interandes

Dra. Ursula OBREGÓN
Peru-Interandes

Sr. Juan Felipe SÁNCHEZ
Building Relations Project Leader
Plan International

Mr. Zvonimir SIKIČ
President
Union of Higher Education & Science
Croatia

M. Conrado A. SURBER
Director
Peru-Interandes

Sr. Patricia VILCHEZ
Assistant Gender Matters
Peru-Interandes

Mrs. Muoy YOU
Human Info NGO
Belgium

ANNEX XX

SECRÉTARIAT

ORGANISATION/ORGANIZATION/ORGANIZACION

I. UNESCO

M.K. Matsuura
Directeur général de L' UNESCO

M.J. Daniel
Sous-Directeur général pour l'éducation

M.A. Sayyad
Sous-Directeur général, secteur des relations extérieures et de la coopération

M.J. Rao
Assistant exécutif, secteur des relations extérieures et de la coopération

Mr. G. Malempré
Directeur, Bureau de liaison, Genéve

Mme C.J. Stenberg
Secrétaire du Directeur général

II. Secrétariat général de la Conférence

Mme C. Bravlavsky
Directrice du BIE

Assistée de

M.P. Luisoni
M.M. Amadio
M.V. Adamets
M.T. Macelli

Assistants du Rapporteur general

M.L. Tiburcio
M.M. Richmond

Assistants des modérateurs

M.A. Sannikov
M.R. Halperin
M.M. Amadio
M.F. Matoko
M.V. Chinapah
M.P. Luisoni

Liaison avec les rapporteurs:

M.A. Sannikov

Assistants des rapporteurs:

Mme I. Byron
M.S. Tawil
M.J. Aglo
Mme M.L. Clérico
M.A. Ouane

Secrétaires/Liste des intervenants:

Mme C. Caparros
Mme G. Canahuati
Mme P. Siméant
M.R. Mariani
Mlle S. Rozemeijer

III. Directeurs des Instituts/ Bureau de l'UNESCO et des bureaux Hors-siège:

Mme F. Chung,
IICBA

M.E. Hernes,
IIEP

M.A. Khan,
UNESCO/Dhaka

Mme A.L. Machado,
UNESCO/Santiago de Chile

M.R. Maclean,
UNEVOC/Bonn

M.A. Ouane,
UIE

M.A. Parsuramen, UNESCO/Dakar

M.S. Schaeffer, UNESCO/Bangkok

M.M. Tawfik, UNESCO/New Delhi

M.J. Werthein, UNESCO/Brésil

IV. Réunions organisées par le Secteur de l'éducation et les Instituts

Mme A. Bah-Diallo
Mme F. Chung
M.A. Parsuramen
Mme K. Kanno
Mme L. Buchert
Mme S. Schnuttgen
M.A. Singh
M.A. Hussain
Mme E. Khawajkie
M.R. Maclean
M.A. Bubtana
Mme C. Harvey
M.K. Grigsby

V. Autres participations de l' UNESCO

Mme A. Naanda
M.Q. Tang
M.N.-Z. Zhou

VI. Cérémonie de remise de la médaille Comenius

Mme N. Sikorsky
M.L. Tiburcio

VII. Médias

M.M. Barton
Mme N. Sikorsky
M.J. Hironaka
Mme I. Le Fournis
Mme T. Murtagh
Mme E. Salas Rossenbach
Mme H.T. Monekosso

VIII. Services de soutien

Administration:

M.T. Zerihoun, Administrateur du BIE

Financiers:

M.M. Milési, Assistant administif
Mme S. Kawakibi
Mme L. Khalouta

Informatique:

M.G. Viollet-Bosson
M.L. Maitret
M.G. Clavel

Secretariat de l'administration

Mme S. Kawakibi

Salles de conférences:

M.A. Perry
Mme N. Iliukhina
Mme S. Ruiz
M.G. Clavel
Mme F-V. Herbert
Mme A. Donnely MacDonald

Accueil/enregistrement:

Mme F. Nacereddine
Mme S. Roux
Mme F. Fahner
Mme J. Thomas
Mlle C. Dafe
Mme T. Workou
Mme M. Lingani Jousson
M.N. Buhlmann

Messages des ministres:

Mlle A. Gorga
Mme J. Bahl

Project "Bridge":

Mme G. Emond
M.A. Anne
Mlle C. Derderian
Mme K. El-Talaoui
M.Y. Gertsch
Mlle M. Lethoko

Internet

Mme F. Nacereddine
Mlle S. Rozemeijer
M.R. Mariani
Mme V. Debellemanière

Liste des participants:

Mlle M. Maguire

Coordination des expositions:

M.J. Fox

Information sur le tableau electronique:

M.J. Fox

Reproduction des documents:

M.C. Leroy
M.L. Maitret

Distribution des documents:

–Documents de conférence:

Mlle B. Deluermoz
Mlle K. Desgeorges
Mme M. Ndiaye Mboup
Mlle Y. Amdeselassie

-Rapports nationaux:

M.H. Bao
M.M. Severino
M.L. Severino
M.C. Brice
M.K. Stanisiere

IX. Services linguistiques

Interprétation:

M.M. Boulares
Mme S. Farchakh
M.A. Bespalov
Mme B. Elas

Traduction:

-Arabe

M.Y. Younes
M.G. Megali

-Chinois

M.M. Yang

-Espagnol

Mme L. Pazos
Mme J. Montejo

-Russe

M.Y. Reznikov
Mme N. Moinov

X. Autres Services de la Conference

Permanence au BIE

Mme C. Bruchet

Service médical

Mlle L Matheson
Infirmière

Part—3

Learning to Live Together: Have We Failed?

---

* Learning To Live Together: Have We Failed? A summary of the ideas and contributions arising from the 46th Session of UNESCO's International Conference on of Education.

Introduction

EDUCATION FOR ALL FOR LEARNING TO LIVE TOGETHER IN THE TWENTY-FIRST CENTURY: NEED, HYPOCRISY OR UTOPIA?

Some ten years ago, the historian, thinker and teacher Joseph Ki-Zerbo posed the dilemma of contemporary Africa (and the whole world) in a book with the provocative title *Educate or perish* (Ki-Zebro. 1990): 'Entry to the third millennium is marked by upheavals that question the certainties of yesterday, thus obliging societies to reinvent a sense of life and create the bases for a newly viable world'. We have now entered that third millennium and, paraphrasing Ki-Zebro, today we could write: 'live together in the twenty-first century or disappear?' Is this not, in fact, the highest stake that quality education should aspire to?

The issue for which UNESCO convened the forty-sixth session of the International Conference of Education (ICE) set the problems of 'living together' at the centre of international debate two years before the events of 11 September 2001 put it on the first page of all the world's newspapers. The Conference was convened by the UNESCO General Conference in 1998 and was held in Geneva from 5 to 8 September 2001. Many of the participants were travelling back to their countries when news broke of the 11 September attacks.

The representatives of all UNESCO's Member States had endorsed and stressed the need to address the fact that they all have problems that conspire against the chances of mankind living together in peace.

Setting out to recognize, accept and share problems represents the first step towards the search for solutions, and to share and disseminate best practices, as well as evaluating their outcomes in order to analyse the possibilities of transferring them to other contexts, represents unavoidable priorities.

The first and chief problem is that the education of the past, inherited from the century of Enlightenment and promising peace based on the exercise and teaching of reading, writing, arithmetic, logic and law, has failed in one of its objectives. In fact, as was often pointed out throughout the forty-sixth ICE, never before had mankind managed to include so many of its members in formal educational processes. However, never before had its members intentionally killed so many of their fellow humans. There are some who reckon that over 180 million people have been killed intentionally during the twentieth century. The initiators and perpetrators of these crimes, who acted in both conventional and novel ways, are usually people who have spent a great deal of their lives in the education systems of both rich and poor countries.

The Ministers, Vice-Ministers and ministerial teams that prepared and participated in the forty-sixth ICE on the issue 'Education for All for learning to live together: Contents and Learning Strategies—Problems and Solutions' maintained a constant balance between: submitting evidence and seeking reasons for what many educational sociologists do not hesitate to consider a resounding failure or a direct consequence of the type of education imparted on the one hand; and the search for solutions that have allowed and are allowing progress in different areas on the other. They can be said to have sustained a perspective that was both analytical and affirmative.

Their analytical perspective made it possible to set out in the Conference's general documents and in many national reports and speeches a series of educational problems and another series of socio-economic and political problems that are at the root of the limits affecting education's contribution to living together. Their affirmative attitude which is an inherent part of politics, led them to demand 'good practices' and analyse them, to present them enthusiastically and to draw conclusions based on inductive work and the analysis of very diverse experiences over decades.

This part is essentially a testimony of the affirmative aspects of the forty-sixth ICE, based on politicians' duty to base action on optimism and their will to succeed. It therefore underlines accounts, ideas and images that help to appreciate, know, want and be able to educate for living together. The primary and secondary school-teachers and high-level decision, makers involved in day-to-day actions have to appreciate that it is possible to educate for living together, know that there are experiences that achieve this, want to advance along this path and have the skills to put their desires into practice.

However, it is also necessary to point to aspect of the analytical and profoundly critical perspective that accompanies that optimism, because we must recognize the origins of the problems and the limits of our sphere of action as well. What is novel about the analytical view of this Conference is the emphasis given to the tension between factors outside education that are obstacles to learning and teaching how to live together and factors inherent in the educational institutions which made it possible to suggest that there is a 'paradigm crisis', that the ways of educating inherited from the past have limitations for achieving the desired objectives.

From this tension a very clear message emerges for the Education for All movement: it is not a question of more of the same education that has failed to bring the world the peace and social cohesion expected in the seventeenth century, or in the post-Second World War and decolonization decades of the twentieth century. It is a different education that will draw what is best from the humanistic traditions of all cultures and may even become a 'counter culture' to some centripetal forces acting in societies and perhaps threatening the future of mankind. These centripetal forces seem to be linked to what could be called the paradoxes of globalization and traditional education.

THE PARADOXES OF GLOBALIZATION AND THE CHALLENGES OF EDUCATION FOR LIVING TOGETHER

The first paradox is between the openness to shared development and the destruction of potential for development in certain specific contexts, particularly in the South and East of the concert of nations. Increased international trade, the opportunities for personal mobility and the progress and speed of telecommunications provided, among other things, a concrete basis for a shared life. However, the way globalization is promoted brings serious problems in many parts of the world, articulated above all in the destruction of the environment, the decline in the quality of life of millions of inhabitants of all continents and the widening of the huge gap between rich and poor.

Then the second paradox is the proliferation of scientific and technological knowledge and the imbalances in the areas where it is applied. In fact, the modes of production and energy consumption in the twentieth century, the modernization transferred from North to South, population growth in a number of regions of the world or less widely discussed aspects, such as the neglect of African urban centres during the decolonization process, have produced serious damage to the environment. In many cases technical solutions are known, for example, cooking using solar radiation in countries as vast as China, but where the appliances are not produced and the techniques or ways of using them are not taught. In the area of biotechnology, progress is being made in constructing knowledge that will make it possible to resolve very diverse problems, but while the applications of some of that knowledge develop very rapidly, in other fields, such as food production in the most densely populated countries in the world, these applications develop much more slowly.

Consequently, *the third paradox* is that the knowledge and tools that would enable a considerable improvement in the quality of life for all mankind are available, but are not applied or learned equitably: 968 million people do not have access to drinking water, 2.4 billion do not have access to basic health care, more than 2 million people die per year due to environmental pollution and 34 million people live with HIV/AIDS (UNDP, 2001, p. 9).

In only two years, the percentage of the population using Internet rose from 2.4 to 6.7; but while in Sweden, the United States, Norway and other countries this figure reaches over 50%, in China, South Africa and Brazil it is well below 10%, and in many regions of large countries, such as Uttar Pradesh in India, or in the poorest countries in the world, it is close to zero. The separation in use of the new information technologies in cumulative with divisions in access to electricity, tractors, the telephone and innumerable other twentieth century technologies. It is simply a milestone along a kind of continum (UNDP, 2001, p. 40/41).

Thus, we come to the *fourth paradox* of globalization in its current form, which is that never before in history has mankind produced so much wealth, but never before has there been such inequality in 1990, 2,718 million people (that is, 45 per cent of the world's population) lived on less than $2 a day. In 1998, the figure had risen to over 2,800 million people (World Bank, 2000, p. 29). It is reckoned that today 1,200 million people live on less than $1 per day.

These conditions mean that increasing numbers of people, and in particular young, educated people, leave their place of origin in search—successfully or otherwise—of a better quality of life whenever they can. Migrations enrich the world and individuals, but they create new problems and challenges, connected with the *fifth paradox* of globalization: the fact that there are increasing opportunities for getting to know 'the other', but at the same time more risks to individual identity, in 'preserving the ego'. Globalization, in principle a synonym of openness, could threaten the world with a cultural uniformity that would endanger the diversity of cultures or threaten a retreat by peoples into their own identity and nationality, with the inevitable consequences of intolerance and rejection of other cultures. The same thing occurs with languages, so important for the formation and expression of cultural identity and so valuable as instruments of communication.

The *sixth paradox* at the start of the twenty-first century seems to be the proliferation and deepening of national democracies and the strength of supra-national institutions and government, mechanisms. Since 1980, eighty-one countries have taken significant steps towards democracy and thirty-three military regimes have been replaced by civilian governments. The presence and influence of non-governmental organizations has become more transparent, as well as their interaction with the spheres of government (UNDP, 2002, p. 10). But voices are increasingly raised regarding the difficulties or even weaknesses of many national governments to withstand the weight of supranational mechanisms and bodies (Stiglitz, 2002) and the tendencies for peoples living within the same nation to take refuge within their own culture. Between 1992 and 1995 alone approximately 200,000 people died in Bosnia and in 1994 in Rwanda, 500,000. Terrorism has again harassed the world, now on an international scale.

Faced with these paradoxes, which in all cases are manifested in their own particular way inside each country, in both North and South, there are two temptations. The first is omnipotence. Education and only education will be able to solve everything. More and better education for everyone and the world will change. The second is impotence. From this standpoint, Education for All for Learning to Live Together would be a hypocritical aim. How, for example, can those people who have much more than they need be educated to live together with those who lack the basic necessities?

The forty-sixth session of the International Conference on Education was not attracted by either of these temptations and adopted the principles of recognizing complexity, diversity, the need for action at all levels (international, national and local) in co-operation and synergy with promising trends, in order to counteract the conflicting aspects of each of the fore-going paradoxes. But it also reinforced the message that in these circumstances people should more than ever want and be able to find ways of living together. Many Ministers of Education, trades union and academic representatives agree that it is necessary to avoid creating expectations and hopes that education will be able to reverse—and moreover on its own—the problems deriving from the paradoxes of globalization in its present form; but that if education does not contribute to a dynamic of 'humanization of globalization', the situation will be irreversible.

GAINS AND LOSSES IN EDUCATION FOR LIVING TOGETHER

There is no doubt that the twentieth century, and particularly the last decade, has witnessed important educational gains. But there is no doubt either that, along with these gains, there are many debts opening and that there debts are intrinsically linked to education's capacity for learning to live together.

Along with decolonization and democratization, almost all countries have laws for compulsory primary or basic education, which oblige national States and the international community to increase their efforts to guarantee educational opportunities for everyone.

The concept of education as an inalienable human right has again taken centre stage. In fact, the more utilitarian conceptions of education have been giving way to more humanistic views. There is more awareness that educating for participation in the economy without incorporating values of solidarity and a vocation for integration can constitute a threat for the economy itself, since no economy can resist the centrifugal forces of disorder arising from violence or the drain of increasing expenditure on war operations and subsequent reinvestments in eternally basic infrastructures.

Education has progressed significantly at the quantitative level. The number of children not receiving schooling dropped from 127 million in 1990 to 113 million in 1998. However, while progress has been marked in certain countries or regions, in others the increase in population, along with complex socio-economic and educational factors, has conspired against greater access. Above all, as recalled by the Dakar Forum, the main shortcomings in the processes of educational inclusion are concentrated on girls and on those living in the poorest circumstances.

The importance of starting the schooling processes at a very early age and of guaranteeing a minimum period of schooling for everyone, particularly for the poor throughout the world, the children of poor immigrants in rich countries (OECD, 2001), and adolescents and young people where there are high levels of unemployment, is being recognized and attempts are being made to honour this.

The available information shows that in some countries and regions progress has been achieved in reducing educational inequalities. More is known about the policies that have made it possible to reduce these inequalities and alternatives are being drawn up to provide move education and more learning resources for those who have less. In the last decades of the twentieth century progress was made in the application of compensatory educational policies in countries as different as Brazil, Uganda and France.

But there are still significant imbalances. These affect, first of all, poor, isolated communities, cultural minorities in many contexts and the 'new poor' in societies in transition or in countries like Argentina where, according to local and international analysts, the application of international recipes out of context and the lack of progress in good government practice have been devastating.

These achievements have been possible because many countries invest more in education than in the past, even when in certain States the decline in GDP, along with other structural or specific factors and the establishment of other political priorities, has annihilated efforts to increase the proportion of national budgets devoted to education. Some countries, even ones where resources remain inadequate, have achieved considerable progress in the optimum use of available financial resources or in channelling resources obtained from debt cancellation into education.

Educating for living together, doesn't that simply mean educating better?

Therefore, in spite of the progress and the investments, the issue of quality of education and relevance of learning remain worrying problems in all regions in the world. In fact, one of the striking issues of the forty-sixth International Conference on Education was the similarity between critical speeches on education in rich countries and poor; in multicultural countries, and in more homogeneous countries; in countries with greater inequalities and in others with fewer inequalities. In the light of this homogeneity there are two alternatives. Either some of the analyses are mistaken or there are problems that are part of the educational model inherited from the past and applied with more or less efficiency and considerable variations in practically all latitudes. It is likely that in some cases it will be necessary to move on to more differentiated an contextualized analyses. But there is undoubtedly a translational educational paradigm associated with modernity that needs to be changed.

In particular, there is now an awareness of the fact that merely better access to education without quality education leads to a 'cul de sac'. Dropping out and failure at school, a high rate of repeated years, inadequate contents, methods and structures, insufficient numbers of teachers, poorly trained and working in difficult physical conditions, the lack of school textbooks and teaching materials, the lack or inadequacy of a serious evaluation of the learning outcomes, inefficient management, etc., are factors that determine the mediocre quality of world education.

The Ministers and their teams present at the forty-sixth International Conference on Education indicated the problems in their programmes and textbooks, in the dynamics of school life, and in the inflexibility and low impact of traditional teaching methods in the new international context. Mention was made of concrete examples of discriminatory stereotypes about neighbouring countries and national minorities appearing in the curricula and textbooks of some countries.

The renewal every five years of practically all scientific subject matter makes it necessary to think of new ways of teaching that will enable us to learn throughout life and of a new profile for primary and secondary teachers so that we can benefit from the vocation and dedication of the immense majority of the world's 60 million teachers. Many presentations during the Conference agreed with the research studies indicating that the expansion in education at the end of the twentieth century was possible in many countries thanks to teachers' invisible investment. The purchasing power of their salaries dropped, but they continued to do their work. However, recognition of this debt should be accompanied by openness to new questions and problems, which will be dealt with in Chapter Eleven of this book.

INTENSIFY DIALOGUE AND REFURBISH APPROACHES TO IMPROVE QUALITY

In the preparatory documents for the forty-sixth ICE it was pointed out that, in the light of these worrying situations and issues for the future of mankind, education is directly committed since it can and should 'make the difference'. It is possible to improve its quality if the true cause of its deficient operation and its inadequacies are attacked energetically and swiftly.

Of these key elements that determine or influence educational quality, it was maintained that undoubtedly improvements in educators' skills and their working conditions come first. But it was suggested that their effects would be useless if a thorough reformation of teaching contents, programmes, methods, structures and means was not carried out. If progress is made at the level of policy dialogue to establish a better connection between education and development policies and a more adequate teaching approach, there... will equally be gradual progress towards identification of the necessary resources for quality education for all.

Throughout the Conference guidelines were developed for this action. These included the proposition that to cover education's debts in relation to learning for a shared life that will guarantee the happiness of peoples and individuals, it is necessary to take into account the complexity of the relations between education and society and of the relations between all the dimensions that must be acted on to promote a quality of education effectively guaranteeing that shared life. The presentations by the academics participating in the dialogue insisted on the importance of recognizing that all boys and girls can be excellent at something (Trier, 2001); of including an historical perspective in the learning of sciences in order to understand their impact (Mittelstrass, 2001), of combining the learning of knowledge, values and standards (Benavot, 2002; Tiana, 2002 and Mockus, 2002), and of moving towards more active ways of learning (Wiltshire, 2001).

The Conference's most important message is the tension between: (a) the concrete experience in each situation due to the efforts of national policies, which are as indispensable now as at the time when the interdependencies between nations were not so clearly recognized; and (b) the need to promote a new educational-paradigm for the twenty-first century so that action can have more impact. Probably one of the key differences between this new educational paradigm and the preceding one will be a new tension between anguish and ambition. The anguish of knowing that at times and in certain contexts this call to action may have a problematical ring—the ambition of wanting to meet the need to learn to live together. Therefore, it is likely that this new paradigm may have the slant of a modest utopia, towards which, simply but steadily, we wish to travel in a continuous manner.

Thanks to the numerous first-hand accounts assembled for the forty-sixth session of the International Conference on Education, the following pages will show that learning to live together' is a fundamental concern of educational decision-makers throughout the world. Questions have been asked, such as: What can education bring to International Conference on Learning to Live Together? What are the local and global conditions that we must create around the school such that it is enabled to provide what we hope from it?

8

Responding to Educational Needs

> The educational legacy of the twentieth century is partly one of unfinished business, combined with a growing questioning of both the means and the purposes of educational provision. [...] One of the most important challenges facing us [is] learning to live together. [...] It reminds us that advances in knowledge and understanding are utterly compromised if they are put at the service of hatred, prejudice, violence and selfishness. Education that would fail to equip us for living together in peace would not deserve to be called education of genuine quality.
>
> Koïchiro Matsuura,
> *Director-General of UNESCO*

Learning to live with other people is in no way a new topic in education. The very notion of 'education' has from ancient time, and in all parts of the world, been geared towards preparing individuals to live in, and contribute to the group and society. However, the notion of 'learning to live together' as understood today was shaped only very recently by the International Commission on Education for the Twenty-first Century, chaired by Jacques Delors. It builds on the lessons learnt from the last decade of efforts towards education for all and emerged in response to the growth of unacceptable inequalities between and within societies.

THE CHANGING VISION OF EDUCATION FOR ALL (EFA)

In 1990, the World Conference on Education for All in Jomtien, Thailand, stressed that every person—child, youth and adult—has the right to basic education and this represented a fundamental human right. The conference set the goal of

Education for All in all countries by the turn of the millennium. Even more specifically, its principle objective was to ensure that all people should benefit from: 'educational opportunities designed to meet their basic learning needs, both essential learning tools (such as literacy, oral expression, numeracy and problem solving) and the basic learning content (such as knowledge, skills, values and attitudes) required by human beings to be able to survive, to develop their full capacities, to live and work in dignity, to participate fully in development, to improve the quality of their lives, to make informed decisions, and to continue learning.

The 1990s saw numerous commitments made by nations and the international community to achieve the Education for All agenda set in Jomtien.

In April 2000, the World Education Forum held in Dakar, Senegal—held ten years after the Jomtien conference—assessed the achievements, lessons and failures of the 1990s. The principal conclusion of the forum was that, while significant progress has been achieved in many countries, unacceptable conditions concerning access to, quality of and equity in education continue to prevail in countries around the world:

- 113 million children, 60 per cent of whom are girls, still have no access to primary education;
- 875 million adults, 65 per cent of whom are women—one woman in four and one man in seven—do not know how to read and write;
- gender discrimination continues to permeate education systems;
- in the drive to universalize primary education, the quality of learning has been sacrificed to quantity and the acquisition of human values and skills falls far short of the aspirations and needs of individuals and societies:
- low quality education has led to high dropout and repetition rates in may countries;
- the situation of teachers (in terms of status, salary, training, etc.) has seen little improvement; talented teachers, who are much needed in education, are leaving for better paid jobs;

- poverty remains a serious problem and is the principal reason why educational goals are not met: it denies schooling, which in turn perpetuates the cycle of poverty.

The World Education Forum adopted the Dakar Framework for Action (April 2000). It emphasizes that, while the vision of Jomtien, developed a decade earlier, remains pertinent and powerful, progress towards education for all must accelerate in order to meet the nationally and internationally agreed targets of poverty reduction and to avoid the widening of inequalities between countries and within societies. The Dakar Framework for Action stresses that education is not only a fundamental human right, the key to sustainable development and to peace and stability within and among countries, it is an indispensable means for effective participation in the societies and economies of the twenty-first century.

It sets new collective goals and commitments for 2015. In particular, the Dakar Framework for Action requests that all States develop or strengthen their national educational policies by integrating them into broad-based national plans for social development and poverty reduction. It further advocates the involvement of all interested parties—all civil society—and calls for clear strategies for overcoming the special problems facing those currently excluded from educational opportunities. Finally, it addresses the chronic under-financing of basic education and affirms that 'no country seriously committed to education for all will be thwarted in its achievement of this goal by a lack of resources', thus requiring national governments and the international community to meet their collective commitments and to underpin political will with adequate resources.

**COMPARED TO THE JOMTEIN CONFERENCE (1990),
THE DARKAR FORUM (2000)**

- Confirms the paradigm shift, replacing a top-down with a bottom-up networking approach based on the reality of localities and networks, and paying attention to the demands of the community and partnerships with it;
- Reinforces the importance of the notion of 'life skills', which broadens the Jomtien concept of 'basic learning needs';

- Pays considerable attention to information and communication technologies (ICTs), which were absent from the agenda in 1990;
- Reaffirms the primacy of national responsibility in the implementation of educational policies, while insisting on international commitment for assistance beyond the level of individual projects to the level of systemic reforms;
- Bases international assistance on the existence of national plans of action that take Education for All into account;
- Pays considerably more attention to the regional dimension, in particular through the six regional Education for All frameworks that refine and adapt the overall strategy to the specific situation and needs of countries in large world regions;
- Identifies particular areas of concern, such as early childhood education, health, education of girls and women, the impact of HIV/AIDS, adult literacy and education in situations of crisis and emergency;
- Affirms that the goal of Education for All goes beyond universal schooling and requires policies focusing on the improvement of the quality of education ('quality' refers to the effective acquisition of the competencies needed to live and work in the community and in the world);
- Insists on the need to support educational policies with global strategies for the development of individuals in political, social and cultural life, and the eradication of poverty; this underlines the strong link between education, sustainable development and peace, and hence the multi-dimensional importance of 'learning to live together'.

LEARNING TO LIVE TOGETHER—THE KEYSTONE OF EDUCATION FOR THE TWENTY-FIRST CENTURY

THE 'DELORS REPORT' AND THE FOUR PILLARS OF EDUCATION

In 1996, the International Commission on Education for the Twenty-first Century, which included educationists, philosophers and policy makers from all parts of the world, drew up a document on the essential role of education throughout life for the future development of individuals, nations and humanity. It emphasized that education had 'a treasure within' and developed a vision (a 'necessary utopia') of education for the twenty-first century based on four pillars:

- **Learning to know** refers mainly to broad-based general knowledge, combined in many cases with a deeper knowledge of some subjects, and includes 'learning to learn' as a condition for being able to benefit from learning opportunities provided at a later stage in life.
- **Learning to do** refers not only to the acquisition of occupational skills but also to the broader competencies needed to deal with different and changing situations and to work in teams. Some of these competencies may be acquired in formal courses, but they can also be learned informally, through the various social and work experiences of young people and adults.
- **Learning to be** refers to the ability to develop one's personality around a set of core values and to act with greater autonomy, judgement and personal responsibility (Faure et al., 1972). It means that education must not disregard any aspect of a person's potential, such as memory, reasoning, aesthetic sense, emotional drive, physical capacities of communication skills.
- **Learning to Live Together, learning to live with others** means the development of an understanding of other people in a spirit of pluralism, respect for differences and peace. Its principal focus is the development of an appreciation of the growing interdependence (ecological, economic and social) of individuals, communities and nations in a small, fragile and connected world. This is accomplished through activities like joint projects or conflict management.

Of these four pillars, the first three had been identified before and are essential for the sound development of persons, communities or individual nations. The fourth pillar, 'learning to live together', is of a different, more global nature: its omission may result in the annihilation of all other educational, health and development efforts through war, civil wars, terrorism, the deterioration of human, financial and natural resources, pandemics, etc.

The 'treasure' within education, referred to by the Commission, remains to a large extent to be discovered.

NEW EDUCATIONAL NEEDS, NEW CHALLENGES FOR EDUCATION

Rapid changes in the world and the entrance into a 'new civilization' have created new educational needs in areas where broadly similar trends have taken place throughout the world:

- To educate and train active, flexible and creative persons able to keep up with rapid change in the world of work, the service-based economy, the knowledge society and the scope of the field where individual and professional destinies are being shaped;
- To counteract the growth of inequality and the poverty and exclusion to which it leads; these powerful factors make it difficult for people to live together and impede economic development—even democracy. This requires educational structures and methods that take into account the diversity of starting points of learners and are designed to prevent the predetermination of educational destinies by such external factors as the lack of access to ICTs;
- To view diversity as a precious resource rather than a mere factor of inequality. The attention paid to cultural diversity in many countries has been growing and has led, for instance, to enhanced opportunities for minority or migrant groups to learn their own languages as an integral part of the educational curriculum;
- To educate individuals who are able to engage in politics and to foster respect for its principles, in particular democratic values and practices;
- To prepare individuals for an ever-broader range of personal decisions, affecting not only choices for one's personal life, but also the ethical, social or environmental consequences.

Most countries are faced with a series of common educational issues and challenges, even though they may vary considerably in their characteristics and scope:

- There is great need for renovation of curricula and teaching/learning methods in the direction of higher quality, defined as more relevant to the needs of learners and society.
- Overcoming the digital gap that is widening between information-rich and information-poor groups and individuals, through the dissemination and sensible use of ICTs in teaching and in learning.
- The need to reduce failure, dropout and repetition rates as well as absenteeism and to address low school enrolment and poor classroom performance; these issues entail the wastage of meager and valuable financial and pedagogical resources.
- To open up schools to all relevant actors (parents, local communities and associations) and to the wider world.

> The new emerging challenges have both positive and negative impacts on our ways of life. The education reform in Thailand is [...] based on the [dual] concept of Education for All and All for Education. [The new curriculum] will be flexible enough to facilitate the community to make adjustments in response to local needs.
>
> Thaksin Shinawatra,
> *Prime Minister and Minister of Education, Thailand*

> There is a digital rift. While in developed countries over 70% of educational centres have permanent access to Internet, this figure is less than 1% in my country.
>
> Nicolas Javier Lynch Gamero,
> *Minister of Education, Peru*

> In the age of globalization, physical access to schools is but one priority. Access to ICTs is the other gap we must bridge. The availability of learning opportunities through ICTs is one influenced by the distribution of economy resources. In today's world, there are no rich and poor countries, only knowledgeable or ignorant ones. [...] Even more important, the intellectual capital of the less-developed countries must be preserved and epitomized through technology.
>
> Raul S. Roco,
> *Secretary for Education, Philippines*

> It is a pity [that] due to lacking funding, educational institutions and administrative bodies have access neither to internal methodological and scientific data nor to Internet [...]. 8% of Moldavian schools have access to Internet. Not being linked up, schools are deprived from information needed in education and from a possibility to share in cultural values of the world.
>
> Ilie Vancea,
> *Minister of Education, Moldova*

> The introduction of ICTs [in education is an] utmost priority [...] both to respond to the needs of the economy and [those] of the educational process, but [also in view of their role] in closing the social gap between the poor and the rich in the Cyprus society. It is seen as a catalyst [for] social cohesion since it is expected to provide to the future citizens of the country the means for social mobility.
>
> Ouranios Ioannides,
> *Minister of Education and Culture, Cyprus*

AN ESSENTIAL ITEM ON THE REFORM AGENDA

Over the last decade, from Jomtien to the Delors Commission and from Dakar to the 2001 ICE, two major, complimentary changes have occurred. The educational and broader social challenges related to quality Education for All have been acknowledge as important throughout the world, and not simply at the local or national level. As a result, it has become increasingly clear to policy makers and educationists that these vital educational and social issues cannot be addressed successfully by countries acting by themselves. They require action at the international level and coherence between worldwide, national and local efforts.

The message of 'education for living together' presented by the ICE in 2001 is increasingly forming part of the educational agenda for regional and national policies and has thus gained more strength and momentum.

> The theme of the forty-sixth International Conference on Education fits well with the [education] policy of Côte d'Ivoire. Citizenship education [...] is an essential pillar of education for all aimed at learning how to live together [as a nation].
>
> Michel Amani N'Guessan,
> *Minister of National Education, Côte d'Ivoire*

> Preventing alcoholism, drug addition, AIDS and smoking [is] the responsibility of the State [...] in spite of hardships in the national economy [...]. However all these issues are of a global nature, and it is impossible to solve them only with the efforts of one country, one education system.
>
> Vladimir Filippov,
> *Minister of Education, Russian Federation*

9

Towards a Shared Vision of Education for Living Together

A number of concerns and issues come to mind in regard to learning to live together and how this challenge (and it is, indeed, a huge challenge) can best be addressed.

The first concern is focused on our awareness of the nature of the challenge and its importance for all our lives. The fact that education is [not] the direct, operative cause of war [...] should not lead us to underestimate its role. After all, education plays a non-insignificant part in how societies transmit and shape beliefs, values, perceptions and understanding regarding many aspects of our lives, including questions of conflict, peace and violence.

[...] More could be done to increase awareness of education's role in conveying messages that weaken or strengthen our capacity to live together. [...] Formal education may be called upon to counteract some of the violent messages communicated by society, but we need to understand more about how this may be done. [...]

At the same time [...], we have to recognize the limitations of education. We must not demand of education what we do not or cannot demand of society at large. How effective can educational messages be if they are contradicted or at least unsupported by the actual conditions for peace and justice in society? [...] we cannot expect schools to be havens of tranquillity if they are surrounded by social turbulence and violence.

[Another] concern is related to the scale on which learning to live together should be promoted. In an increasingly globalized world, learning to live with others cannot be confined to relations with ones' immediate neighbours. [...] Environmental education, an

> important component of approaches towards learning to live together, can offer countless examples of how actions in one corner of the world may produce effects very far away.
>
> Learning to Live Together should not be based on a false presumption that we can create a conflict-free world or that difference will not elicit a negative reaction in at least some cases. We must achieve better knowledge of the nature of conflict and acquire improved skills for handing conflict so that it does not degenerate into violence or oppression. We must learn to accept the reality or other people's distinctiveness and the fact that they are unlikely to change themselves just to please us. Learning to live with others implies the right for people to remain 'others'.
>
> John Denial,
> *Assistant Director-General for Education, UNESCO*

Over the last few decades, the notion of 'right to education' has changed significantly.

The Universal Declaration of Human Rights proclaims that everyone has a right to education, that elementary and fundamental education should be free and that elementary education should be obligatory. The declaration adopted by the World Conference on Education for All in Jomtien in 1990 proclaims that each person—child, youth and adult—should benefit from an education responding to basic learning needs. Since the Declaration of Jomtien, the right to education has not been measured in terms of the provision of education, but rather in terms of what society should make available to people without them having to ask, in other words, that which people need and that which is required to satisfy this need.

> National unity has been the primary agenda of the Malaysian government in working towards the integration of a multiethnic and multicultural society. Education has been instrumental in bringing together Malay, Chinese and Indian young people. [...] The practice of teaching ethnic languages has ensured the preservation of traditions and cultural identities of the various communities. [...] Values such as tolerance, humility, neighbourliness, love, honesty, public-spiritedness and understanding are taught throughout the school years. These values cut across religions, traditions and cultures [in Malaysia] and are congruent with universal values.
>
> Seri Musa Bin Mohammad,
> *Minister of Education, Malaysia*

> To live is to live together. Therefore the ability to live together is undoubtedly one of the most important for human development. [...] learning to live together is learning to live, and this can be learnt. The big challenge in educating [individuals] to live together is to mobilize the participation of all actors.
>
> *Mariana Aylwin,*
> *Minister of Education, Chile*

Even though the human being has been defined as a 'social animal', 'living together' does not appear natural, innate or even capable of being acquired once and for all.

A consensus appears to be emerging regarding learning to live together in the twenty-first century, and this includes not only 'learning how to live together', but also, and just as importantly, 'wanting to live together', peacefully.

Wanting and knowing how to live together imply:

- **knowledge,** since intolerance and rejection of others often stem from fear, which is nurtured by ignorance, and by unbearable injustice access to knowledge.
- **emotions and sensitivity,** since they influence the necessary knowledge to build and shape values attitudes and beliefs that are not inherited 'naturally' human beings.
- **self-esteem,** since at the individual and societal level it is a prerequisite for listening to others, dialogue, the peaceful resolution of conflicts and an attitude towards co-operation rather than confrontation. Psychologists, teaching specialists and educators know that a positive self-image, as well as one's culture and community, are preconditions for the development of acceptance, respect and empathy for others and, hence, for solidarity.
- **attitudes and behaviours,** grounded in a number of elementary codes, such as respect for the common good and community life, form the foundation for the existence of society. Above all, a 'civil education' must be developed or rebuilt.

A major question with respect to learning to live together concerns the responsibility of schools in the development of attitudes and beliefs that favour or impede living together.

Education alone cannot be held responsible for wars, violence or exploitation, nor is it able to prevent them in the future. History and current events demonstrate, after all, that educated people are capable of using their knowledge for the purpose of promoting political or religious intolerance and war or other forms of dominance. Yet, education does have an important role to play in questioning and challenging beliefs and attitudes that make it difficult for people to live together and in proposing an alternative to them.

> Education is an immensely powerful tool, one that could be used to shape the younger generation's attitudes in a positive way. [...] Education is essential if we are to increase children's understanding of the similarities among all human beings and their interdependence [...]. We must seek to promote a way of life without conflict, without negative attitudes—not only within national communities but also in respect of other nations, linguistic groups, [...] and cultures. We must be able to accept and respect people and cultures in our present interrelated world even in the face of substantial differences.
>
> Eduard Zeman,
> *Minister of Education, Czech Republic*

> Learning to live together is one of the principle challenges of the Balkan region. The mission of our schools is to prepare the new generation as citizens of a democratic society, equipped with the right concepts of coexistence with different groups and minorities, respecting other nations and other cultures.
>
> Ethem Ruka,
> *Minister of Education, Albania*

> Burundi is striving to reacquaint itself with the values of peace, tolerance and living together [...], the values that the new schools [...] need to convey. Relearning how to live together is an imperious educational need and a necessary antidote to the virus that has so deeply torn the social fabric of Burundi.
>
> Prosper Mpawenayo,
> *Minister of Education, Burundi*

Another important and closely related question concerns the ability of education to transmit messages different from those prevailing in the broader society and/or in the media. This is particularly important in countries and regions that have suffered from wars or civil wars and need to restore peace with neighbours as well as within society.

At a time of global interdependence and interaction, learning to live together is not only about living with close neighbours. Demography, environmental needs, the need for peace, export-driven economies, as well as worldwide instant communication, mean that all people are becoming neighbours. Of course, at the same time geographically close neighbours ought not to be neglected, whether they live in the same society, in a nearby minority community or just across the border. Another important factor is that the fast-growing number of long-term migrants (estimated at over 150 million people in 2000) is transforming distant people into close neighbours. Education for learning to live together is therefore primarily about living day by day within a group, a community and a society in which one encounters diverse situations and aspirations.

> Living together is not a new concern for schools, but its main focus has moved from international peace to civil peace within countries.
>
> Francois Audigier,
> *Professor at the University of Geneva, Switzerland*

> A big challenge in education is to find and to value a dynamic balance between human differences and similarities. Unavoidably, both [...] will always be part of human lives. We should build our collaborative efforts on similarities, but we should simultaneously fully respect differences.
>
> Yahya A. Muhaimin
> Minister of National Education, Indonesia

> I believe that for nations to learn to live together in harmony in the era of globalization, the pursuit of universally shared values and the encouragement of pluralism, especially the promotion of cultural and linguistic diversity, are vital
>
> Atsuko Toyama
> *Minister of Education, Japan*

> Learning to live together is only one aspect of a larger discipline, namely 'education in human values' UNESCO should actively work toward the elaboration of a common code of universal values that will be accepted around the globe, [...] attempting to harmonize the differences of the participants in the fields of religious faith, economical and political thinking, knowledge systems, living styles and so on. [This would] effectively promote the right of every human being to choose between different alternatives [...] without being compelled to do so under threat of force.
>
> *Delegation of India to the ICE*

Education for learning to live together could find itself being torn in seemingly opposite directions. On the one hand, its principal purpose could be seen as identifying and promoting a set of fundamental values shared in common by all the individuals, communities and nations of the world. On the other hand, its principal mission could be seen as educating individuals to appreciate and respect the difference of others, whether linguistic, ethnic, religious, social, etc. The vision developed at the 2001 ICE is not grounded exclusively in one or the other: Learning to live together needs to build on whatever ground for common understanding there may be, but it also needs to respect and promote diversity and solidarity across different groups and nations.

Learning to live together should not be understood as learning to accept all ideas, beliefs and behaviours in an uncritical manner. Education, and particularly education for learning to live together, is not a value-neutral endeavour. Its purpose is not to promote in an equal way all possible values but rather to promote a select group: those favouring solidarity, living together in peace and the respect for individual and collective rights.

In the knowledge society, education in the broadest sense is at once the following: the principle instrument for the preparation of new professions; a protection against social and professional exclusion; a key giving access to communication; and the tool for shaping personal and cultural identities as factors against uniformity and the levelling out of society. The boundaries between these various dimensions are becoming more blurred, but their respective weight in the educational mix varies. Cultural aspects and vocational training are no longer seen as opposing educational alternatives but rather as complementary, and bridges between school and employment are increasing in number. The new labour market demands go beyond specialized professional knowledge and encompass skills and competencies that may be acquired and exercised at school, for instance, autonomy, the ability to work on group projects, taking responsibility, working in English and in other (foreign) languages, learning by doing, etc.

Adapted from the National Report of Switzerland

Access to digital technologies is a necessary precondition for [the success of] policies focusing one equal opportunities for all (access to job markets, access to information, etc.); in fact [the

> need for this access to digital technologies] is equivalent to the right of democratic participation, [that is,] for full participation in world economic, political and social life. Digital technologies can radically change the way teachers teach and students learn. Thus schools are [...] the privileged agents for promoting equal access to all, for transforming the digital divide into a digital opportunity.
>
> Efthimiou Petros,
> *Minister of Education and Religious Affairs, Greece*

> [Overcoming] the rift between the knowledge-producing and other nations [is a] huge challenge. For a long time now, the main priority of our education policy has been universal schooling-something which we achieved [...] before Jomtien. Now our priority is to provide equal post-school opportunities for all, through enhanced quality Education for all.
>
> Moncer Rouissi,
> *Minister of Education, Tunisia*

'Learning to live together' is a multifaceted agenda with many objectives, including: the acquisition of knowledge, values and attitudes necessary for active citizenship; preparation for professional life as a means of entering society and contributing to it; the development of an awareness of global interdependence and the ability to respond positively to diversity; promotion of the acquisition of moral values and a commitment to solidarity as a means of combating exclusion and hence violence, etc.

All of these dimensions are essential for sustainable economic and social development in rich as well as in poor countries. The acknowledgement that a link necessarily exists between education, social inclusion and sustainable development represents a major step forward in the shaping of the worldwide educational agenda.

Furthermore, 'learning to live together' is not a new discipline to be added to existing curricula. Rather it is a concept that must permeate education systems as a whole. The time for educational structures designed to select an elite for a stratified, but integrative, economy has passed, while curricula designed for the preservation of culture and for the reproduction of a paradigm of civilization has reached its limits. New orientations are necessary for the education of individuals if they are to carry out long-term change, counteract inequalities and combat

EDUCATION FOR ALL FOR LEARNING TO LIVE TOGETHER: CONTENTS AND LEARNING STRATEGIES—PROBLEMS AND SOLUTIONS

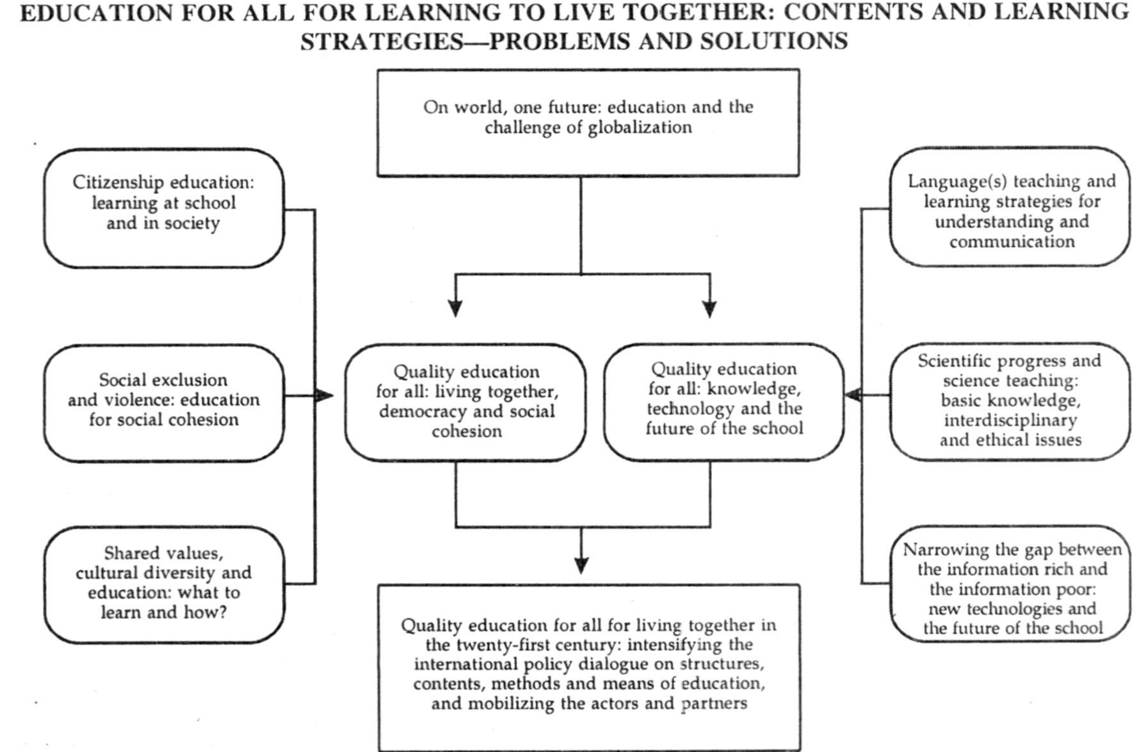

violence, at the same time as accepting technical progress while reducing its paradoxical consequences.

Learning to live together is only possible when special attention is paid to the needs of those individuals or groups who run the highest risk of being excluded from education and society. This concerns in particular the risk for young people and adults of being excluded from professional life, which tends to entail exclusion from other social activities (e.g. culture) and systems of protection (e.g. health care). The 2001 ICE enhanced the awareness that exclusion generates violence—irrespective of its sources or reasons. A basic requirement for learning to live together is that all have equal opportunities to access quality education meeting their particular needs—a challenge made both more essential and more difficult over the last decade, in particular with respect to equal access to information and communication technologies.

Contents and Strategies for Learning to Live Together

During the forty-sixth session of the International Conference on Education (ICE), the ministers and educationists underlined the importance of the challenges set out in the previous chapter and expressed their willingness to overcome them. However, these challenges require significant changes in the content and the methods of education. The ICE made it possible to share and disseminate considerable experience acquired from all regions of the world. In this way it contributed to a better identification of the components of education for learning to live together and the development of a more coherent paradigm for education for the twenty-first century (see figure on page 286).

Education for learning to live together concerns numerous domains:

- citizenship education;
- education for social cohesion: combating exclusion and violence;
- education and cultural diversity;
- language learning strategies;
- science learning;
- ICTs and the digital divide

Each of the following sections deals with one of these content areas. These sections, corresponding to the thematic workshops of the ICE (see Annex 2), present the main lines for future developments, illustrating them with case studies, examples of good practice or reforms presented during the Conference, national reports and expert opinions.

The final section integrates the six content areas and explores overall strategies for curricular reform for learning to live together (in terms of content, teaching material and methods).

These orientations may guide efforts to improve education at individual schools, in each community and nation, and even at the international level. They are the core of the vision (or the 'necessary utopia') of what the nations of the world want for and from education in the twenty-first century.

CITIZENSHIP EDUCATION: LEARNING AT SCHOOL AND IN SOCIETY

Individual and collective development were promoted exclusively in turn, yet they constitute the two sides of the same coin in today's world. The first refers to the knowledge society, the second to citizenship education. [...] School is the first place where solidarity and the rights and duties linking each individual to others can be learned. Citizenship cannot be decreed, but it may be stimulated.

Hervé Hasquin,
Minister-President of the French Community of Belgium

New history textbooks: history teaching plays an important role in the building of citizens' vision of the world; the Council of Europe plans to step up assistance activities concerning the design of new history curricula and the establishment of new standards for history teaching, including the production of new textbooks in the Russian Federation, the countries of the Caucasus, Southeast Europe and the Black Sea region.

Meeting of the Council of Europe's Standing Conference
of European Ministers of Education,
Cracow, Poland, 15-17 October 2000

Fighting poverty is [...] the very beginning of the process of learning to live together. Programmes to eliminate illiteracy and to teach adults are [...] important: illiterate adults (both men and women) teach values to their children [...].

ALESCO, Arab League Educational,
Cultural and Scientific Organisation

Learning to live together requires the development of democratic citizenship education. This has been a growing concern in nearly all education systems and should be seen in light of the progress over the last decades toward democracy as well as gender equality around the world. This 'civic' or 'citizenship' education is based on the acquisition of knowledge, the shaping of attitudes and the building of appropriate values, a process requiring much time and attention.

How do we introduce the practice of citizenship education in such different social and economic contexts? How can the educational community contribute in the most efficient way possible to citizenship education? These questions raise specific challenge, particularly concerning:

- The new roles and responsibilities of the teachers;
- Participation in and actual practice of civic life in various educational situations;
- The coming together of the educational messages and the values communicated by the school and by society in general and particularly by the channels of social communication.
- The possibilities and the limits in the use of new information and communications technologies (ICTs).
- The importance to be given to the construction of user-friendly social networks.

The principal orientations identified by the 2001 ICE show that schools in particular and education in general should:

- Encourage the participation of pupils in internal school decisions and student associations.
- Create an institutional methods encouraging dialogue, co-operation and democratic relations, and establish co-operation with families, communities and the whole society.
- Promote a whole-school approach to citizenship education; it requires not only the transmission of values, but also the acquisition of knowledge and the development of a direct experience with democratic practice.

What will the role of education be in the development of a universal form of citizenship? Universal citizenship requires that responsibilities be shared and a sense of belonging to a single entity that goes beyond the national, at the same time as a 'common future'. However, it is not always easy to reconcile this vision with history and the daily realty of countries and communities. The Conclusions of the ICE provide some answers.

> The 'civic path', France: Citizenship education and the democratic functioning of schools have attracted growing interest in recent years and several reforms have been adopted in this area. While civic instruction has traditionally been a theme for teachers of history and geography, the current trend toward it is becoming more and more a topic in all disciplines and for all teachers. Secondly, a growing number of special events dealing with a particular theme (women's rights, children's rights, hunger in the world, environmental issues, combating racism, freedom of the media, etc.) have come to involve all teachers, and many have been co-organized with local media organizations or partners. Thirdly, the regulations adopted by each school have been revised in the direction of a stronger organized involvement of students in democratic representative bodies. Finally, the 'institutional project' developed by each school now always includes a strand on citizenship education and draws on activities involving all relevant local actors and organizations, such as health care professionals, police officers, judges, social workers and informal educational and youth organizations. This 'civic path' leading from pre-primary to upper secondary school aims to equip students with skills, attitudes and experience needed to become critical and active citizens.
>
> *Adapted from the National Report of France*

> Improving gender equality and co-education: the Sultanate of Oman has ensured the provision of educational opportunities for all citizens regardless of their gender—something which did not exist before 1970. Students are unconditionally enrolled in schools. Since 1991, increased emphasis has been placed on improving the efficiency and quality of general education for all and on the elimination of regional and gender disparities. Instructional materials take account of international views for the twenty-first century, the needs of Omani society and overall educational goals, in particular: eschewing violence and extremism; establishing understanding and co-existence with others; developing the active role of citizens in maintaining peace and development through mutual co-operation and understanding; and emphasizing individual and children's rights.
>
> *Adapted from the National Report of Oman*

Pupils' Parliament, Lithuania: After the restoration of Lithuania's independence [...], a civic education programme was inaugurated in 1991. We decided that [t] must be multi-layered, that is, civic issues must be integrated into all subject syllabuses as well as taught as a separate discipline. We place great hopes in the Pupils' Parliament established in 2000. Pupils may draft laws and submit them to our Parliament. The Pupil's Parliament now has ties to similar institutions in other countries.

Vaiva Adasta Vebraite,
Minister of Education, Lithuana

The APNIEVE network brings together people from many countries in the Asia-Pacific region committed to values education for living together in a globalized world. It has published teacher source books and conducts workshops on teaching values, principles and ethics, using highly participative methods. APNIEVE's experience has taught that: teacher training is a vital prerequisite, since teachers must first learn to critically explore their own values, identity and culture; the teaching/learning methodology for values education is more important than intellectual knowledge; and values for living together are best integrated across the curriculum rather than as a separate subject.

Vice-President of APNIEVE,
Australia

Swedish schooling is not neutral when it comes to values. The idea is that the curriculum should clearly state the basic value system [...] that permeates all school activities [...]: respect for a person's dignity, individual freedom and integrity, gender equality, appropriate care for special needs children, an intercultural perspective and taking responsibility for one's actions are such fundamental values. The challenge of equity is to provide to all students, regardless of their backgrounds and where they live, a learning environment enabling them to reach the national objectives with respect to values and knowledge. Lessons on law, regulations, values and attitudes along cannot impart a living sense of democracy. Learners must be able to practice it themselves in everyday school life and in the teaching and learning of all subjects.

Adapted from the National Report of Sweden

In Japan, the enrichment of moral education is a priority in elementary and secondary education. Moral education aims at nurturing in children such morality as will provide a sound foundation for ensuring a better life for them on the basis of their proper awareness of how human beings should live. In recent years, the environment surrounding children has been changing, and moral education should be further enriched to make children aware of the preciouseness of life, consideration for others and norms such as right and wrong and good and evil, as well as to future sociability. For these reasons, the new curriculum is one that has been improved to make children learn through personal experiences in moral education in co-operation with the home and the community.

National Report of Japan

EDUCATIONAL FOR SOCIAL COHESION: COMBATING EXCLUSION AND VIOLENCE

The 'Forty-school project' in South Africa: The Centre for Survivors of Violence and Reconciliation operates a programme in South Africa designed to prevent and cure violence at school in the wake of the abolition of apartheid. Activities involve teachers as well as students and include, for example, theatre, the cleaning-up and upgrading of school premises by those who attend them and care provided to the victims of physical and psychological violence.

Video presentation introducing Workshop 2 at the ICE

'Tackling Violence in School' (Norway and European Union): In combating violence, school plays an essential role (since it) is the best way of reaching young people and their parents. A specific programme or campaign alone cannot solve behavioural problems at school. Work against violent behaviour, including bullying, racism and discrimination, demands a continuing and long-term effort. The heads of schools play a key role in creating a positive environment in their schools. However, specific action is also needed. Violence is a growing international phenomenon: international co-operation is (therefore) of growing interest. An example is the EU project 'Tacklng violence in schools', which was shown that a broad-based approach combining school, parents, the local community and pupil activity has positive effects.

Fact sheet on combating school violence,
Ministry of Education, Norway

The project 'Comunidade Solidaria' fights poverty and social exclusion in the poorest regions (of Brazil) though the co-ordination of civil society with public administration. It includes in particular an action programme against illiteracy ('Alfabeticao Solidaria') based on community education and a scheme mobilizing thousands of university students to work in disadvantaged communities.

Universidade Solidaria, Brazil

The 2001 ICE debated the question of how the content and processes of formal education relate to the process of social exclusion and the patterns of violence associated with the breakdown of social cohesion. This theme has become a major concern of policy makers and educationist over the past decade. Yet, the role of education in strengthening social cohesion is still interpreted in various ways: for some, social cohesion is primarily an issue for economic and social policies and addressed to society in general; others think that, even if education alone is not enough, the objective of social cohesion is part of its fundamental mission and that educational policies should serve as counter-weights to the effects of family and social background, which still remain the most powerful determinants of school destinies in most education systems.

Orientations for the future taken at the 2001 ICE address three principal questions.

- What are the consequences of societal violence on education? While many countries express the view that social cohesion presupposes peace, there is also widespread consensus that peace in turn can only be based on justice. The institution of school is no longer an ivory tower and, in numerous cases, violence at schools reflects the climate of violence and of injustice that characterizes the environment in which these schools function.
- How does format education relate to the wider processes of social exclusion? The family, the home, the immediate environment as well as the media play a central role in socialization from a very early age. Television, in particular satellite television, is increasingly important in the education of young people in today's societies around the world. The limits of schooling ought to be recognized. There is no conclusive evidence regarding the ways in which individual and interpersonal skills and attitudes transmitted through formal and non-formal education shape group behaviour, particularly in settings of acute social and political tensions.
- How can education contribute to the strengthening or rebuilding of social cohesion? The principal thrust of

the educational agenda for social cohesion lies in efforts to reduce school failure and dropouts, in full awareness that exclusion from school usually entails exclusion from other areas of social life (often starting with employment) and that exclusion generates violence.

There are examples of successful initiatives based on a complementary strategy combining cultural, economic and political components. Their common features are that they develop a civic culture through raising awareness of the need for minimal rules for living together and that they draw simultaneously on formal and informal approaches, including schooling, adult (and parent) literacy and psycho-social support in societies emerging from conflicts.

Critical factors include effective networking for dialogue and the sharing of experience between educational institutions, between teachers, between teachers and parents, between school and community-based organizations, and between donor agencies. These partnerships may help education to promote social cohesion and prevent (or at least reduce) social exclusion.

EDUCATION AND CULTURAL DIVERSITY

Multiple cultural identity is like the accordion, which needs to be pushed open and closed to play a melodious musical phrase; in the same way, cultural identity in today's world is not a choice between local roots and openness to the world, but rather the ability to combine both in an appropriate way.

Cecilia Braslavsky,
Director, UNESCO's International Bureau of Education

According to Fleming (1993) three broad educational and social values which cross provincial/territorial boundaries have shaped the attitudes of Canadians towards public education, the first is the elimination of obstacles to access related to language, gender, race or a physical or mental handicap; the second is the conviction that the quality and choice of education should be the same irrespective of place of residence and local availability of resources; the third is cultural pluralism, which was adopted in the 1970s and meant for the First Nations of Canada the end of the dark period of 'residential schools' during which the school system was used as a means of assimilation.

Adapted from the National Report of Canada

> Self-esteem as a foundation for multiculturalism: The current focus given to international dialogue on education for living together [...] indicates a recognition that [...] this pillar of education is critical to the establishment of a sustainable social order. There is an ever-growing demand on our citizens to increase their knowledge and appreciation of other societies and cultures while being reassured about the value and viability of their own.
>
> *Bruchell Whiteman,*
> *Minister of Education, Jamaica*

In many countries or communities the transition from cultural uniformity to cultural diversity and exposure to other values has occurred only recently as a result of globalization, migrations, ICTs and the greater mobility of people and ideas. Education for cultural diversity is therefore in many respects both a new challenge and an urgent need. The 2001 ICE focused on an essential issue: to determine what should be taught and how.

To what extent should education be focused on common values shard across cultures or rather on the ability of diverse cultures to co-exist and engage in a dialogue? While harmonization seems both undesirable and unfeasible, the growing interdependence of regions, countries and communities should be underlined in curricula, in particular in history geography, civic education, social studies, religious or ethical education, as well as in the learning of the mother-tongue and foreign languages. This concerns both the production of new textbooks and teaching materials providing different interpretations of the same event in different countries or communities instead of a single, usually ethnocentric one. It also involves the development of curricula and teaching methods adapted to the diversity of cultural and social contexts. Yet, the principal question about the value of certain cultural characteristics remains unanswered: are they all positive, do they all deserve respect, are they all worth being transmitted to the next generation as factors fostering living together? How can common values be promoted in contexts of fear or discrimination?

The content of education for cultural diversity should emphasize the transmission of the cultural heritage, a degree of autonomy from globalization, learning relevant to the community and to the learners, the promotion of gender equality and, above all, the learning of the mother-tongue. This learning seems to be a new or renewed priority in a considerable number of countries, but it is not articulated in the same way everywhere: sometimes the trend is towards the strengthening of the rights of minority cultures to a cultural identity of their own in combination with the learning of the majority's language and culture; other countries want to open access for all citizens to all cultures, both the minorities, and the majority's, in order to allow them to share in the same cultural and linguistic diversity, and co-exist in a constructive way. This implies, in particular, the absence of a hierarchy among the various languages spoken in a country or community.

For the purpose of intercultural education, the boundaries between formal and non-formal education should be removed. School alone cannot be expected to solve the problems and conflicts resulting from political, economic, historical and social factors. Hence, the involvement of all school actors and partners (teachers and trainers, learnings, parents and families, peer groups, local communities and local, regional and national.

New meaning of education in Nunavut, Canada: Canada's latest autonomous territory, Nunavut introduced a new school curriculum in 1999 based on these search for a balance between traditional Inuit values and knowledge and the requirements of modern life. It aims to build up a strong communal identity through the teaching of the Inuit language, Inuit culture and Inuit traditions, combined with the active involvement of families The underlying principle is that enhancing self-respect through increased respect for one's own culture is the best way to develop a positive awareness of the impact of technologies on local life and integrate both dimensions

Video document introducing Workshop 3 at the ICE

From black and white to colour: Research carried out in Belarus explored factors that may inhibit the development of pupils' capacity for international understanding. Among the many psychological factors involved is the tendency for children to develop a simplified, 'black-and-white' notion of the world, dividing people and nations into 'good' and 'bad' idealizing one's own behaviour and completely dismissing the opinions of others.

Lucie-Mami Noor Nkaké,
Education for international understanding,
Geneva, IBE, 1996

LANGUAGE(S) STRATEGIES FOR UNDERSTANDING AND COMMUNICATION

> Most countries (...) are faced with the same problems and the same challenges, irrespective of their level of economic development and of the political and social conditions prevailing in their part of the world. Language learning [is] a precious tool for living together. [For the purpose of citizenship] in ever more multicultural and diversified societies, [...] the native language, the local language, the neighbour's language [and] the world communication language are as many challenges if one accepts that a language is not only a means of communication but includes a strong cultural component combined with the dimension of identity.
>
> *Martine Brunschwig Graf,*
> *State Counsellor for Education,*
> *Republic and Canton of Geneva, Switzerland*

> In primary education in Latvia, one model of educational development is proposed for schools with Latvian as the language of instruction and four models of bilingual educational curricula are proposed for schools serving minority populations so that the pupils of such schools many acquire in their native languages, bilingually or in Latvian the same educational content as the pupils of schools [offering instruction] in Latvian and can begin their [secondary] education in the Latvian language.
>
> *Adapted from the National Report of Latvia*

The fundamental importance of language learning and language communication in 'learning to live together' was underlined by the 2001 ICE.

The Conference provided an opportunity for a large number of countries to confirm their multilingual status and to acknowledge that instruction in the mother-tongue is of crucial importance for pedagogical, social and cultural reasons. The monopoly position held by one 'global; language (or by a restricted number of 'international' languages) in international communication may be perceived either as a threat to linguistic and cultural diversity, because it discourages the learning of other languages, or as a simple tool for communication whose danger should not be overrated since it tends to be used only for specific purposes or in a restricted number of language-use situations. The ICE underlined that there are no superior and inferior languages for the transmission of knowledge and values and for the creation of a dialogue.

Mother languages and national and international languages are more than just means for communication. They serve also to facilitate understanding and appreciation of one-self and openness to differences. Hence, they allow a dialogue with others and contribute to peaceful conflict resolution. This is particularly true for the learning of the mother-tongue, which has been recognized as a top priority in many education systems. This often remains a politically sensitive question, primarily in countries where numerous languages coexist. It is sometimes difficult to obtain a national consensus on the choice of language of instruction and parental approval requires large awareness-raising and information campaigns. It seems, however, that the priority given to the native language of students constitutes the best basis for further learning (including for the learning of other languages) and fosters positive emotions needed for the building of a personal and cultural identity, as well as the sentiment of belonging to the community.

How can language teaching and learning strategies be made effective? The ICE stressed the need for language learning throughout the period of education. The usage of methods privileging communication gives interesting results but there is an unfortunate relative lack of pedagogical research about the comparative efficiency of various language learning patterns or strategies. This question concerns in particular the best time for introducing foreign-language learning in school curricula and the impact of early instruction in foreign languages, including on the learning of the children's own language.

> 'Speaking more languages makes one more human' (Czech proverb). The language teaching priorities in the Czech Republic are to ensure that children are able to communicate in their own language [Czech], to awaken their interest for other languages at an early stage (starting the teaching of English in pre-primary and the first year of primary education), and to offer a real choice from a significant number of other foreign languages in later schooling, including those of neighbouring countries, national minorities and the European Union. Foreign language teaching pays considerable attention to cultural aspects such as music, etc.
>
> *Video document Introducing Workshop 4 at the ICE*

Valuing migrant children's languages in Germany: Intercultural learning should also include a comprehensive range of foreign languages on offer. The intensification of foreign-language learning [...] has been promoted in recent years by the increased inclusion of foreign languages in primary school teaching in the spirit of a first encounter with a foreign language. It also include bilingual teaching with parts of subject lessons in the foreign language. The secondary school exist examination (Abiturpiüfung) can only be taken by those who have studied at least two foreign languages over a minimum period of time, Children who arrive in Germany at the lowest secondary education level, who in any case have to learn German intensively and cannot catch up in the second obligatory foreign language, such as English or French, may choose the language of their country of origin or have it recognized. Pupils who enter directly into upper secondary education may replace the compulsory foreign language with the language of their country of origin or with Russian. Thus, in North-Rhine/Westphalia in 1998 7,000 foreign pupils were successfully examined in their native languages instead of a second foreign language. Examinations were held in a total of thirty-five languages.

National Report of Germany

Croatia launches a reform of its education system-structure, standards, curricula, methods—in order to develop a system compatible with those of developed democracies based on the principles of pluralism, co-existence, tolerance and democratic standards.

Vladimir Strugar,
Minister of Education, Croatia

Convergent teaching gives priority to the child's own language, which serves at the same time as a means of communication and expression and as a tool for structuring through and personality. The introduction of a second language should be contemplated only when the most important types of behaviour, especially those concerned with writing, have been mastered in the mother-tongue. A child's mother-tongue, in our view, is the only language that can develop in the child the behaviour, attitudes and aptitudes needed for all types of learning. It generates trust and harmony between pupils and their teacher and amongst themselves. It provides the children with a better opportunity to perceive and query the world around them. It frees them of their inhibitions and develops their imagination and creativity. A child who has learned to read, write and calculate in his own language will use the same skills when learning a second language, which in turn will give him a clearer awareness of his own tongue, his culture, and the world around him. According to convergent teaching, initial learning should start from the child's personal experience and should use his awareness of his socio-cultural environment as a reference. The opening to the outside world will occur gradually as the child progresses through school. This also enables the learner to incorporate the school as part of his daily life.

Adapted from: Samba Traoré,
Convergent teaching in Mail and its
impact on the education system.
Geneva, IBE, 2001, (INNODADA monographs, no. 6.)

SCIENCE LEARNING: BASIC KNOWLEDGE, INTER-DISCIPLINARY AND ETHICAL PROBLEMS

The 2001 ICE stressed that the universality of science, both in terms of content and a common reasoning method, is an important dimension of learning to live together: it develops a common notion of the world and values such as sharing, co-operation and interdependence. Access to universal scientific knowedge is a right of all, rich and poor, male and female, irrespective of ethnicity or religion, and is hence closely linked to citizenship and democracy. At the same time, science is a key contributor to economic growth and sustainable development and the gap in science learning between developed and poor countries is an impediment to living together more harmoniously on the planet.

The development of science education is impeded by a series of factors:

- inadequate teaching methods and the obsolete contents of natural science curricula;
- the lack of resources for, and the consequent poor quality of, science education in many countries;
- the perception of science as an instrument of dominance or exploitation of the poor by the rich in large parts of the world;
- the diminishing attractiveness of science disciplines among young people, especially girls;
- and the widespread shortage in teachers of these disciplines at all levels of education systems.

What kind of science education do we want and for what

purpose? The acquisition of scientific competencies must allow citizens to better understand the world and to know how to act in it for economic growth and sustainable social development, in full awareness of the ethical values and citizenship models linked to scientific progress and to its consequences.

The principal orientation taken for the future emphasize that science learning needs to be profoundly renovated and should, in particular:

- answer the need to improve the quality of science education at all levels and to avoid discrimination between genders or against disadvantaged groups;
- adopt, active real-life learning methods as a source of learning;
- stimulate critical thinking and curiosity as a stimulus to intellectual discovery of the universe, focusing on both boys and girls;
- alleviate curricular overloads in scientific disciplines and adapt them to what students are effectively able to learn;
- link curricula to the human and social context by stressing the ethical dimension of science in terms of human values and responsibilities with respect to others, the environment and future generations;
- favour an interdisciplinary approach as a means of putting science into context;
- develop learning to learn with others' and links between formal learning at school and informal learning in the community as a means of ensuring the sustainability of science learning (media, multimedia, museums, scientific parks, etc.);
- recognize that ICTs have an important role to play in science education, but cannot and should not replace real-life learning experiences.

For the ICE, the feasibility of the above orientations depends strongly on science teachers. As the key actors in the process, they should enjoy higher social status and the time and resources for ongoing quality training in keeping with new discoveries and methods. Their special role in combating HIV/

AIDS in countries and communities affected by this epidemic was also underlined.

Awareness of energy and renewable energy, Cuba: This experiment run by the Cuban Ministry of Education in conjunction with the NGO Cubasolar aims to educate children about renewable energy and to teach them respect for the environment. The equipment of rural schools with photovoltaic cells makes it possible to watch television in the evenings. This creates a clear link between the investment effort made and the benefit for individuals and the community. The role of teachers is crucial in explaining that there is no sustainable development without respect for the environment as a means of making possible living together.

Video document introducing Workshop 5 at the ICE

Hands-on learning ('La main à la pâte'), France: The pedagogy of science is being renewed in the light of an experiment introduced a few years ago at the initiative of Nobel Prize winner Georges Charpak with the support of the Academy of Science ('La main à la Pâte', that is, 'hands-on' learning of science). Its primary aim is to develop reasoned investigation starting with the observation of objects or processes of the world of life or technology. It requires a global, multidisciplinary approach to science and serves as a stimulus to the desire to know and learn. It signals a significant departure from the traditional French approach to science teaching more based on abstract reasoning than pragmatic experimentation. In addition to increased effectiveness, it is also expected to be more democratic, by creating an alternative to the traditional selection of elites on the basis of their capacity to deal with abstraction.

Adapted from the National Report of France

EDUCATION, ICTs AND THE DIGITAL DIVIDE

Information is one thing; education is another. Access to information alone is not enough. The cost of hard- and software is a major issue.

Elie Jouen,
Education International

Hardware and software are expensive and very quickly become obsolete. Hence, partnerships with private companies are indispensable to equipping schools. But equipment and access to data are not enough; the real issue is to develop critical thinking and an ethical dimension.

Vaiva Radasta Vebraite,
Vice-Minister of Education, Lithuania

> The Bahamas Education School Technology project (BEST) is based on a contractual agreement with Fujitsu-ICL [...] and will be implemented [...] in all 110 primary schools throughout the Bahamas.
>
> Technology should provide 'equity in quality education', especially for students and teachers of our remote islands and cays [and for] under-achievers and under-motivated students.
>
> *Dion Foulkes,*
> *Minister of Education, Bahamas*

> Our aim is to offer opportunities to all citizens to acquire the basic ICT skills [needed in the information society, for example, through] in-service training [as well as] in libraries, in liberal adult education and in voluntary organization. Finland's comprehensive and popular library network provides an opportunity to access on line information networks. This is the only way to ensure that the new technologies benefit everybody, irrespective of age, gender, educational and cultural background, etc.
>
> *Delegation of Finland*

The message from the 2001 ICE was that the future role of education as a factor contributing to living together is closely related to its ability to help narrow the gap between the information rich and the information poor. The impact of ICTs ought to be assessed on the basis of how effectively they contribute to the expansion of humanity's knowledge base all over the world.

While every society has a wealth of information and a rich knowledge-base of its own, the power to own, structure, decide upon and control the technology for coding, transmitting and using information is determined by economic means, with the dividing line following economic, linguistic, ethnic and gender barriers. The huge imbalance of access to ICTs carries an intrinsic risk of fostering inequities among and within countries, communities and workplaces, and this 'digital divide' between the knows and know-nots goes along the same lines as the older divide between the haves and have-nots.

> The Internet Mobile Unit (IMU), Malaysia: The IMU project was conceived as a means to bridge the gap between the information-rich and the information-poor and to democratize access to ICTs in Malaysia. The project started in 1999 when a 'cyberbus' was

equipped as an Internet Learning Centre able to visit even remote rural areas of the country and provide children with initial opportunities to use computers. The project first targeted students and their teachers who were invited to use the Internet and to prepare their own homepages, in 'order to make them more than just users'. Since 2001 families and communities have also been involved with a view to enhancing the benefits of the IMU at the local community level.

Video document introducing Workshop 6 at the ICE.

India has developed the SIMPUTER, an ICT device enabling basic education to be taken to remote locations and to disadvantaged sections of society through education and self-learning.

Comment by the Delegation of India

RENOVATING CURRICULA, TEXTBOOKS AND METHODS FOR LEARNING TO LIVE TOGETHER

Among the elements in position to help ameliorate the quality of education, the Dakar Forum stressed the importance of organizing basic education content in order to meet the needs and values of society:

> The economic, social and other changes sweeping through human society in recent years have forced a reconsideration of what knowledge, skills and values are needed for successful living. The movement, toward more open and democratic societies has created a need for learning that goes beyond the academic curriculum and factual knowledge to emphasize problem-solving and open-ended enquiry. The expansion of communication and information technologies necessitates more interactive and exploratory forms of learning, and the increased pace of change has put a premium on the need to engage in continuous learning over a lifetime. There is also a new urgency to ensure that education at all levels and in all places reinforces a culture of peace, tolerance and respect for human rights.

The renovation of the content of education in the light of the new needs of learning to live together entails change in curricula, textbooks and other teaching materials and, inevitably, in educational methods, for teaching, learning, assessment and evaluation. Change may mean simple adjustments or updating in some countries or disciplines, but in many cases the need is for much more radical and comprehensive change, that is, for the 'renovation' or even 'recasting' of education systems and the curriculum.

REMODELLING CURRICULA

There is a widespread trend in curricular reforms to introduce change in four converging directions:

- to gear programmes towards the acquisition of competencies;
- to reduce their fragmentation into disciplines through cross-disciplinary work;
- to leave more choice to students rather than retaining monolithic curricula;
- and to revive project-based learning.

Contrary to structural and quantitative reforms that are sometimes 'imposed' on education systems, the characteristic of 'qualitative' reforms (that is, those reforms dealing with the very essence of education) is that they can only be successful if they are able to convince and mobilize teachers.

> How can we [get out of] degraded versions of eighteenth century encyclopaedism that often create a gulf between education and personal needs?
> [...] How can we avoid an exaggerated emphasis on congnitive development to the detriment of emotional and social aspects of personal growth?
> [...] What kind of curriculum design and educational practices can best help us to deal with the strong emotional component of the prejudices and stereotypes that often obstruct the process of living together?
>
> *John Daniel,*
> *Assistant Director-General for Education, UNESCO*

FLEXIBILITY, DECENTRALIZATION AND EVALUATION

> Secondary education as a sub-system has failed to [clarify] the ends and objectives it pursues. In the past [it] bowed to the demands of higher education and more recently to those of the labour market. [This] is no longer thought to be the correct approach. Secondary education has [its own] aims to achieve, such as the personal and social development of young people and their education for citizenship, democracy, tolerance, acceptance and understanding of other. [A] wide-reaching debate in 1997-1999 revealed:
>
> - a significant difference between the curriculum proposed by the Ministry of Education, the curriculum actually taught in schools and the curriculum effectively learnt by students;
> - a lack of adjustment between content and assessment methods [...];

- a lack of balance in curriculum development, over-estimating the teaching and learning of purely academic contents to the detriment of skills development, particularly those running throughout schooling such as education for citizenship.

Adapted from the National Report of Portugal

Curricula should be re-adjusted periodically and all items constituting an unnecessary and inhibiting burden should be removed. Curricula ought to be flexible and built on concrete notions that can be assimilated by learners because they are relevant to their daily lives. These are factors that could stimulate the children's desire to learn and their curiosity.

Jean Bio Chab Orou,
Minister of Education, Benin

One of the primary aims of the educational reforms [in progress in Pakistan] is to raise the quality of education through a massive programme of curricular revision and teacher training. In addition, we are devising a system of assessing the outcome of these measures through an objective system of testing [..] at two level: on completion of primary education and at the stage of secondary-level education.

Tariq Farook,
Head of Delegation, Pakistan

With reference to curricula, the major issue emerging from the debate that took place at the 2001 ICE concerns their flexibility. Flexibility is widely seen as an important dimension of education for living together. It has been growing in tune with the decentralization of school administration, in particular when it has been possible to adapt certain parts of the curriculum to local issues. There seems to be a broad consensus that curricula need some kind of common core defined at the national level and other elements that are flexible enough for regional authorities, communities or particular schools to adapt them to the specific needs of their constituencies. Curricular flexibility may concern both contents and methods.

It has led everywhere to increased attention to school and system evaluation, both internal and external. The call for a 'culture of evaluation' permeating all aspects and institutions of education is largely associated with the need to ensure that more flexibility leads to higher quality education rather than to degradation. Indeed, several examples of what has taken place in recent decades have shown that decentralization or greater autonomy granted to schools has sometimes resulted in an impoverishment of education and not to an enhancement.

It is interesting to note that in many countries the dilemma of flexibility vs. constituency seems to be particularly acute at the level of lower secondary education. Experiences with a single curriculum for all seem to reach their limits as the diversity of learners increases and teachers are faced with 'an impossible challenge' in the classroom: a growing variety of studies.

EDUCATION: A SERVICE NOT LIKE ANY OTHERS

In spite of significant progress, the quality of learning and the acquisition of competencies and values [...] remains far from expectations and from responding to the needs and aspirations of individuals and societies. Crucial new challenges have emerged [with] globalization and we need to pay all the more attention to [...] the protection of the Public Service of Education, in order to avoid the diversion of its content and substance as a result of the most negative effects of globalization. There is a real risk that education may become just a service like any other, [...] Our 'Strategy 2020' is based on the following principles: education concerns the entire society and must therefore be founded on the basis of strong participation of society in its planning, administration and funding. This calls for a genuine partnership [...] between educational institutions and the other circles of society.

Ali Abdul Aziz Al Shartan,
Minister of Education, United Arab Emirates

Most countries see education as a key governmental responsibility. This idea is deeply rooted in culture and society. Some country representatives underlined this by pointing out that education is and should remain a public service; it should not become a service like others or be traded as a commodity.

GLOBAL QUALITY

Quality education for living together in the twenty-first century is definitely not education confined to reproducing existing curricula and structures [...]. The quality of education should be assessed in accordance with its ability to integrate scientific knowledge and technological skills with universal and humanistic values and to prepare for moral and cultural as well as economic well-being.

Najib Zerouali Ouariti,
Minister of Higher Education and Research, Morocco

Curricular renovation for learning to live together, as well as all innovative projects introduced to prevent failure, early dropout inequality and exclusion, give rise to concerns about their impact on the overall 'quality' of education. The quality of education is a relative notion and is hence difficult to evaluate and monitor. With regard to Education for All for learning to live together, the notion of 'quality' needs to be understood as 'global' quality: it needs to take into account not just the 'academic level' achieved by a group of students but also the relevance of what is learnt to the needs of learners, their starting point (which determines the 'value added' by education) and a whole series of indirect effects of a non-academic nature, such as the diminution of violence or greater acceptance of cultural diversity.

THE IMPACT OF CURRICULAR CHANGE AND INFORMAL LEARNING

The pertinent evidence, from rather thin comparative research, lends little credence to claims that textbooks have significant non-cognitive effects. Textbooks, to the extent that they are available, may dominate the contours of classroom life, but they are not necessarily authoritative socialization tools that shape pupils' attitudes and worldviews. [...] Under such conditions external forces [like the decisions made by international textbook publishers] have especially powerful effects on chool curricula.

Aaron Benavot,
Educational Researcher, Israel

The liberalization of the school textbook market in Poland led to the availability of a much broader range of textbooks and a general increase in their quality. Publishers now offer full packages including exercise books, methodological handbooks for teachers and often also computer software CD-ROMs or cassetters.

With new textbooks and learning materials, pupils and teachers are forced to [...] apply more active teaching and learning methods. Pupils are encouraged to look for solutions by themselves instead of reading ready-made answers. In this way textbook change contributed to promoting innovation in education, usually coming ahead of actual curricular change, for example, through integrated teaching (with no division into subjects) in elementary school. Innovation came also as an outcome of the increasingly intensive co-operation of publishers with teachers, who are both authors and reviewers of new textbooks.

> In history and geography textbooks, the work of a specific bilateral German-Polish commission resulted in the removal of sections containing inaccurate history claims. This contributed significantly to establishing closer co-operation between the two countries. Following that example, other such bilateral commissions were set up. These efforts were also successful in the case of the Polish-Israeli Commission.
>
> *Adapted from the National Report of Poland*

> In this increasingly interrelated and complex world, where differences need respect and the mixture of cultures needs understanding and acceptance, learning to live together requires international co-operation and exchange. Since it is much more difficult to experiment in education than in other areas, the world should be seen as an education laboratory allowing the comparison of performances between various education systems and to analyse the factors explaining them. Such a worldwide international comparative approach is a powerful instrument for the evaluation of where we stand with education. Although each country may learn by itself, the learning process will be much enhanced if shared with others.
>
> *Adapted from a presentation by Alejandro Tiana, Professor, Faculty of Education, UNED Madrid*

While policy makers tend to expect direct positive consequences from changes in curricular content and textbooks, the actual impact of such changes is not clearly confirmed by educational research. This may be seen as a confirmation of the crucial importance of informal learning that remains largely unaffected by change in official curricula or textbooks. This may also mean that the impact of curricular change is more indirect than direct, e.g. when the renovation of textbooks entices teachers to adopt more innovative teaching methods or to work in teams.

Some External Conditions for Teaching on Learning to Live Together

The previous sections have emphasized the visions, contents and expected benefits of Education for learning to live together. The reform of educational contents, methods and practices is important in distinguishing between education that teaches learning to live together and that which does not. However, education will only deliver what we expect of it if certain conditions are fulfilled enabling it to fulfil its destiny. This chapter tackles some of these key conditions: training appreciating and mobilizing teachers; the development of partnerships which civil society; policy dialogue; and the movement to humanize globalization, None of this can be achieved except through visions and policies that go beyond the education sector and also imply a new international commitment.

VALUING, TRAINING AND MOBILIZING TEACHERS AND TRAINERS

> Educationists the world over are a beleaguered species, threatened not so much by extinction as by exhaustion as they seek to perform their routine work while also responding to virtually incessant change derived from reforms, improvement programmes and new policy initiatives. In recent decades there has been a growing awareness of the importance of mobilizing and gathering together all the social actors [...]. It has been recognized that curriculum reforms sometimes fail because they have not enjoyed sufficient backing from society in general and teachers in particular. Within curriculum contents and methods,

the theme of learning to live together is one which stands out as requiring an approach that is thoroughly consultative and participatory, involving all interested parties.

John Daniel,
Assistant Director-General for Education, UNESCO

Internationalization and globalization, the explosion of knowledge and communication, the pace of technological progress and the complexity of living together in an organized society are challenges for the future. The world will soon require from our children a formidable ability to deal with change, communicate, solve problems and innovate. Hence, the necessity to update current curricula. [...] Numerous initiatives concerning curricula are taken and implemented in a hurry without [enough] consultation of teachers and stakeholders. Furthermore, the time and resources for the training needed by teachers to implement them are often missing.

Adapted from the National Report of Canada

For a curricular reform to be effective it should be coupled with a structural reform. Otherwise conservative teachers resisting the reform might wave proposals for curricular changes aside and continue to teach their pupils as they had for many years, following exactly the same patterns. However, a structural reform could hardly pass unnoticed. It would be difficult to teach the old way in a new school. Thus the idea [of the polish reform] was to provide an impulse to deep reflection in teacher communities and to bring actual changes in teaching contents and styles. Schools were to build their own curriculum within a predetermined general framework while balancing three dimensions of education: acquiring knowledge, developing skills and shaping attitudes. [Beyond] change in the contents and the methods, the curricular reform was designed above all to change the teaching philosophy and the culture of schools. Instead of passively following instructions of the education authorities, teachers were expected to come up with their own curricula that would be best suited to the needs of their pupil. Teachers were thus faced with entirely new tasks.

National Report of Poland

The 2001 ICE devoted considerable attention to the decisive role of teachers in promoting the quality of education and, particularly, in training for living together. The myths that planning, teacher-proof texts or information and communication technology (ICT) education could henceforward happen without teachers need to be opposed. The processes of systematic and ongoing innovation and qualitative reforms of education, as well as those required for learning to live together, need the proactive support of teachers and trainers and are doomed to fail if they are not able to find it. However, this support can only be achieved if teachers are associated with the process of devising educational change from an early stage, if they contribute to such processes and if, as a consequence, they see the reasons for change rather than only its costs in terms of perceived disruption and inconvenience.

Mobilizing teachers is one of the key factors leading to effective action for change both in and for education. Throughout the forty-sixth session of the International Conference on Education, it became clear that education is far from just a means of simply passing on wisdom, and that while the role of teachers may be changing, it remains as indispensable as ever to help young people to progress from information to knowledge, and to develop their sociability, values and will in the face of many challenges, particularly that of living together. Mobilizing and guiding teachers is at its core dependent upon three aspects: their training; their working and living conditions; and their recognition in society.

Teacher training often consists of repeating information, mastering uniform teaching techniques and working in one language-the country's language or one of them. The ICE stressed the need for change in initial and in-service training, and also the need to plan radical processes of change in the profession that go far beyond the idea of courses and partial policies for teacher support. For change in the profession to act as a genuine focal point for promoting educational quality and relevance there should be an informed and systematic process of self-change, in which all teachers are agents of educational innovation, with humanist and family values, and with communities and students accepting the required changes.

In this sense, all teaching staff need to strengthen their ability to deal simultaneously with features of local culture and the opening-up to universal values and horizons. Also noted was the importance of reinforcing the cultural wealth of teaching staff and to make progress in training language teachers so that they may be better equipped to take up the dual challenge of cultivating identity and inculcating universal values.

The training of teachers in learning to live together should aim to overcome new and diverse challenges, such as the lack of sufficient teachers in the face of growing populations in many regions of the world, the losses of life due to AIDS, preparing for self-change, empathy for those who are different and planning ongoing change in available teaching technologies. For teachers to face the challenge of education throughout their lives, it is essential that there are radical changes in curricula and teaching practices.

As regards the working conditions of all teaching staff, this is not limited to the matter of salaries. In many countries of the world, a teaching salary is totally insufficient. However, there is evidence that shows that there is no genuine and unequivocal direct correlation between the level of teaching salaries and the ability of teachers to teach more effectively. Although it is evident that a minimum level of salary dignity is required so that teachers can carry out their work, this is also true for other aspects, such as justice in the constitution of salary scales, the need for a teacher career structure that does not oblige teachers to take up a management position with better salary conditions, the existence of incentives, policies for encouraging the best teachers to work in the poorest areas, in rural areas and at primary grade level. But also, there is clear evidence that social recognition of teachers has a significant impact on their ability to teach living together.

Teaching how to live together involves training in human dignity and in recognizing others. Consequently, those who do not feel recognized in their own dignity cannot make a meaningful contribution in this area. Social recognition of teachers is indispensable and this includes the recognition of the quantity and the quality of their teaching. But, at the same time, respectful interaction with some of the representations and practices of teachers with might be contradictory with those of meeting the challenge of teaching how to live together is also necessary. Teachers are not unfamiliar with human weaknesses and difficulties, and developing appropriate professional resources for dealing with new situations is still limited

[Ghana seeks to] improve teachers' competencies and their working conditions through reform of the contents, curricula, methods, structures and means of teaching. Teachers need to be motivated to perform effectively. Apart from increased salary, we make our citizens aware of acknowledging the work of teachers. The provision of accommodation and praise for a job well done could contribute to this, [for example] the 'best teacher prize' [or] accelerated promotion to reward outstanding teaching performance.

C. Ameyaw Akumfi,
Minister of Education, Ghana

A major task for China's education system is to improve the qualification of teachers. Some of the measures taken in this direction are:

- efforts to raise the social status of teachers, gradually turning teaching into a truly most respectable and admirable profession, and by creating a social tradition of respect for teachers and for teaching. China has proclaimed 10 September as Teacher's Day. This has given an opportunity for the whole of society to show its respect for teachers and for education, which teachers appreciated as a concrete form of encouragement;
- national events to acknowledge the efforts of outstanding teachers and educators;
- a new wage system to make the remuneration of teachers more competitive, through a general increase in salary and the introduction of various allowances for special or extra activities;
- an accelerated construction programme to improve the housing conditions of primary and middle-school teachers and educational administrative staff;
- considerable effort to provide in-service training in ICTs in all teacher-training centres, including demonstration broadcasting of model teaching courses selected for their pedagogical value.

Adapted from the National Report of China

Indian teachers, who have traditionally stood for universal brotherhood and unity irrespective of diversity, inspired by the Gandhian school of thought, have played a crucial role in efforts to reduce social and economic disparity [...]. This can be achieved only when educational institutions provide environments conducive to the inculcation of the attitudes, values, skills and competencies needed to deal with discrimination, segregation and inequality. The role of teachers is critical. Out of a total of 4.5 million teachers, nearly 3 million are teaching at the primary level. The success of the entire effort hinges on their acceptance by and credibility in the eyes of the community. Education for social inclusion in India [...] is based on flexibility, universality and tolerance. The imposition of a homogeneous curriculum on teacher education programmes throughout the country is counter-productive. It has caused tremendous waste and stagnation in India as in other developing countries. A large number of dropouts and academic failures can be attributed to this entrenched, though unsound, practice. The curriculum framework for quality teacher education [will] offer only broad guidelines, with detailed curricula being formulated by educators at individual institutions. [...] In addition to the conventional roles of the teacher, the following additional roles are envisioned:

- [...];
- inculcating a sense of value judgement, value commitment and value transmission;
- understanding the import of inter-relationships between culture and education, and 'culture and personality';
- understanding the aspirations and expectations of the community and establishing mutually supportive linkages between the school and the community.

Adapted from 'Teacher education for social cohesion: the Indian context', J.S. Rajput and K. Walia, Prospects (UNESCO), No. 119, September 2001, pp.367-375.

In some cases they have preconceptions and find it difficult to devise teaching techniques for social inclusion, for mediation and the peaceful resolution of conflicts, respectful confrontation of ideas and respect for a multitude of viewpoints. The work of trade union and professional organizations is fundamental in overcoming these difficulties.

PARTNERSHIPS WITH CIVIL SOCIETY

In the 1990s, involving communities in contextual planning and implementation of programmes to meet basic educational needs was found to be more productive than centralized planning with decentralized implementation. In India, a new ambitious countrywide education-for-all movement called Sarva Shiksha Abhiyan has been launched. Its objectives are [...] that all children should complete five years of good quality primary schooling by 2007 and eight years of schooling by 2010, bridging all gender and social category gaps. The approach is community-owned and village education plans will form the basis of district education plans. The scheme accords highest priority to community monitoring [...] and a mission-based approach.[...] The social mobilization generated by literacy is having a tremendous impact on other social sectors, notably women's empowerment, health and environmental awareness

Adapted from the National Report of India

Botswana has increased educational expenditure to about 30% of the national budget. Although we support the idea that education is a basic human right, which means that it should be free and compulsory, we are aware that sustainable quality education requires cost sharing with all stakeholders, including government, parents/guardians and the private sector. Cost sharing will be introduced [in a way] mindful of the needs of the poor.

Kgeledi George Kgoroba ,
Minister of Education, Botswana

With the support of its partner for development, Senegal has put in place an important ten-year programme for education and training. [Its achievement] requires the active participation of all categories of the population, i.e. an effective transfer of the responsibility for education to the basic communities. The myth of standardized knowledge dispensed to all children of a country is being replaced by a school that is diversified and adapted to the needs of each basic community.

Moustapha Sourang,
Minister of Education, Senegal

Some 98% of the 400 pupils of Rinkeby School, Sweden, come from non-Swedish backgrounds. When a parent-teacher association was created in 1989, the school was facing serious problems. Parents responded to the invitation and asked for a quiet, completely finished, clean and positive learning environment. They had been interested before, but could not express their interest in any way other than dissatisfaction. It was no trouble getting parents to help with school on evenings and weekends. For a year and a half, students, parents, teachers and the principal worked at cleaning, caulking and painting the entire interior of the school. Parents said they began to like their school. At the same time as working on the physical appearance of the school, class councils and a school council were restarted and adults were present at every meeting to provide support. Now pupils see the teachers more as leaders and the school is open not only during the day for classroom activities but also in the evening during youth's spare time. There the concept of school has undergone change: it is now the place where adults in the community meet school activities and see what solidarity and respect can be all about.

Adapted from the National Report of Sweden

The experience of Madagascar concerning partnerships and the mobilization of actors has shown that activities undertaken within the framework of 'contract programmes' with the communities led to improved access to school. This is all the more interesting in that it allows communities to feel responsible for educational projects and to thus reduce their need for external aid, which may constitute a factor of dependency

Simon Jacquit Nivoson Rosat,
Minister of Basic and Secondary Education, Madagascar

Koïchiro Matsuura, Director-General of UNESCO, as chair of the special session on the relationships between education policies and civil society at the forty-sixth session of the ICE, stated:

> *Civil society organizations (CSOs) cannot replace the State in the area of its core educational responsibility and authority. [...] it is increasingly apparent that the role of CSOs cannot be reduced to that of merely complementing the efforts of the State; moreover, such a narrow conception ill-serves the needs of the EFA movement. I shall now out line the four main roles performed by CSOs in regard to EFA: [...] as alternative service providers where state-provided services are either absent or insufficient; as innovators and sources of new thinking and new practices, especially concerning the impact of globalization on education; to lobby for free and compulsory education of good quality for all children, as well as education programmes for out-of-school youth and adults; but now also to be strategic partners in informed criticism and advocacy.*

The debate during the session once more highlighted that in order to learn to live together the mobilization of all actors is as important as the proposed content of reforms. The World Forum on quality education for all held in Dakar (April 2000) called on countries to move beyond the recognition of the importance of civil society in the shaping of education policies.

All of civil society—not only teachers—needs to be fully and actively involved in all aspects throughout the teaching processes, by means of 'renewed partnerships'.

The involvement of civil society, in particular parents and community organizations, serves not only the purpose of enhanced relevance and quality of teaching. It is also crucial for the democratic functioning of schools and for providing a model of fruitful dialogue to children and their parents and relatives. It is also essential for making greater progress in terms of consistency between the values in and outside school. The partnership between school and families opens the door to a wider partnership, which includes, among others, means of communication. Children and young people spend a lot of time with new and traditional means of communication; a stronger partnership between schools and families would serve as a better mediation point for these and other cultural consumer goods and would generate a greater demand towards achieving the necessary consistency between school messages and media-related messages, as well as having a greater impact on training in learning to live together.

Local festivals, private companies, the social services, religious groups and other community societies may offer opportunities for exercising empathy and solidarity which can be associated with school practices in their efforts to teach how to live together.

Such 'renewed partnerships' at the local or community level seem to develop hand in hand with the growing decentralization of school management in the fields of both administration and practical teaching techniques. They seen also to favour the educational outreach of school to the community for certain important tasks, such as adult literacy and integrating migrant families.

POLICY DIALOGUE

School, can only perform their complex and important role properly if they co-operate with other social agents as well: parents, the social sphere, health institutions and other partners of the local environment. Education [is] best capable of promoting social cohesion. However, not only governmental measures and adequate funding are necessary, but also the development of social dialogue.

Jozsef Palinkas,
Minister of Education, Hungary

The school cannot achieve the desired quality if it only transmits knowledge. It must also play its role in educating for social and moral values and must be active in the community. [...] Education as a whole is not only the mission of the school, but also that of the authorities and society at large [...] Only dialogue can ensure that all partners and stakeholders of educations are involved. Political dialogue is not adopting resolutions: true dialogue means a partnership in the decision-making process with a view to achieving consensus.

Najib Zerouali Quariti,
Minister of Higher Education and Research, Morocco

Education for all [requires] the promotion of dialogue on educational policies and strategies. Cambodia has just reviewed with donors and NGOs its Education strategic plan and its Education Sector Support Programme. Their preparation involved a large number of stakeholders in the formulation of priorities, strategies and programmes.

Im Sethy,
Minister of Education, Cambodia

During the 1970s, the trend was to consider that the mobilization of civil society organizations, and in particular that of communities, could substitute the educational responsibilities and obligations of the public authorities. The outcome of numerous decentralization experiments that have taken place between the 1960s and the present have shown that this is not necessarily true. In reality, the decentralization processes that reduced the need for the public authorities to intervene at all levels (national, provincial and municipal) and in all sectors (executive, legislative and judicial) found themselves unable to satisfy their population's educational needs.

The 2001 ICE highlighted that, along with promoting new partnerships with society, education policies also have to promote new forms of policy dialogue, which include society, but do not abandon the challenge of building and following up on education policies in the long term at national level.

The concept of policy dialogue during the ICE was used to greater effect than on other occasions to pass on the idea of the need for promoting ongoing and informed dialogue between those responsible for public policy at high levels, social organizations with national representation and-also-local communities and their representatives.

Better linkages between educational practices, new partnerships between schools and the community, as well as a renewal of public policies intending to take into consideration the technical, social and political dimensions in the search for better quality Education for all—and in particular those aspects of this quality that are critical for learning to live together—clearly become a necessity.

HUMANIZING GLOBALIZATION

Poverty, especially extreme poverty, is the most effective means we have invented to undermine the right to education and hinder the enjoyment of educational opportunities.

John Daniel,
Assistant Director-General for Education, UNESCO

Humanity everywhere in the world is being haunted by problems and challenges which are, in effect, manifestations of poverty—humanity's single most deadly problem. Poverty is not only the absence of income or limited consumption, it has non-monetary dimensions: Lack of access to public services and ways to make one's voice heard, lack of opportunities, vulnerability, insecurity, powerlessness, etc. Our [education policy] cannot be effectively implemented without the involvement of the rural masses—especially the poor and the women. An agriculture-oriented educational system is needed in Ethiopia not only to increase agricultureal productivity but also to minimize urban unemployment and thereby alleviate poverty

Gennet Zewdie,
Minister of Education, Ethiopia

How can a sizeable proportion of the children of the global village understand the importance of school when they are dying of hunger, illness or drought? The rift is enormous between the daily reality of part of humankind and the fundamental notions drawn up by the Delors Commission; this rift becomes even more profound with the introduction of ICTs in education. learning to live together is achievable only if each country is allowed to develop economically. Learning to live together is objectively only feasible if each individual in the global village can enjoy a decent life. Learning to live together also requires that no culture dominates and no civilization excludes another one.

Boubakeur Benbouzid,
Minister of National Education, Algeria

Kenya is a multy-racial and multi-ethnic society. [...] Understanding and appreciation of the diversity of our culture [with forty-two ethnic groups] removes prejudice and fear of others, thus empowering our children to learn to live together. [...] The impact of HIV/AIDS on education is seen in the loss of trained teachers, increased number of orphaned children and a lowered capacity for parental support for education. HIV/AIDS information has therefore been included in our syllabi.

Henry Kosgey,
Minister of Education, Kenya

What kind of common future can be envisaged when some live in a context of generalized poverty? Nothing good and sustainable seems to be achievable in common until a solution is found to the growing deficit affecting the poor.

Ibrahim Ary,
Minister of National Education, Niger

One of the concerns of UNESCO and of the community of the United Nations is to find a way in which the liberalization of international contacts plays a part in improving the quality of life for all.

The forty-sixth session of the ICE did not question whether globalization was desirable or not, but how to find ways for advances in wealth creation, science, technology and communications to be at the service of the world in its entirety and not only for a small part of the richest and most powerful regions.

In this sense, the **General Rapporteur of the ICE, Philippe Renard (Belgium)** took up the message of participants by stating

One model which we do not want to promote is that of economic empires dominating the markets and information technology that deepen the rift between North and South, foster the brain drain and sometimes [set financial conditions] resulting in the decrease of educational quality in certain countries. This is not the kind of globalization we want. The priority must be to educate the individual for 'living together', empowering him/her to become aware of what is unique in each human and to benefit from the diversity of others.

During the ICE it was underlined that education is central in giving globalization a human face and in contributing to peace and growth. It also underlined that globalization had the potential to open the door towards a more intense and more open exchange between cultures provided it does not lead to what is known as the 'brutal force of indifference'.

Indeed, as shown in the introduction and in the of this book, the rift between nations and communities keeps widening and deepening, dividing humankind into many different worlds, which are developing at different speeds and partly facing the same problems, but partly also facing very different ones. Some of these problems at certain times have greater visibility, while others, however, can remain in the background with the risk that some people become indifferent of them.

No sooner had the forty-sixth session of the ICE come to an end than on 11 September 2001 some 3,000 people were killed in a series of terrorist attacks. But also, some estimates suggest that, on the same day, some 35,000 children died of hunger and poverty in the world, and over 7,500 people died of HIV /AIDS and approximately 14,000 people became infected, the majority of them in poverty-stricken nations. The possibility of learning and teaching living together depends on the recognition of every-one of these problems, the ability of presenting them side by side and on making headway in understanding their specificities and also their interconnectedness.

This gives rise to educational, economic, social and political challenges for every professional group, communities and the world as a whole. Additionally, a further significant of the forty-sixth ICE was the need also to share development, to finance quality education for all on a permanent basis as an indispensable—but not sufficient—component of peace, international understanding and development, and to design shared strategies for this financing at the international level. This would fulfil the need to find common models and strategies for improving the quality of education, rather than promoting uniform models or formulas for different realities.

The Conclusions and Proposals for Action in the illustrate how the forty-sixth ICE reflected the complexity of the reality on the ground and the necessary actions to improve them.

Finally, the Postface continues the thinking on this subject, one year later.

> The prospects for those living under the weight of the scourges of our present day world are far from being bright. Unfortunately it will remain so unless we stop paying just lip service to international solidarity and co-operation and give true meaning to the idea of our common destiny
>
> *Abraham B. Borishade,*
> *Minister of Education, Nigeria*

> There is no such thing as a ready-to-use magic formula to be applied in all circumstances; rather a set of ideas, experiences and innovations that may be used, whenever we learn to listen and think together.
>
> *Koïchiro Matsuura,*
> *Director-General of UNESCO*

Agreement on the Guidelines for Learning to Live Together

The forty-sixth session of the ICE unanimously adopted Conclusions and Proposals for Action that constitute valuable indications for a plan to renew education that takes into account the need for better learning to live together. The circular and structural reforms envisaged are, of course, only orientations pointing in suitable directions. They may nevertheless guide initiatives taken by governmental authorities as well as other stakesholders in the education system at the national and international levels.

These conclusions built on previous developments in the wake of the Jomtien Conference, and they in turn have been reinforced by a recent series of convergent international initiatives which underline the importance of the questions of living together for the worldwide agenda.

CONCLUSIONS AND PROPOSALS FOR ACTION ARISING FROM THE FORTY-SIXTH SESSION OF THE INTERNATIONAL CONFERENCE ON EDUCATION

Preamble

1. The International Bureau of Education, in its capacity as a UNESCO specialized centre for the contents and methods of education, organized the forty-sixth session of the International Conference on Education in Geneva from 5 to 8 September 2001.
2. More than 600 participants took part in the discussions, of whom eighty were ministers and ten vice-ministers of

education, coming from 127 Member States of UNESCO, together with nine representatives of intergovernmental organizations, thirteen non-governmental organizations and three foundations.

3. The objective of intensifying and strengthening dialogue at the level of educational policies on the problems and prospects of solutions with a view to improving the quality of education for learning to live together has been largely achieved. This conclusions and the resulting proposals for action present the key features of the debates and preparatory work (Netforum, ministerial messages, national reports, good practices, etc.). The entire collection will be made known through the Final Report, the reports of the workshops and the other documents to be published after the Conference.

4. These conclusions, adopted on 8 September 2001, have been drawn from the Major Debates, the Plenary sessions and the six worldshops that took place during the Conference. They are intended for governments, international intergovernmental and non-governmental organizations, teachers and organizations of the teaching profession, the media and all partners in civil society whose efforts improve the quality of education, encourage dialogue and develop the capacity to live together.

A. The Challenges

5. Given the enormous complexity of the problems all societies have to face, particularly globalization, and unbearable inequalities between and within countries, learning to live together, a concept created by the International Commission on Education for the Twenty-first Century, has become a necessity in all regions of the world.

6. One of the major challenges confronting education systems remains that of guaranteeing and respecting the right of education for all. However, the right of children to have free access to schools is far from being respected everywhere in the world and particularly in those countries experiencing situations of war, occupation, violence and intolerance.

7. The plea for education to overcome these challenges facing societies is not a new phenomenon. Yet, today, the expectations have become far more urgent, giving the impression that education can by itself overcome the problems that exist in countries and at the international level.
8. Both formal and non-formal education are essential tolls for launching and promoting sustainable processes of constructing peace, democracy and human rights, but they cannot alone provide solutions to the complexity, the tensions and even the contradictions of the present world.
9. It is essential, however, as was stressed in the Jomtien Declaration and the Dakar Framework of Action, that efforts at the national and international level to develop education be complemented by global strategies to eliminate poverty and to promote participation in political, social and cultural life.
10. Achieving the objective of education for all goes beyond the effort of universal schooling. Within each country, the search for social cohesion, the struggle against inequality, the respect for cultural diversity and access to the knowledge society, which may be facilitated by information and communication technologies, will be achieved through policies that focus on improving the quality of education.
11. These policies must overcome the obstacles posed by inequalities of access and risks of exclusion in the fields of languages, science and technology.
    - As far as languages are concerned, it is possible to note that numerous countries are multilingual even though a single language appears as the official language of communication.
    - Concerning science and technology, particularly those of information and communication, the gulf is growing wider due to inequality in access to the most recent advances.

B. Educational Policies and Practices

12. Throughout the world there is a strong political will on the part of numerous governments and teachers to adapt educational contents, structures and methods in order to respond to the above-mentioned challenges.

13. The experiences of educational policies and practices indicate that it is necessary to consider reforms more as processes than as products. These may arise as such from governmental decisions as from the initiatives of other stakesholders. The way in which they are implemented, involving the mobilization of all actors, is as important as the content.
14. Basic agreements within the international community already exist concerning lines of action for promoting the ability and willingness to live together. Those responsible for education policies at the national level have clearly expressed their will to pursue the implementation of these agreements.
15. The evaluation of the outcomes of the reform processes, and particularly "good practices", enables us to highlight both some conditions unique to each cultural context as well as to pinpoint some common characteristics.

C. **Proposals for Action**

16. The entire range of teaching and educational practices for living together should be better known, disseminated and exploited with a view to strengthening the endogenous capacities of each country.
17. Training for policy dialogue is essential in order to achieve the major objective of improving the quality of education for all.
18. Reform processes should be continued or undertaken in the following domains:

Contents

- Adapting curricula and updating contents in order to reflect:
  - — economic and social changes set in motion, in particular, by globalization, migration and cultural diversity;
  - — the ethical dimension of scientific and technological progress;
- The growing importance of communication, expression and the capacity to listen and dialogue, first of all in the mother-tongue, then in the official language in the country as well as in one or more foreign languages;

- The positive contribution that may result from integrating technologies into the learning process;
- Developing not only disciplinary but also interdisciplinary approaches and competencies;
- Supporting and nurturing innovations;
- Seeking, in the development of curricula, to ensure relevance at the local, national and international levels at the same time.

Methods

- Promoting active learning methods and teamwork;
- Encouraging all-round and balanced development and preparing the individual for active citizenship open to the world.

Teachers

- Facilitating genuine involvement on the part of teachers in decision-making within the school, through training and other means.
- Improving the education of teachers so that they can better develop among pupils behaviour and values of solidarity and tolerance, so as to prepare them to prevent and resolve conflicts peacefully and to respect cultural diversity.
- Changing the relationship between teacher and pupil to respond to the evolution of society.
- Improving the use of information and communication technologies in teacher training and in classroom practices.

Daily Life in Educational Institutions

- Creating within the school a climate of tolerance and respect encouraging the development of a democratic culture.
- Providing a way for the school to function that encourages participation of the pupils in decision-making.
- Proposing a shared definition of projects and learning activities.

Educational Research

- Stimulating research that clarifies the concept of learning to live together and the implications for policy and practices.
- Promoting research on the development of contents and teaching methods relating to learning to live together.
- Stimulating comparative studies in the sub-regional, regional and trans-regional contents.

19. Partnerships

- Since education is not the sole answer to learning to live together, its improvement requires the contribution not only of the school but also of all concerned actors. It therefore implies the introduction and the strengthening of genuine partnerships with the entire society: teachers, communities, families, the economic sector, the media, NGOs, and the intellectual and spiritual authorities.
- Partnerships are also requried to expand access to and effective use of new information and communication technologies.

20. Learning to live together requires policies for the development of lifelong learning beginning with early childhood education, and paying particular attention to the period of adolescence (12-18 years).

D. International Co-operation

21. The Development of international co-operative activities to improve the quality of education for learning to live together for all should be based on six main principles:

- Strengthening the function of the IBE as an observatory of trends, as well as its role in the development of easily accessible databanks and information systems.
- Collecting the results of educational research on the development of contents, undertaking comparative studies at the sub-regional and regional levels, and their worldwide dissemination.

- Setting up co-operative networks at the international, regional and sub-regional levels facilitating the exchange of experience and promoting joint projects in order to strengthen endogenous capacities.
- Training educational decision-makers in policy dialogue so as to encourage the definition of common objectives, the search for consensus and the mobilization of partnerships.
- Experimenting with new modalities of technical assistance provided by bi- or multilateral co-operation agencies, in order to emphasize not only North-South but also South-South collaboration.
- Strengthening of partnerships between UNESCO and other relevant intergovernmental organizations.

E. The Role of UNESCO and its Socialized Institutes

22. The conclusions of the forty-sixth session of the International Conference on Education are communicated to the General Conference of the Organization in order to be taken into account in the process of reflection and to reinforce, in the short, medium and long terms, the programme of action of UNESCO, the International Bureau of Education and the other specialized institutes with a view to improving the quality of education.

13

Postface: 'Learning to Live Together': Have We Failed?

The question is directed first of all to political decision-makers and to all the national partners in the education system. And there is no doubt that the answer must be moderated: yes, we have failed to a certain extent, or perhaps not yet succeeded? No, we have not failed completely, at least not everywhere. In the world numerous model exist of positive and promising policies and practices. There are millions of teachers who ensure every day that their classroom becomes a place where one does really learn to live together.

This question can also be directed to international organizations and particularly to UNESCO. Has the action already carried out been appropriate and does it correspond to our present concerns? In his introduction to the work of Commission II, at the thirty-first session of the General Conference of UNESCO, John Daniel, Assistant Dirctor-General for Education reminded us: 'the events of 11 September lead us to reconsider the relative importance of the ultimate objectives of our work. In particular, we ask ourselves if the ambition of learning to live together is now more important than the construction of the learning society.'

There seems to be considerable agreement on one point: more of the same education is unlikely to improve its quality and it will be necessary to carry out a thorough review of the very objectives of education throughout the world.

The Conclusions and Proposals for Action of the forty-sixth session of the International Conference on Education (ICE) reveal the advances made in the last few years in the Ministries of Education of many countries throughout the world. In fact, at the beginning of the twenty-first century, it can be stated that there is a new consensus regarding some of the characteristics for an educational paradigm that will help to foster education for peace, development and social cohesion, the pillars of 'living together'. Contents for international understanding in dynamic interaction with contents for the construction of local and group identities, active institutional methods and practices that promote civic responsibility and various ways of participating democratically in society now have a much more solid presence in the declarations and proposals for education of a much large group of countries and of the community of education ministers. Even thorough civil society did not participate in this Conference as activity as required, very important non-governmental organizations, in particular Education International, are contributing to increase this presence.

On the other hand, during the forty-sixth session of the ICE, it also become evident that on all continents there is a considerable capacity for innovation in pursuit of the desired characteristics. That capacity for innovation is reflected in policies, programmes and projects at different levels of education: national, provincial, local or institutional. However, it is still restricted to a limited number of educational establishments. Although some innovative feature or other can be detected in many educational establishments in line with the type of education the conclusions of the forty-sixth ICE desire to foster, in the great majority there is a prevalence of the features characteristic of the education conceived in the nineteenth century and whose limitations were exposed by the twentieth century. In fact, none of the participants in the forty-sixth session of the ICE would hesitate to recognize that there is a significant distance between the consensus over certain characteristics of the education required for living together and its slow implementation.

THE CHALLENGE OF CONCEIVING EDUCATIONAL POLICIES FOR QUALITY EDUCATION

Consequently, the challenge for the first decade of the twenty-first century is to find ways of turning the consensus constructed in the last decades of the twentieth century regarding 'an educational utopia' into reality. It seems necessary to update contents, simultaneously giving them an international and local character, active methods that recognize the central role of learning processes and the importance of active intervention by primary and secondary teachers, a dynamic institutional life that will educate in civic responsibility and educational institutions associated with local communities, without being enslaved to them.

Although the debates at the forty-sixth session of the ICE placed more emphasis on further explaining the consensus on what education for learning to live together should be like in the twenty-first century and on what advances can already be recorded as concrete moves in that direction, political and educational practice at the start of the century allows us to predict that in order for the kind of education mankind needs to survive and develop to become universal, progress is required in understanding and in the capacity to manage what could be called policies for promoting quality education.

There are many kinds of policies for promoting quality education. Some of them were presented at the forty-sixth session of the ICE and many more appear in countries' national reports. The most important of these presented at the Conference are: some curricular reform processes; policies for pupil and teachers participation in the day-to-day life of educational establishments; policies to promote teaching for access to scientific knowledge and its connection with ethics; policies for access to learning to learn and for access to economic production; policies for promoting the use of the new information and communication technologies in association with interactive and collective teaching methods—instead of promoting interaction of each individual pupil with computer screens; incorporation in schools of each cultural group's artistic and cultural practices; the promotion of multilingualism; and others.

But as important or even more so than knowing what policies for promoting quality education for learning to live together exist is knowing how they are advancing and what difficulties they are encountering. Enormous tenacity and energy are required in the day-to-day action to achieve Education for

All through the fostering of educational inclusion and improved quality. Therefore, those responsible are not always in a position to systematically communicate more information or elaborately systematize how it is done.

Some national reports presented at the forty-sixth session of the ICE, the results of some—still very few—research studies on the dynamics of educational chance (Tyack & Cuban, 1995), and many, many diaglogues between the participants at the Conference allow us to pose the hypothesis that the design, implementation and permanent, systematic support for policies to promote quality education require much more time. Politicians with expertise in education and with years of experience know very well—as they state in the Conclusions of the forty-sixth session of the ICE—that changes in the quality of education, and in particular in those of its dimensions most closely associated with the possibility of learning to live together, as much slower than the community of man would like.

These expert politicians also know that implementation and permanent, systematic support for policies for promoting quality education for living together require great skill in navigating a secenario fraught with many tensions—both old and new.

POLICIES FOR PROMOTING QUALITY EDUCATION IN THE LIGHT OF NEW TENSIONS IN THE FIELD OF EDUCATION

In fact, educational policies for promoting quality in Education for All for learning to live together are confronted by a number of tensions which are different from those arising from the expansion in education system. This new set of tensions can be classified into three groups: the first is that of 'institutional' tensions; the second 'teaching' tensions; and the third 'cultural' tensions.

Institutional tensions are associated with expectations and the fostering of innovation in a system and in a set of practices and mechanisms that were invented for reproduction. That famous phrase of sociologist Emile Durkheim defining education as the purposeful activity of the adult generations to transmit culture to the younger generations, based on the assumption that knowledge, values and social practices are lasting, captured better than anyone else the 'reproductive' nature of education and of traditional education systems. Government and monitoring bodies, for example, were set up to control the quality of the reproduction of practices and contents considered to be permanent in closed systems. Suddenly, those same systems are being asked to innovative, to be creative, to give way to diversity and not to withdraw into themselves. In some countries, primary teachers trained to teach the same lessons each year according to inflexible curricula and to transmit the idea of 'nation' are now being asked to respond to flexible curricula that are both global and local, and in which the world and the community take on a new dimension in an unstable, complex balance with the country or the nation. In post-colonial contexts or in countries in transition, on the contrary, the education systems are being asked to contribute to the creation of new 'nations', recovering traditions of peoples subsumed in political units that ignored them, but also in interaction with local and global contents. These institutional tensions are intrinsically linked with teaching and cultural tensions.

The teaching tensions are, in turn, associated with the fact that knowledge is obviously important, but at the same time quickly becomes obsolescent. At the end of the twentieth century, information was already being renewed at a much greater speed than is necessary for acquiring what is already available. However, there is no possible knowledge without rigorous management of updated information. This situation obliges education on the one hand to facilitate access to information, but on the other to educate in the awareness of its obsolescence and in the exercise of learning practices that will last beyond the information. But these learning practices also differ at different ages, according to individual characteristics and in different cultures, and should be increasingly authonomous. In this sense, calls to focus education on the learners merit particular attention, as do those that stress that there is no possible access to knowledge without professional intervention by a new type of primary and secondary teacher.

The cultural tensions are the backdrop to the other two. They are associated with the civilizing movement of the new diversity, quality and depth of world interdependences. Formal education processes, the main centre of interest at the forty-sixth session of the ICE, are one of the focal points of inter-generational relations. From Durkheim's statement it also stemmed that in their usual form those processes were invented at a time when adult generations desired and were able to transmit their own culture and that of their ancestors to their children and, through them, to their grandchildren and great-grandchildren. They were confident that by transmitting that culture they would guarantee future generations a better quality of life. That confidence, in turn, gave them energy to educate and that energy was exploited by educational policies as legitimization for initiatives for educational expansion.

At the start of the twenty-first century, on the other hand, the tendency, towards social marginalization and division, and the increasing labour problems referred to in the introduction cast doubt on education's effectiveness to improve the quality of life. In other words, when large contingents of the world's population wonder whether any improvement to their quality of life is possible, they also wonder it is worth while being educated and educating their children. Actual experience shows that, although in that context education does not guarantee the indefinite progress people aspire to, without education there is no change of integration into ways of life that allow development and peace. Quality education for learning to live together is therefore a necessary though not sufficient condition for the survival or mankind.

Navigating to construct an education for living together requires a compass and navigatonal skills. The compass is the vision, and the ability to navigate consists of certain competencies for carrying out action. But the vision is richer and more relevant if it is also developed through a specific kind of action: policy dialogue.

THE IMPORTANCE OF RESEARCH AND POLICY DIALOGUE TO PREPARE POLICIES FOR PROMOTING QUALITY EDUCATION

The last but one decade of the twentieth century was characterized by confidence in mechanisms for regulating and controlling education as an ideal means of constructing quality education. In effect, the 1980s set the construction of standards and evaluation of pupils' learning achievements, particularly in languages and mathematics, at the centre of educational initiatives. The spirit of the decade was strongly influenced by the idea that, to achieve better quality in education, more and better definitions about the quality and quantity of knowledge were required, and more and better examinations introduced, enabling the acquisition-or not—of knowledge to be measured exactly.

It is of some interest that, at least during the forty-sixth session of the ICE, the top ministerial teams seem to have paid much less attention to these issues. Top-quality academic presentations stressed the need to base oneself on the outcomes of research (Audigier & Bottani, 2002). But the delegates gave priority to other themes. In fact, when it came to making its contribution to 'living together'—the focal point of the definition of quality education—the issues of standardization and evaluation were apparently no longer so highly valued as levers for promoting change.

Research, good practices and, above all, dialogue on edcuation policies, both nationally and international, compete with those two issues or complement them. Certainly, the priority given these topics by the ministerial teams is proportionate to the scant attention paid to them in the preceding decades and to the fact that the vision developed in the forty-sixth session of the ICE has a global orientation and is therefore not sufficiently elaborated.

In fact, a vision that includes the importance of diversity and the local dimension—that is each context—requires a great capacity for reconstruction and for appropriate recreation. It requires solid historical knowledge and a great ability for comparison in context to avoid uncritical transfer of inappropriate models. This historical knowledge and great ability for comparison in context can only be achieved if research results are available and if there is dialogue marked by critical skill and mutual respect.

As shown in a recent study by the OECD (2001), the role of research for promoting innovation in the education sector lags far behind in comparison, for example, with the health sector. The availability of series of comparable valid, reliable data for the analysis of qualitative trends, research into processes, the promotion of 'designed experiments' (De Corte & Verschaffel, 2002), evaluation of programmes and projects and universally accessible databases of 'good practices' evaluated according to agreed and systematized criteria are an exception in the education sector. Their availability to schools, their use in basic and in-service teacher training and in training activities organized by trade unions are not frequent enough either. In this training, the normative approach continues to prevail over 'empowerment' of the actors through the availability of valuable, well-selected information and instruments that help reflection.

Policy dialogue in education is simply the interchange of ideas on relevant educational issues to achieve agreements and to contain disagreements and only regarding what should be done in each particular context but also, and very particularly, how to do it: in what order and with what methodology should one address the different dimensions of change, what implications each decision involves and what price each individual is prepared to pay to achieve shared progress. But there is increasingly frequent interchange between the actors specifically from the educational sphere (primary teachers, secondary teachers, parents and pupils) and the actors who exert influence on education (professional politicians, entrepreneurs, trade union and religious leaders, among others) on how to promote quality education for learning to live together.

Their achievements, however, are still not as fruitful as desired. On occasion, the processes are very long and, despite the goodwill of the participants, fail to produce powerful, long-term agreements. The novelty of the forty-sixth session of the ICE was the shared recognition of the need for training to improve the quality of this dialogue. This recognition, like the warning regarding the limits of educational change and the need for social changes to enable the educational change to take place, are a declaration of modesty and a demonstration of balance on the part of the participants. They are at the same time a demonstration of coherence between the demand for promoting education throughout life and acceptance of the need for training at the highest levels of educational decision-making.

To construct more solid partnerships it is indispensable to improve the capacity for communication and negotiation